CANNIBALS TO CONDORS

CANNIBALS TO CONDORS

Breaking Bread with Serial Killers
while Working as a Soldier for Jesus

Jimmy Winters

AN ADVENTURE TRAVEL MEMOIR

Printed in the United States of America

ISBN: 978-0-578-67329-5

Disclaimer:

This book is written with the specific intention to describe some of my personal life experiences for your entertainment. Some of the people and places that I have encountered proved to be the most dangerous, perilous, and unsafe experiences imaginable. Do not attempt to repeat or reenact any situations described herein, since your experience will most probably be very different than mine, with a high probability that you will not live to tell about it.

With deepest gratitude and appreciation,

I thank all of my Guides on the other side of the veil.

CONTENTS

PREFACE

S ome of you may have acquired this book with the desire of pursuing your missionary calling, raising your personal level of empathic ability, taking an armchair spiritual travel adventure, piecing together facets of modern-day anthropophagi, and others just for nonfiction entertainment or curiosity. Whatever the reason, regardless of understanding the true motivation of your interest to read this, your completion of the reading of this book will elevate awareness of your vibrational being and potentially enhance a deeper level of comprehension and connection with God, Jesus, Source, Angels, and Spirit. Most likely, this also will favorably impact your future life choices by helping you recognize your clair abilities and reception to intuitive guidance, thereby presenting you with more creative options to use for your benefit. Maybe you're being called to spiritual service and aren't exactly sure what you want to do or where to go, but after finishing this book, you will undoubtedly have more choices available than you originally thought of before picking this up.

Written in a general chronological timeframe, my development reflects progressive spiritual awareness, which allowed more in-depth truths to be learned through my deep interest in ancient origin. Although specific details and disclosure of humans' beginnings remain closely guarded, for various unknown reasons, I surmise this is true to enable continuance of our relatively slow, controlled, methodical pace of evolution. I have found that our race has apparently experienced a half-dozen wipeouts, restarts, and major modifications, which have substantially delayed the "Master Plan," and "all hands on deck" now seems to be the prevailing MO to see us through to completion (i.e., developmental integration with a higher order).

This book is primarily a compilation and account of many actions, situations, and events that have manifested throughout my life as a result of spiritual influence. By no means is it a complete account of every daily occurrence that I have experienced, but an overview of how more significant Divine authority has affected my life path over the course of the past fifteen years, which comprises the bulk of my descriptive adventures. It took me many years of study to get a grasp on the powerful spiritual and metaphysical concepts that I describe herein, and hopefully in the future, you will benefit as I have, by leading a more effective and rewarding life in alignment with Jesus and his army of assistants. With the bulk of my travels throughout the Western Hemisphere having taken place after my retirement in 1996, a few parts of this book may seem to flow other than in a typical story format due to a substantial time lapse between my living a "linear" life and periods of significant, spiritually aligned events that have changed the course of my life. The thread of intuitive guidance ties it together.

There will be those whose vibration raises just enough to cause interest to initiate their study of personal spiritual development and enlightenment, and those whose spiritual development will be enhanced and solidified, who may appreciate particular situations with more in-depth humor and relevance of events described herein. Whatever the case may be, know that powerful God-Sourced angelic and Spirit entities will assist you at whatever comfort/knowledge level you are currently operating in. Remember, Angels usually don't interfere or assist unless you ask, and our physical, emotional, and spiritual well-being is their utmost priority.

My references to "hearing" messages comprise terminology used to explain where certain thought, information, and ideas originate.

No sounds or voices are actually heard, since it is a "knowingness" and powerful "feeling," with occasional visuals. I do not literally "hear" any words or voices, since clair abilities identify the expression and often the Source. A person is intuitively clairvoyant (seeing), clairsentient (feeling), clairaudient (hearing), or claircognizant (being aware) when they are aware of imparted knowledge and information that is projected and provided to them by Spirit.

Several situations in this book require that I change the names of the persons involved, due to the nature of their actions or offenses against humanity, or others in respect of their privacy. The exact locations of some village names and locations have been slightly changed in order to prevent overly enthusiastic investigative journalists from getting themselves robbed or kidnapped, or more probably, having their heads cut off. Every incident contained herein is the truth and nothing but the truth. I don't read or write any kind of fiction, so help me God. No fake news here! I see absolutely no purpose in life whatsoever to waste my valuable time, energy, and brain capacity derailed off into unproductive fantasy entertainment.

However, to the nonbelievers of truth, I say: continue with focus and persistence on your personal journey, wherever it may lead, because eventually you will grow and come around to face your fear. Once you understand and clear out your clutter, not only will you exist in joyful truth and freedom with enhanced comprehension of consciousness, but you also will possess the ability to fathom your connection with God and your place within ultimate reality. I have learned to see life more through the eyes of Spirit, instead of just my own, and hopefully this widens your visionary horizon as well. The learning curve starts off slowly until you have a solid foundation, but then you will eventually learn of, and accept, the true being that you are. But for now, if you fit into the category of denial of God with narrow- or close-minded, self-centered, narcissistic, or immature stories of fantasy thought, excuses, or fanatical criticism, please don't waste your time reading this book as it's not for you, and I prefer that you not hear my story.

Thousands of exciting, thrilling, adventurous, and joyous experiences have regularly occurred throughout my life but have evaded inclusion herein, or I would have needed to write at least another thousand pages. I don't describe any extended periods, circumstances, or personal relationships in my life that were spiritually deficient or deviated from an expected wholesome course of society. Nobody is perfect—not here on this planet anyway! We'll also save for another time my numerous awesome days as a kid catching frogs down by the creek or playing football or soccer, or short stints during my late teens as a truck driver, cement mason, landscaper, painter, and factory worker. Family vacations later in life, my addiction to roller coasters and race cars, fabulous deep-sea fishing trips, mountain construction projects, and day trading will be kept for another time as well.

Thank you.
Namaste.

INTRODUCTION

Attending Sunday School was mandatory for me and my sister until we were old enough to rebel. We grew up in the Lutheran faith, to which one of my great-grandfathers switched from our long heritage of Roman Catholic a few hundred years ago in Germany. I was confirmed in our Lutheran church as a young teenager and then drifted away from the church, in line with the generational mores of most others. Our church pastor was great, but I just didn't buy the story line, and playing baseball, building tree forts, or fishing was a lot more exciting.

By the time I graduated high school, I knew that something was substantially different with my perception of life, understanding of reality, and general overall circumstances. There were just too many instances of coincidental experiences that subjected my crossing paths with assassins, death, and unknown subjective phenomena. They say the average person during their lifetime walks past sixteen killers, but I was already nearing my quota by the time I turned eighteen. The few questions that I asked our local church pastor indicated to me there was no reason to continue discussions with him, other than he was just another regular nice guy. Preachers often refer people to "professionals" when they don't have the answer, but for me, there was no asking anyone anything for fear of being confined.

Having first retired from the business world very early, at the age of forty-two, I had the time and resources to make a difference for good. Little did I know the extent to which I would make an impact, since the furthest thing from my mind was teaching serial killers how to pray. My life's experiences have prompted my desire for increased knowledge of spirituality, while raising the level of my awareness of working for God, as a Soldier for Jesus, and it has been the most rewarding aspect of my current incarnation. It has been the highest privilege imaginable for me to have been shown the most phenomenal concepts working alongside Archangels in expansive spaces, and to have worked with elevated-vibration interdimensional Beings, Entities, and Energies in service to God. My rewards of being taught, by a most loving quadriplegic boy, the basics of telepathy and interdimensional travel are indescribable. We are all on a lengthy human mission designed to ultimately reach enlightenment and collective ascension. Everyone plays a part, and with Jesus's continued guidance, I pray my wonderful life continues with creative manifestation and intuition of the highest order that provides, guides, secures, and reinforces my path.

During my younger years, I thought that bizarre life was just normal—growing up in a New York suburb in the sixties with high school gang fights and drugs, and seeing people broken and killed in car wrecks, bank robberies, drownings, teachers getting beaten up by students in my classroom, and getting beat up or blown up, or throwing up after drinking with my high school friends on Friday nights. School acquaintances who murdered a store manager one late Saturday night over a hamburger were a sampling of my classmates at the time.

The series of my life events continually prepared me for greater challenges as I got older. Many events of my younger experiences would be considered outrageous and unacceptable by an educated society, but each one that crossed my path effectively prepared me for more intense future encounters to benefit mankind unserved by others. These future challenges then became a combination of difficult previous occurrences, necessitating creativity to integrate and resolve for the highest good. Initially, I was unaware of the subtle game, but with a thorough footing and assistance from the most powerful order of spiritual Beings, I've gotten pretty good at it. I just wish that I had figured it out much sooner in life, so as to more effectively utilize the knowledge to benefit myself and others. Considering that many people never get it figured out, I consider myself lucky and recognize my gift of awareness and connection to our God-Source Creator, a most wonderful blessing. Thank you, God!

Remembering before I was born, my Guides worked with me to help me choose the best place for me to reincarnate. There are many other choices, and a half-dozen planets like us, with two others very similar to us. I agreed that I would be most useful here, at this time, and remember my Spirit accelerating from "far away" to occupy my new body, with my memory blocked moments before entry. I was twice delayed momentarily until reprogramming was completed: once, in order to avoid having me meet two other copies of "me" (one in southeastern Colorado, which was a major concern, and the other in a different part of the world to where my Creator knew I would not travel), and the other delay was to ensure that I enter the correct body.

Certain concepts discussed herein may be misunderstood by the reader simply due to their lack of training, knowledge, or experience with the subject matter. I encourage you to research and learn phenomena currently unknown or lacking definition by you, so that you will always have an additional wisdom compartment in your toolbox. I am unable to explain the functionality of some perceptions or conditions due to the extent of their complexity, which, after years of study and practice, I am still continuously learning. Theoretical positions are stated based upon my personal experience and beliefs.

Thank you to all who have encouraged me to put this information on paper. I never considered creating this hard copy, let alone author a book, until I realized how many people told me that I have lived an incredible life, incomprehensible to many folks, and that I need to share my story for the benefit of all. Following that advice, I finally pulled out all my old travel journals and diaries to help me see my life in a rear-view mirror. Reliving several situations at times was painful while documenting it all, but I had spiritual guidance of the highest order to help me write this work. I hope that when you are finished reading this, you are more consciously aware of life paths available for you to follow, and options to choose for a more productive and fulfilling incarnation in harmony with God's plan.

CHAPTER 1
ADAPTING TO MY NEW BODY

"You've been prepared for this," I heard so many times, but taking 150 rounds of machine gun fire into my motel room window, or teaching serial killers and cannibals how to pray, was not what I signed up for. Long Island set a great foundation to prepare me for my amazing life ahead, but a methodical series of uncommon, and sometimes shocking, events ensured my alignment with a predefined spiritual path. My childhood was blessed with the best of worlds, having the ocean and beautiful beaches nearby, given the freedom to roam as a kid on my bicycle all day with friends, building forts and tree houses in the woods, digging in the creek for buried treasure, chasing fire trucks, fishing, and getting into mischief like most other kids. Unbeknownst to me, the groundwork was being well set.

I was brought up with the best mom ever and a dad who, after surviving Omaha Beach, worked fifteen hours a day, seven days a week, to provide for us by working in our family's luncheonette. Dad made, in his lifetime, over a half-million sandwiches (of which the tuna fish was the best in the world), over one hundred thousand pounds of chocolate, and four hundred thousand gallons of ice-cream. Working in our busy luncheonette and candy store, I learned how to make ice cream, roll candy canes, mold chocolate Easter rabbits, decorate cakes, change out seasonal window displays, and, of course, to wait tables, wash dishes, and mop the floor—when I wasn't planting my face into a big pot of tuna fish salad or freshly made whipped cream when nobody was watching!

I enjoyed anything involving fresh air: mowing the grass, raking leaves, painting, and shoveling snow with my friends, which generally became seasonal routines. My preferred activities were anything outdoors, having sensed and known that I had been there and I'd seen this all before. How was it that I could feel some type of unseen energy outside penetrating my body, which made me feel different? How come nobody else felt it, saw it, or talked about it? It seemed like some type of information was available "in the air," but I just couldn't seem to locate or identify it, thinking at that time it must be a really big super secret.

With fun-filled days as a kid, my nightly dream state was just as active—how exciting—until my first powerful nightmare around age three or four. Prior to then, I knew there was something in dream state going on—not all good, but, of course, I had no idea. I had several visitations of the same invader "walk-in" Spirit, the first two about a year apart, and the third occurrence two to three years later, with a slight reminder several years afterward that "it" was still there, deep in the background. It was the second visitation when I woke up screaming and crying out of sheer terror, running around the house, trying to escape the monster in my brain at one o'clock in the morning. I specifically recall clearly seeing *through* the front door of the living room, as if it was a hazy apparition, out into the lawn of the dark front yard. Something tempted me to run through it to escape, so full speed ahead from the other side of the living room, flat out, I tried to run through the front door but bounced off and fell to the floor. I lay there on the floor totally exhausted before Mom and Dad took me back to bed. They didn't understand and therefore had no explanation, so they couldn't help. That was a brain-changing, life-altering experience, as my core awareness was then formally introduced to some other force/power/aspect of another dimension. Little did I know at the time, that experience prepared me to accelerate my learning later in life of interdimensional energies, and it helped train me to teach children and their parents how to escape and prevent that kind of terror.

My mom must have spoken with my grandfather about the event, because I recall my pop teaching me about Angels and Spirits at a very young age. Pop emigrated from Germany to New York around 1905 and opened a bakery in New York, where he and my grandmother worked for about fifty years. Although proficiently intuitive, Pop faithfully studied astrology daily for over seventy-five years, thoroughly reading and interpreting the daily charts of all our family members with amazing accuracy. He combined intuitiveness with astrology and was extraordinary in every detail. When I was a young teenager, he explained many details of my future, and also those of all our family members, under the condition that I promise never to disclose to anyone their predicted outcome. Every single one of the fifteen family members' circumstances that he mentioned, came to be—exactly. Pop taught me that all the answers lie in the stars and I just had to figure out how to access them.

From a young age, I always knew that things were other than how they seemed to appear, and I had always felt that we were just one big experiment. Spending a little extra time under the stars with my telescope that Mom and Dad gave me for Christmas, I knew there was something more, much deeper and more complex than we could imagine here on this miniscule speck of a planet spinning around out in space in the middle of nowhere. I strongly felt that *Only Truth* accelerates our human race on the most direct path into whom we are destined to become by God. Fast-forward fifty years, and now I found out that it's true. Even as a kid, I was stupefied at the thought that information suppressed and hidden from society under a veil of secrecy was because it's for their own good. Who's running the show here and automatically assumes we are all insufficiently competent to know the truth?

I was about six or seven years old when one day out of the clear blue, I first asked, while she was doing the dishes, "Mom, where is Peru?"

She turned, perplexingly looked at me, and asked, "Where did you hear the word 'Peru'? They aren't teaching you that in school yet. How do you know that? It's a country in South America, very far away," she said.

"I don't know, Mom; the name just came into my head, but I want to go there. Can we go there, maybe this summer on vacation?"

"I don't think so, honey, because it's very, very far away, but when you get older, you'll be able to go someday if you still want to," she replied.

I had an interest in aliens from a young age and always looked to the stars, wondering who among us actually knows—and why won't they tell? Did they have anything to do with the fact that sometimes I identified things that escaped the attention of others? I thought that eventually, we would learn in school as we got older, because teachers are smart, and that's why they teach, right?

As a kid, I thought that it must be a secret advanced class I would get to take in high school or college, so that's why nobody ever talked about it, but the class never came. Math was always my favorite subject due to my underlying inquisitiveness and analytical nature, always having a desire to figure things out. English, history, and art class were my worst, year in, year out, feeling that every moment I spent in class was wasted, that someone was stealing time from my life, which I could have been using for a higher and better purpose, but I didn't know how to get out of it or stop it. I felt that the ones teaching just didn't understand, or else it was a big cover-up, because there were much more important concepts to teach, and to me, those classes were at the bottom of the barrel. Of course, it never occurred to me then that at some future point in my life, I may want to document for my family, friends, and future ancestors a written account of interesting highlights that occurred in my life. By the time high school history class rolled around, I realized they weren't teaching me anything near what I felt should be taught, and I could never grasp the relevance of learning why some jackass caused something or other to happen 286 years ago. I always wondered why people who taught useless stuff were told by God to do that, and to this day, I still haven't figured out why. I sensed there was a vast amount of valuable, ancient information to be accessed and taught, which would ultimately result in permanently contributing to the betterment of my life, and that also of society, but it never came.

After school and on weekends, my friends and I would often chase fire trucks on our bicycles, with baseball cards attached to the spokes with clothespins, like lots of kids did back then. One Saturday while we were playing in the woods, Danny and I heard the firehouse horns go off, looked at each other, and said, "Let's go." So off we ran out to the street, looking in the distance to see a massive smoke column billowing high into the sky. It was two to three miles away, and with the amount of smoke at that distance, we knew it was a big one. Pedaling as fast as we could, we finally got there to see a dozen fire trucks already there fighting the fire. The blazing plastics factory was just across the street into the adjoining town, but our town's fire trucks were called for backup.

Of course, we wanted to get as close as possible, so we rode over toward the big ladder truck that was extending and positioning the ladder upwind to the smoke. With a fireman on top as the ladder went way, way up high, he hollered down, "Give me water!" as we watched the guys on the truck turn the valves to send the water. At that moment, a police car pulled up in front of us and parked his front tire directly on the hose, cutting off the water supply to the ladder. Danny and I looked at each other, thinking the same thing as any other eleven-year old kid—"What an idiot"—as the guy on top of the ladder was looking down and hollering for the water that never came. When they finally saw the problem, they told the cop to get his car off the hose, which he did quickly, and the water instantaneously shot through the hose up to the guy on top of the ladder holding the nozzle. The instant pressure caused the hose to whiplash and sent the fireman flying off the ladder through the air and falling to his death right there in the parking lot in front of us. A few nearby firemen tried to catch him, but their efforts were no match for a two-hundred-pound man free-falling from one hundred feet up. For another hour or two, we continued to watch the fire blaze out of control from a different spot, but the disturbing nature of viewing what had occurred stayed on our minds for a couple of days. Was that cop responsible for negligent homicide? Regardless, I imagine that his psychological guilt was carried throughout his life.

I began to occasionally know ahead of time, or at the same time, something strange would happen. For instance, when I was fourteen years old, riding my bike down the middle of a quiet street in our residential neighborhood of Levitt houses around 2:00 p.m. on a Saturday afternoon, all of a sudden, my leg hurt, and I mentally knew something happened to my buddy Tony. I continued three blocks more to his house, but nobody was home. When we met at the school bus stop Monday morning, he was on crutches.

I asked him, "What happened, man?"

"I was working with my father Saturday, and a transmission fell on my leg."

"What time?" I asked, while explaining the reasoning of my question.

"Somewhere around two o'clock or so," he said.

Premonitions had begun to catch my attention and awareness more frequently; however, they failed to help me in any way I could identify. My first out-of-body experience was at fourteen years old in my bed, where I floated around the room looking down at myself resting, late one Saturday afternoon. I had heard about what happened to people like me getting institutionalized. Better not tell anyone, or they might lock you up in the nuthouse and give you drugs. I never did care for drugs, but then again, pot is a natural herbal remedy. Smoking pot not only suppressed my back pain but also obscured the confusion that I could not process or understand,

and it helped to quiet my brain from receiving messages from unknown sources.

A typical Long Island winter would usually provide us with at least one good storm, dropping enough snow to close schools and businesses for a day or two. Waking up to Mom saying, "There's no school today because of the snowstorm, honey," was music to my ears. I jumped out of bed and looked out the window to see a raging blizzard.

While I was having breakfast and planning out my free day, my friend Jerry called from his house a few blocks over, and he asked, "Do you want to go shovel?"

"Sure, we can probably pick up some cash today, so let's do it," I replied.

Agreeing to meet on a nearby corner in a half hour, I got dressed in warm clothes; put on my boots, heavy winter coat, hat, gloves, knitted face mask, and goggles; and then headed out the back door of the garage with my dad's snow shovel. Reaching our meeting point a few minutes later, we decided to walk several blocks up to the main street in the village. There wasn't one other person we saw outside, and no cars were on the streets because they hadn't been plowed yet. By the time we reached town, we were beaten up fairly well by the storm, and we decided it was probably a good idea to rest and recover in the firehouse, which was only a couple of hundred yards up the block.

We got inside, appearing as living snowmen, and brushed ourselves off a little before talking to one of the volunteer firemen that was on desk duty. It was obvious that the third door inside parking space was empty. "Where's the new engine?" I asked.

"Down at the taxi office. Roddy and a couple other guys are standing guard in front of the building. There's a gas leak inside, and they're waiting for the gas company to show up." Jerry and I just looked at each other, knowing that the taxi office was our next destination. After bundling up again in our hats, coats, gloves, and goggles, we headed back out again into the raging storm, and ten minutes later, we turned the corner to the taxi office across the street from the train station.

There in front of us was the new fire truck parked in the middle of the street, in front of the old two-story wood building that housed the taxi office and a closed bar next door. We walked over and briefly spoke with the three firemen milling about in the street, before going over to look inside the huge storefront window of the waiting room. At the moment Jerry and I walked over to stand five feet in front of the giant plate glass window, looking inside the waiting room with a dozen chairs and a desk in the middle with an old-style black rotary phone sitting on top, the phone rang. Also, at that split second, one of the firemen was telling us, "Boys, you really shouldn't—"

Instantly, the building exploded with a massive ball of flames shooting out the front of the building, blowing us up, sending us airborne through the blizzard, with a hard landing forty to fifty feet across the street, before tumbling and sliding to a stop in the two to three feet deep snow. The landing hurt more than the blast!

After recomposing my scrambled brain, I checked to see if all my body parts were still attached. With a moment of internal silence, other than the nearby roaring inferno, both of us peered up out of the snow at about the same time, while looking around for each other. I hollered, "You OK?"

"I think so!" was Jerry's response, who landed about fifteen feet behind me.

"Me too!" I answered.

"Run!" he yelled.

As I rolled over in the snow to look back, I saw that a high-voltage power line had fallen, with the end of the bare wire causing massive sparks and welding itself to the back platform of the fire truck. Roddy jumped inside the cab, put it in gear and floored it, breaking the wire loose while the huge truck momentarily roared off slowly with the engine wailing and wheels spinning, and then it slid sideways on the snow-packed street before coming to a stop. With the entire building engulfed in fire, and flames shooting out what was left of the roof, I took Jerry's advice, and we retreated to the corner to watch the inferno, while checking ourselves in disbelief that we were both still alive. Roddy radioed for help, and the firehouse horns began blaring nonstop, but the storm substantially impeded the response because many volunteer firemen were unable to get to the firehouse. The fire raged through a half block of buildings before it was brought under control later that afternoon. Thanks for those goggles, Mom and Dad! Jerry and I continued to pick little pieces of glass out of our clothes for the rest of the day.

Or how about knowing where there would be a car accident? I thought, "Neat, I'll just go there now and watch it happen." The first couple of incidents were cool to watch, but then the problem was that I would be awakened in the middle of the night and be told to get dressed, sneak out of the house, and go wait at the corner. So that's what I did and waited for fifteen minutes with no cars in sight, at 2:30 a.m. in the middle of the night. The last time I did that, I went to the wrong corner, and the cars crashed six blocks away, so forget it—I'm going back to bed, and maybe I'll go see a shrink next week. Wait! There're headlights! A car is coming from a mile away, but where is the other car? Poof! Another car appeared coming up the cross-street, and yup—*crash!* A pickup truck ran the stop sign across the street from where I was standing and crashed broadside into the other car, a Volkswagen with two girls. I saw the lights go on inside the corner house as I ran over to the VW, where I offered comforting words and assurance to them that help was on the way. Both crying girls were stuck inside their car and in shock. Then I heard sirens coming from whoever called for help, so I knew I had to get out of sight before the first cops showed up, or I would have some explaining to do as to why I was there. While running away, I passed the driver's side of the pickup, realized he was drunk, cursed at him, and disappeared into the night. It wasn't until later in life that I realized I was awakened and sent to the car accident for the primary purpose to verbally comfort the victims after the crash.

Another good premonition was walking home from high school one afternoon with Tony. We both lived a few blocks from each other, about a mile and a half from the high school, and we got out of class around the same time. Rather than wait two hours for the bus, we usually walked home, with our common route through the village. "Hey, let's get a soda at the stationery store," I said.

"What?" he replied.

"Something is going to happen in town, so let's go watch."

"What's gonna happen?"

"I'm not sure, but I want to see it, so walk faster."

Of course, as a teenager, Tony said, "You're just freakin' crazy."

"I know, but come on," I answered.

So we walked quick and got to the stationery store across the street from the bank in town, around ten minutes before 3:00 p.m. We were standing on the sidewalk, leaning on a tree near the curb while drinking our sodas, when Tony looked at me and said, "So?" There was nothing going on, other than a typical lazy afternoon in the village.

"What time is it?" I asked.

He checked his watch, looked at me with a bit of bewilderment, and said, "It's three o'clock, and I'm going home."

At that moment, a loud banging noise caught our attention from directly across the street. There was a guy locked inside the bank, kicking out the glass of the front door. He crawled out and stood up with a brown paper bag in one hand and a gun in the other. At that exact moment, a police car slowly drove by on routine patrol down our narrow two-lane main street. The driver saw the bank robber, stopped his patrol car fifteen feet directly in front of us, jumped out, and hollered, "Stop or I'll shoot!" The robber pointed the gun at the cop, which was also straight at us, and *bam!* The cop shot the guy right there on the sidewalk in front of the bank. We ran across the street laughing so hard, thinking that couldn't be real and that it must be a movie or something, so where were the cameras? Then we realized it wasn't so funny as we stood hovering over him, because the man wasn't moving. When a crowd began to grow around the guy lying there on the sidewalk, the cop told everyone to move back, and within minutes, a bunch more cop cars showed up. Lesson learned? If you're going to rob a bank, make sure you get out before the security guard locks the door at closing time!

I was fifteen years old and was hanging out with my friends one night down near the bay. I had a feeling that I just needed to leave, as it was time to go home right then. After saying good night and hopping on my bicycle, I was ready for the three-mile ride back home that evening and took my normal route through quiet residential neighborhoods. With only a few blocks to go, I saw light emitting out to the driveway from an open garage door up the street on the right. *Hmmm, that's unusual,* I thought, so, of course, I looked in while riding past. There I saw a woman hanging by a rope from the rafters with a noose around her neck and her feet dangling a few feet above the concrete floor. Instantly, with the superpower of survival mode kicking me in gear, I ran up the half stairway to the landing where she had jumped off, pulled out my six-inch Boy Scout knife from my boot, hung by one arm from the rafter, and cut her down with the other. She fell to the floor like a sack of potatoes, coughing and then rubbing her neck, after which she then stood up and began to curse at me. Just then, as she was cussing and pointing her finger in my face, about to punch me, a car pulled up in the driveway with a guy getting out and asking, "What's going on?" I pointed to the rope tied to the rafter while she stood with the noose piece in her hand that I had just cut. I said, "Ask her," and then got back on my bike and left. This is another example that timing really is everything, and we are all connected but need to learn how to recognize it.

One beautiful summer afternoon when I was about eighteen, while lying with my girlfriend on our beach blanket near the water's edge, I had dozed off after a light lunch. The waves on that particular day were huge, due to an offshore hurricane about two or three days away causing a rough surf with powerful riptides. From a sound

11

sleep, while gently waking me, Mary said, "Honey, there's a guy out there drowning, and nobody is helping him. Look! Everybody is watching him drown, all these people up and down the beach here [there were thousands of people], and he's been yelling help for a long time! Can you help him? No, I don't think you should because it's just too rough, and he's way too far out. That's why nobody is going in after him."

Whoa, this is a big one, I thought, *but let's do it or else this guy dies right here right now.* I saw him go under the water again and again. I said, "I'm going in, but you have to go right now, fast, and tell the lifeguards they have to come help me too because I can't do this by myself!"

"I love you," she said and took off running.

"Could somebody help her find a lifeguard?" I hollered to the crowd near me before I dove into the waves. I was wondering if anyone was going to help her get the lifeguards, and when I looked back, I saw a couple of guys running with her. Of course, what guy wouldn't follow a real cute blond chick in a bikini when her boyfriend was about to drown?

After a brutal attack on the waves, I finally reached him way, way out, a couple of hundred yards off the beach. He was totally exhausted, as I was, and in panic. After ripping his arm off from around my throat, I told him that help was coming, and all we had to do to survive was stay above water for five minutes more and we would both get to live. There was other conversation, redacted for foul language. We both eventually calmed down. Help arrived and got us both back to the beach, and they pumped his stomach out while I lay collapsed at the water's edge. Of course, Mary was there with me and then helped me back to our blanket. At various times for an hour afterward, a dozen people came to me expressing their appreciation and thankfulness and giving me their blessings. Although I never saw the guy again, an intuitive medium told me during a reading about twenty-five years afterward that his mother was coming through, and she always wanted me to know the appreciation, love, and gratitude she had for me for saving her son's life. The intuitive and I hardly knew each other, and she had absolutely no prior knowledge of the event. That's pretty cool. Talk about paying it forward. Thank you, God!

Due to my slightly taller physical size compared to most, I had many friends and acquaintances a few years older than myself, several of whom went off to Vietnam and never came back. In our town with lots of motorheads, there were a half-dozen junkyards, one of which was built up and owned by two friends that had fabricated themselves a huge, powerful car crusher. While we were hanging around the junkyard office chewin' the fat over a few beers on a late Friday afternoon, up drove a big black Lincoln with three men in trench coats who got out and entered the office.

"Who owns this place?" belted out the first big gorilla.

As we all looked at each other and sank in our chairs, Billy finally answered, "I do."

Then they told the other few of us to get the hell out of there. As we left, we were all thinking the same thing: "Bye-bye, Billy." The next day I saw Billy in town, where he told me they gave him five hundred dollars and ordered him to teach them how to operate the crusher. Before closing the yard that afternoon, he had to load the crusher with a car ready to compress, and then give them the keys to the gate, while being told that if he returned to the yard before Monday morning, he would be put in the crusher. Checking in with Billy the following week, he showed me the crusher with the dried floor stain from a large pool of blood.

Hanging around our town's small marina was a meeting place to pass time and keep up on local news with the "boys." A good acquaintance of mine owned a delicatessen nearby, where Ralph always made a great sandwich. He was a socially outgoing and likable kind of guy, with a good business. One day I went in to buy a sandwich to take out fishing with my buddies, who were waiting at the dock.

After paying him for my sandwich while no one else was in the store, Ralph said, "Jimmy, eat this," while sticking a toothpick into a plate of a few small, bite-sized chunks of gray meat.

"What is it, Ralph?"

"Don't worry, just eat it, and someday you will thank me for it."

"OK, thanks," I said, as I chewed the unknown substance on my way out the door.

A week later, I asked him if that bite of different-tasting meat was what I thought.

"Yes, because knowing what it tastes like now will help you later in life," he said.

I asked him to explain, as I couldn't understand how or why.

"Someday, you will be in a place or situation where it will be served to you as a message," he continued. "It's cooked, has just a little seasoning, and won't physically hurt you or get you sick or anything like that. Nothing will happen to you; it's like any other meat in your stomach, like roast beef, but it just tastes different."

I told him, "Fine, just don't put any more on my sandwich!" and we both laughed. Little did I know at the time, at some point in my future, that I would have a thankful flashback to that experience.

Life as a teenager on Long Island was fun to a certain extent, but the fact of living on an island with a million people never sat well with me, and it was getting old, especially since you had to pay to get off the island by car, train, bus, or plane. Although after high school I began attending community college, I couldn't tolerate being forced to retain any more useless information. Why was I having these thoughts and feelings when none of my friends were thinking this way? I began spending more time in bars than in the library studying.

Drinking a Friday-night beer at an old-time local bar with a full house and no available seats, the bartender cut off the guy sitting next to me, Jamie.

"You've had enough; you're done. I'm not serving you any more tonight," she said.

He was really mad, cursed at her, and said, "I'll be back," while he turned and sternly told me, "Don't let nobody take my seat, you understand?" and walked out the door.

It was a bit of a rough place, and I knew that I had to defend the seat, since Jamie's nickname was "Animal." He could bench-press 350 pounds and was a wild man, although generally a regular, very nice guy when he wasn't drinking. His seat had better be there when he got back, or I knew I would be in trouble.

Five minutes later, Jamie came back inside. He sat down, looked at me and said, "Don't worry, Jimmy, you'll be OK, just don't go nowhere," and he pulled a .357 Magnum pistol out of his pants.

While he pointed it at the bartender, who started screaming, I asked him, "Sure you wanna do that?"

He said, "No, I ain't gonna hurt nobody, I'm just tired of her bullshit in this place." And then he started shooting the bottles of whiskey off the backbar like an arcade duck shoot with mirrors and bottles exploding and glass flying everywhere. Actually, at the time, I thought it was pretty awesome entertainment. Everybody scattered, and Jamie asked, "Would you stay here for a few minutes with me?" Obviously, this guy needed some help, so I said, "Sure, let's have a beer!"

He answered, "Yeah, good idea, cause it's probably gonna be the last one I'll have for a while. They don't serve no beer where I'm going." We both laughed.

I reached over the bar and drew a couple beers from the beer tap spigot in front of us and passed one to him. We knew the cops were going to be there real soon, so we just talked quietly while drinking our beer, and then, of course, the place was surrounded with police looking in the windows. We talked for a couple minutes more while he was calming down, and then he decided to go outside peacefully, so he wouldn't get shot, saying he would probably only get six months or so.

"Come out with your hands up!" we heard. I negotiated a peaceful outcome, he left the pistol on the bar, no more shots were fired,

I went outside, and Jamie went off first to jail, and then to the state mental institution. I went home thinking to myself that if I stayed there, I was going to end up the same way, so I needed to get out of that place and go away, far away.

Lacking in-depth understanding or answers to my discomfort, I thought that talking to a shrink would help set me straight, but when I did, he didn't believe what I told him. He was just trying to figure out why I made up these crazy stories. *How is such a narrow-minded, shallow jerk of a person going to help me?* I thought. I realized that he couldn't, when all he could say was, "Make sure you get help later in life when they will have more modern drugs to help you, or you will most likely end up in one of three places: a hospital, prison, or a cemetery. Why don't you go take a couple aspirin and get some rest?" he said. "You'll probably feel better tomorrow."

Of course, I wanted to slap him hard, for being such an incompetent moron and wasting my time. I was really pissed, and to myself I just thought, *You freakin' idiot; I'm not going to either one of those three places, you worthless jackass.* And then I got up and walked out. So what's a young man to do? I dropped out of college, bought a motorcycle, and headed out West on vacation in July. I had the address of a friend in Colorado, where I eventually ended up. It turned into a very, very long vacation.

CHANGE OF DIRECTION

Living in campgrounds and rest areas was a whole new concept of the lifestyle to which I had become accustomed. All of a sudden, survival became my priority, being around really bad people living on the road, outrunning tornadoes on my motorcycle, seeing bad wrecks on the highway, and lots of new phenomena to which I needed to rapidly adjust. Thank God, growing up in New York and having been a Boy Scout gave me quick-witted survival benefits that were on call when necessary. I visited lots of neat and interesting places, riding down through Texas, through the summer desert over to the Grand Canyon, and then up into the Colorado mountains. A few experiences are mentioned here below.

Strolling through some boulders in a remote Texas canyon one hot afternoon, I suddenly heard a rattlesnake's rattlers shaking, so I instantly rerouted my path down through the riverbed. Wandering along, splashing my feet in a few inches of water, all of a sudden, I began sinking in quicksand, and before I could even think straight, I was already down past my knees, unable to escape, in sheer panic, slowly sinking. I instantly had a flashback recall to the page in my Boy Scout manual that I had read one day ten years earlier. After mentally locating the page heading of "Quicksand" and rereading the paragraph with escape instructions, word for word (in one to two seconds), I threw myself on my back, doing a backstroke, and got myself out. Shaken from the event, I turned around and went back to my campsite, where I took a nice siesta under a shade tree. I realized that something unexplainable by me had just occurred. Some type of intervention instantly took over my brain, something that I had never experienced before. The Boy Scout manual instructions seemed to have been presented to me without thinking and was different than memory, but I can't explain it. Hello, Guides! Thank you, God!

I continued on my journey and made my way to the Grand Canyon, enjoying the scenery on a peaceful and relaxing ride after my near-death episode a couple days before. I spent the following few days exploring a small part of the most enormous hole in the ground that I had ever seen, and I wrote several postcards while sitting in a dinosaur footprint on the precipice of a cliff overlooking the spectacularly scenic canyon. The sweeping view from my cliffside perch was captivating and brought to my attention some powerful (and previously unknown-to-me) energies of what I thought to be of earthly origin. There was something different about that place, other than the expansive scenery, but I just couldn't put my finger on it. Fast-forward forty years to learn that this day's "energy" has been with me all my life. I could have "connected" at the time, but

I wasn't listening because intuitive and spiritual understanding escaped me.

Several hours after leaving the canyon on a brutally hot day in northern Arizona, I spotted two Harleys with Texas plates in front of a desert bar, so I stopped in for a beer, where I met Gary and Dilbert, both my size, from Corpus Christi. We exchanged some short road-travel banter, which gave me a funny feeling about them, but Dilbert seemed like a generally decent kind of guy.

Big and mean, with his Texas drawl, Gary asked "Where're you headed?"

"Colorado," I replied.

His firm response was, "Good. Then you're ridin' with us. You ready?"

"Finish your beer," I said, as I polished off mine and headed for the door. We rode for the afternoon, stopped a couple of times for gas, and went into a diner around suppertime. There, just as we finished our meals, while Gary was in the restroom, Dilbert told me that Gary had just killed a man in a highway rest area bathroom the day before.

"All I heard was a couple gunshots, Jimmy. Then Gary walked outside, stopped in front of the trash can, took money out of a wallet and put it in his pocket, and then threw the wallet in the trash can, and said, 'Let's go.' Gary says he ain't goin' back to prison, and he'll kill anyone that gets in his way, including me if I try to leave him, so be careful, Jimmy."

Gary walked out of the bathroom and headed straight to the front door of the diner and left without paying. I left my money on the table and ran out when the waitress started hollering to her coworker, "Ethel, call the police!" The three of us hopped on our bikes and hauled ass. I knew I could outride these guys' Harleys with my 650 Triumph Bonneville on a Colorado mountain road any day, so I figured then was the time to make my escape. I left them in the dust, and after a few miles, I was about a quarter mile ahead of them when I saw a sign pointing to a four-wheel drive National

Forest road. I hit the brakes and turned up into the forest, but unfortunately, one of them saw my tail end just as they rounded the long curve behind me, so they followed me up through the trees on the rough four-wheel-drive road.

After finding a nice level area, we pitched our tents and made camp, while no one said a word. We had a nice spot along a small creek a few miles up in the forest, and since darkness was near, I was determined to get a fire going. I wandered off into the trees twenty or thirty yards to gather firewood, came back with an armload, and dropped it nearby my tent, and I went back for more. With the second armload, I did the same thing, and when I went back for more, Gary arrogantly hollered, "What the hell do ya need all *that* for?" I instantly realized that Gary had never spent much time in the mountains, nor probably was he ever a Boy Scout.

"It's going to be a long night," I said.

GARY. What the hell are you talkin' about! What 'r you gonna do, sit up all night a keep the fire goin'?

ME. I just might do that, Gary.

GARY. (*Approaching me and blocking my path*) You tell me right now what the hell you're doin'!

ME. Well, Gary, it's like this: a picture is worth a thousand words, right, so why don't you follow me over here so I can show you something. (*I turned and walked around him.*)

He followed me over to the edge of the clearing by the trees, where I pointed to the ground and said nothing. Gary just stood there, looking at the biggest pile of bear crap that you, I, or he has ever seen.

GARY. What the hell is that?

ME. That's from a bear, Gary, a really *big* bear, Gary.

GARY. How do you know it's a bear?

ME. 'Cause it looks real fresh to me, and I don't think there's any man alive big enough to leave a pile like that. I know that when I go, my pile is only a quarter size of that one. *(I poked a stick into it.)*

He thought about it, looked at me, and realized he and I were both about the same size. Gary was beginning to freak out and began to sweat, as if in fear for his life. The change in his disposition was like night and day, as if he had just been introduced to his worst nightmare. I knew then it was an opportunity to capitalize on his phobia to create a situation allowing for my escape, but realized I had to wait until morning. He asked me a few more questions until I explained to him that it was best we keep a fire burning all night to keep the bears away. He quickly began scavenging firewood and helped me get the fire going, which we built directly in between our opposing tents ten yards apart. I retrieved a long, skinny pole to continue occasionally pushing it into the fire all night, for a fire weapon at-the-ready in case any wandering visitors came into camp. I got one for Gary, too, to make sure he was occupied and had something to do, instead of fall asleep. The fear in Gary reminded me of my first night sleeping in a tent at Boy Scout camp. I was so scared that I didn't sleep a wink all night long. Lying in my tent on my sleeping bag, I knew that he wasn't going to sleep that night, either, so I peacefully passed out exhausted from a long day on the road. I knew I had an up-all-night security guard watching for bears.

When I woke up early at the crack of daylight, all I heard was two guys snoring away in their tent in front of a dwindling fire. I quietly rolled up my pup tent and sleeping bag and tied them on to my prepositioned bike headed down the trail. I hopped on, fired it up, hollered, "See ya!" and took off. Thank you, God. Little did I know at the time, this would be only my first direct experience crossing paths with a killer.

With road life, the people I met were other than the kind of those whose lifestyle that I was comfortable being around. My objective quickly refocused, with a sense of urgency to reach my buddy's place in Denver without delay. Less dillydallying on the highway and a more resolute itinerary became my new priority.

After my escape from the last two boneheads, I found two more replacements the next day, when I rode with two guys from California who were overly proud of their brand-new shiny Hondas. They wanted to show me how much better they could outride me with their new bikes, while we raced a dangerous cliffside mountain road with no guardrails, until one of them took a turn too wide and smacked head-on into an oncoming car. He flew up over the car and landed in the boulders alongside the road, while I saw in my rear-view mirror that his bike ricocheted off the car, crossed the road behind me, and disappeared out of sight. With long hair, a New Jersey license plate on my bike, and the cops to be there shortly, I didn't hang around to answer potential questions of where I had been the day before.

Finally, I made it to Denver and crashed on my buddy's couch for a couple weeks, where I had time to recollect and mentally process my recent experiences. I took various construction jobs; rented my own place; hung around bars, bikers, and billiard players; witnessed a couple of gun fights/shoot-outs; and generally floundered along until I recognized messages telling me to get creative and change my life. I played billiards well and always seemed to get "the extra roll" that skewed the game in my favor, but it was never enough to pay the bills.

Ignoring occasional intuitive messages, I quickly deteriorated to homelessness and ended up in a creek-side camp living in a re-frigerator box among other brilliant people. As long as the weather was nice, it was survivable, since humans are the most adaptable creatures on the planet, right? One early morning just after sunrise, someone kicked my box and said, "Get the hell outta that box, dirtbag."

Wondering who it was, I responded, "You better be big, or have a gun, 'cause I'm coming out!" As I poked my head out, I saw two men in suits standing in front of me.

One said, "We're both big, and we both have guns; what else do you want to know?" Without saying another word, I got up and handed them my ID when they asked for it. They were investigating a guy found murdered three hundred yards down the riverbank. After ten minutes of questioning me, they declined my request to take me for coffee and a doughnut but advised me that if I stayed there, I would most likely end up in one of three places; a hospital, prison, or a cemetery. Gee, seems that I had heard that somewhere before, and I certainly wasn't enthused about hearing it a second time.

Totally depleted and without hope, I deeply meditated that afternoon, calling on Jesus to intervene in my existential crises, or I needed to check out and start over again. *This life must be a mistake,* I thought. *But if not, and you're the real deal, show me, so we can work together and get with the program, or I'm outta here, and you can restart me all over again, because this is bullshit.*

I figured Jesus would probably kill me anyway just for talking to Him like that and save me the trouble of doing it myself. The following morning, a guy walked into camp just after sunrise, stood in front of my box, and asked, "Anybody here want to work today? I need three guys." I jumped up, and two minutes later, we were on our way to a concrete job. I then got hired on full time, rented a room, and went to night school at a local community college, taking a class in income tax preparation. I then used those skills to prepare taxes for a few months at night and on weekends to generate some extra cash. My life turned on a dime, and a new reality offered me a way to reintegrate into society.

A NEW ROAD AHEAD

Neighbors and new friends were spiritually aware, and while visiting with new acquaintances one afternoon, I was introduced to seances and Spirits, which were new to me. "Come meet Sam," my new friend suggested. OK. So upstairs to the bedroom we went. We sat on the end of the bed, and Samantha began to call her Spirit friend to appear in her mirror. After fifteen minutes without a response, we returned to the living room downstairs, where our other friends were visiting and talking. I sat on the couch next to an end table where there were a few items such as an ashtray, lighter, scissors, roll of tape, and a ruler. When others in the room asked if I had the opportunity to meet Sam, I sarcastically replied, "I think Sam only exists in someone's head." Apparently, Sam didn't like my response since everything on the end table was instantly swept off the tabletop onto the floor! In a perfectly lighted room, no one nearby, along a wall nowhere near a window, and my hands were in my lap! Whoa! Sorry, Sam! That introduced me to a whole new realm of Spirit entities. Then renting an apartment with my new girlfriend a few months later in another old house a few blocks from Sam, Jeannie and I also had Spirit visitors and nonphysical residents that frequently turned on the radio, bathtub water, or lights, or turned off the television. Interesting.

On weekends, a group of friends and I would hike with our camping gear twenty minutes up the side of a mountain and sneak in a side entrance between the boulders into an enormous cave system. It stretched for miles under the mountain, where you could walk all afternoon without passing anyone else, even when twenty to thirty others were in the cave at the same time. On the way to one of our weekend expeditions, we stopped at Ben's house to pick him up last because he lived closest to the cave. With a carload of guys in my car, and a carload directly behind me, I drove up to the house on the wrong side of the street, jumped out, ran up to, and firmly knocked on the door.

His girlfriend opened the door, looked at me weirdly, and said, "Benny won't wake up."

So I replied, "Get his lazy ass up. Where is he?" and she motioned for me to come in the front door while pointing to the couch. The moment that I first saw him, I knew something was critically wrong. I went over to the couch hollering at him even though he was out cold, shook him, slapped him, and then I saw the needle, torch lighter, baggie of white powder, and a big piece of rubber strap on the end table. It quickly set in, what none of us friends knew before then: he was using hard drugs. The rest of us only smoked pot (as far as I knew) because I, like other friends, never liked any of that chemical stuff. I found no pulse in him. He was cold, and then I hollered at his strung-out girlfriend to call an ambulance, because "I think he's effing dead! Call! Now!"

She slowly responded in a spaced-out tone, "That's what I was thinking too." I dialed 911 from the wall phone, handed it to her, and told her to speak her address into the phone, as I flew out the front door, mentally freaking out while hollering, "Ben's not coming!" I jumped in the car and hauled butt outta there, with the other guys close behind. When we got to the cave, I explained, and we all said a prayer for him. The next day, we found out that he was officially pronounced dead shortly after we left his house.

After Jeannie went back to California, I took a bus back to New York to visit for a week. Since I had more time than money, I hitch-hiked my way back to Colorado, and, of course, met lots of interesting people on the road. Outside of Oklahoma City, two guys around my age stopped their van at the entrance ramp to the freeway where I had my thumb out, and I hopped in the back. After some small talk, I sensed something odd about those guys, but I couldn't ascertain exactly what it was. We talked briefly, until ten minutes later, we saw a single girl hitching on the side of the freeway and stopped to pick her up. She got in, handing me her backpack first, and then climbed in the back of the van with me.

We drove about fifteen miles when the driver and his buddy began talking quietly and whispered among themselves, until I heard one of them say, "Hey there's a rest area comin' up. Pull in there, off to the side."

As the driver parked off to the side at the end of the parking area away from other cars, the driver's buddy said, "I'm first," and jumped in the back with us while he told the girl it would be easier for her if she cooperated. He pushed her on her back while ripping her blouse off and jumping on top of her.

At that moment, the van came to a stop. I said, "You can let me out of here because I don't want any part of this." I opened the side door, threw my bag out, and then threw her bag out.

One of the guys asked, "What are you taking her bag for?"

"Because she's coming with me," I exclaimed, while I pulled the guy off her. I threw him into the side wall of the van, then got out, taking the girl with me. The van sped off back on to the freeway, and then the girl asked an older woman from the rest area to help her. After they drove off to the bus station, I continued hitchhiking my way back to Colorado.

I fell back into my normal daily routine of working a menial job, and on weekends traveled around to various interesting places. While visiting an old historic fort in the plains of southeastern Colorado during the 1970s, out in the middle of nowhere, I learned of a nearby site where a slaughter of Indians occurred many years ago, in error. I drove out there and sat along the expansive dry riverbed, contemplating visions of the old battle, the Sand Creek Massacre. I felt a pervading sadness of many Spirits in the area. An hour later, I knocked on the door of the only house visible for miles around. During our five- or ten-minute visit, the grandson of the only nonmilitary white man to view the battle told me the story of how it all went down. Awfully sad, to say the least.

On my way home, I stopped in a local convenience store, where a woman approached me and excitingly said, "Wow, Tommy, you're out, it's great to see you!" and wanted to give me a big hug. (I was thinking, *Hmmm, she is kind of cute; go with it!*), but after a minute or two of talking, I still couldn't answer any of her questions about mutual friends, nor convince her that we had never met. She was adamant about it, got mad at me, told me to quit fooling around because it wasn't funny anymore, and then she felt very hurt, while she walked away crying and asking what happened to my brain.

Life seemed to be a continual discombobulation of strange events, so I eventually figured out that I needed to return to living in mainstream society to get a chance at having a normal life. Some type of state-recognized profession could be my bridge to return, so I decided on real estate for its timeliness, potential, and ease of licensing.

CHAPTER 2

MOVING INTO
THE MOUNTAINS

I continued returning to college classes in order to upgrade my work environment into an office setting, and I earned my real estate broker and appraisal license. After interviewing with a well-known national real estate firm, I was accepted as a sales associate trainee, so I showed up bright and cheery Monday morning to begin training with the office manager, whose desk was immediately behind mine. An hour and a half into on-the-job training, I began returning personal items back into my briefcase.

The boss asked, "What are you doing?"

"You're no different than the scumbags I used to live with under the bridge, except you've got a suit and tie. It'll be a cold day in hell before I ever work for you or anyone like you!" I authoritatively replied in his face.

As I walked over to the wall where all real estate licenses were pinned on a board, I removed my license while the boss said, "You can't do that!"

"Watch me," I replied, while my piercing eyes tried to burn a hole in his face, and with my license in hand, I headed out the door and never looked back. Working for a bloodsucking, deceptive real estate company was not in the cards for me, as I was determined to earn an honest living by providing some type of intelligent service to help society without capitalizing on someone else's expense or ignorance. So obviously a national real estate company wasn't the answer, and working for myself was the only option.

I met an older gentleman in a mountain bar one day who offered me a job selling land out on his ranch in the Colorado mountains with some other guys, including Jerry (who just got out of a Texas prison for killing his brother). Tom was wearing a ten-thousand-dollar Rolex, so I figured that I'd give it a shot. The job was fun by day, trying to find survey pins, coming across wildlife, and exploring the rugged mountain backcountry, but on weekend nights, it was a bit different. Friday nights in a one-horse mountain town two blocks long consisted of getting drunk and shooting up the countryside with our pistols. It seemed like I was working with some of the same type of guys from under the bridge again, so I began looking for another source of income to support myself.

Luke, being a nice family man, also wanted to open a small mountain real estate office like I had been contemplating, so we did just that. Timing was the worst, going into winter, but we were determined. There was a lot of slow office time that we used to trade great stories of our younger days. Mine were like running from the Pagans motorcycle gang from a Long Island gas station that I worked in at two o'clock in the morning, but his were the absolute best, especially ones about flying small planes into the Colombian jungle to meet a guy named Pablo.

Until late one morning, six unmarked police cars surrounded our little office on the highway, and a dozen men jumped out, sighting down their machine guns, rifles, and pistols at the front door while hollering for us to come out.

"You got two minutes, and then we're coming in" was hollered over their bullhorn. I was freaking out, while Luke was calm, cool, and collected. He said, "Go tell them I said hello, and ask them where they've been. Tell them I've been waiting for them, and I'll be out in a few minutes."

Standing outside in front of the door with my hands raised high, I told them there was no need to shoot because we were peaceful guys and had no weapons. "And Luke said to tell you he has been waiting for you, and he'll be out in a couple minutes." I was the intermediary, bargaining for more time before they would rush the office to come in for us. Every time they said, "You got thirty seconds," I went back in to ask my buddy if he was ready yet.

"No. Tell them I am calling my daughter in school to say good-bye. Now go back out and tell them I'm calling my wife. Now go tell them I'm going to the bathroom." It got to be ridiculous until seven to eight minutes passed, when I told them all I was quitting my job as intermediary, and they needed to quit pointing their guns at me. Then they trusted me, realized I was reasonable, and lowered their barrels. I went back in and brought Luke back out. Now I got the idea of why he used to have a lot of friends in South America and owned three planes, two fishing trawlers, a few yachts, a fleet of fast boats, and a few mansions in Florida and elsewhere. Old cool-headed Luke headed off with his new acquaintances, and with winter setting in, I closed the office for good.

Snow skiing then became an obsession for a few years, drawing me to ski forty or fifty days a season, or more, until it became less each year as work responsibilities intensified. Working with mountain real estate made for a flexible lifestyle, so praying for a foot of fresh powder overnight and clear blue skies in the morning was a frequent wish. I was unaware of anything that could surpass the feeling of free-falling a fourteen-thousand-foot mountain covered in fresh powder on an off-tourist season weekday under a clear, crisp blue sky. It was clearly addictive! The scenery was most spectacular and almost mesmerizing, with the magnificent glittering peaks in the distance. Floating down the mountainside was as close to living in God as one can get.

As I grew into my twenties, my interest in ancient history also began to emerge, and anything of prehistoric nature began to catch my attention. Having a few days of extra time, I threw my sleeping bag, pillow, and some warm clothes in the back of my Jeep Cherokee (sporty Wagoneer old-style, black, with chrome wheels and tinted windows) and headed out on the highway one morning. I followed the "dinosaur highway loop" of northwestern Colorado up into Utah, stopped at a few roadside attractions and other places of interest, and the second day found my way to my anticipated destination of Dinosaur National Monument, where I spent most of the day. The visitor's center was informative and interesting to view the fossilized remains of giant creatures that roamed so long ago, and offered one the opportunity to contemplate the vast expanse of time that had elapsed since one of their last heartbeats occurred. Heading back home was a long drive, of course, and being totally exhausted, I pulled off the highway into a rest area at around 2:00 a.m.

There was one open parking space left next to a camper in a dimly lit area, toward the end of the single row of about twenty-five parked vehicles. I pulled into the space, used the restroom, and then crawled into my sleeping bag. With my head on the pillow directly behind the driver's seat, I flipped open the rear vent window to its three-inch maximum, secured my pistol within arm's reach, and began to pass out. "Don't go to sleep," I "felt." *Wow, I guess I'm really tired*, I thought, so I rolled over on my stomach. "No, turn back over, you can't stay on your stomach," was the message, so I again rolled over onto my back, thinking that this really sucked because I was so tired and really wanted to sleep. "Get ready, sit up, and look out the window, *now*," is what I heard, so I did just that. There was a guy approaching the back of my truck from the woods across the street, while waving to another guy to come with him. He walked straight up to my side vent window near my head, where he stuck his face directly in front of the open vent to see inside. At that deadly silent moment, the six-inch barrel of my .357 Smith & Wesson quietly found its way through the window into the guy's mouth, and the sound of my cocking the trigger was deafening. He freaked out and hollered "*No!*" and took off running. I soundly slept the rest of that night and made my way home the next day after enjoying my visit to Dinosaur.

Wintertime in my hundred-year-old, dilapidated rented house (which I eventually bought) in Cripple Creek was rough but was a survivable experience cutting firewood and plowing snow to make ends meet, while cat Spirits kept me company in the house when my girlfriend was working. Limited-stakes gambling had just passed a state ballot initiative in the general election, so many new faces were showing up in our small, old, one-horse mining town with their sights set on hitting it big in the new gold rush. One day while sitting in my living room, I subtly received a message to open my reception to a higher vibrational channel of communication.

Kicked back in my chair, gazing out the living room picture window to the mountains late one snowy afternoon, I heard, "You need to go to the courthouse and look through the files. There is something there for you." *What the heck could this be?* I thought. Listening more intently, I felt the same thing a few minutes later repeat the message again, and again. So, the next morning, with a notebook and pen in my jacket pocket, I braved the blizzard and walked three blocks to the county courthouse into the assessor's office. Having been an acquaintance of my neighbor who worked in the office, I said good morning and asked to look through some of the files.

Deena asked, "What are you looking for, Jimmy?"

At a loss to explain what I was looking for, I just responded, "I'm not sure, but I'll know it when I find it."

"Well, the first six cabinets [they were four-drawer, legal size] starting here are the city, and the rest are the county," said the clerk, pointing to the double row of twenty-four legal-size file cabinets.

One folder, one property—thousands of them. I chose a drawer in the middle, took an armload of files out, put them on an old rolltop desk used by visitors, and began opening each one, one by one, armload by armload, until breaking for lunch. I found nothing that struck a bell, but I returned after lunch and continued my search. I knew I was supposed to continue looking for something but didn't know exactly what. Hundreds of files later, at a quarter to 4:00 p.m., I was told it was time to wrap it up as it was almost closing time. Feeling empty and bummed out, I put on my coat, hat, and gloves, and walked home. There was something telling me to give it up, but a more empowered gut-feeling message told me to continue until I found it. So I went back the next morning and started all over again.

Again, all morning, I repeated armload after armload, one by one until just before noon, *Jackpot! I've got it.* I felt the energy shoot through me like a weak electrical shock, along with a mental confirmation. It was a file that showed a bulk transfer list of tax deed properties. *But what's so special about this?* I wondered. I wasn't sure until I analyzed the list and found the last legal description on one page did not follow the transfer to the new page of the intended new owner. The title company clerk doing the transfer either overlooked it or probably figured it wasn't worth the paper it was written on. Understandably, as the property's legal description was something like: E5'9L5B2 Dooly Addition, 1893. In a transfer of many individual hand-typed legal descriptions, comprising dozens of acres and larger parcels with houses and barns, who cared about a five-foot-wide piece of a lot that was probably just a useless old easement on the side of a mountain somewhere that nobody wanted, and let it go at tax sale? I cared. Why? I had no idea, but I was determined to find out.

I researched the location and found it to be in a strategic location in the middle of another large property zoned for recently legalized gambling. I contacted the legal owner, who vehemently denied that it was his and insisted that I stop bothering him and wasting his time, until I offered him five hundred dollars if he would just sign and return a quit claim deed to me, and then I would go away and quit bothering him. He agreed to that. He was a lawyer. I spent the afternoon running around town acquiring the paperwork and bank check, and shipped it off express mail from the post office.

The following snowy morning, while anxiously awaiting the return of my signed deed, I drove my old F-250 snowplow pickup, chained up on all four, down to the most popular (and only) break-fast café in the old mining town for coffee with the "boys," as usual. With everything under a foot of fresh snow, the fifteen-foot flames shooting out of the chimney of an old house on the corner, with smoke coming out from underneath the shingles, caught my instant attention, and I knew the place was about to blow (been there, done that!). I saw a snow-free car parked in front on the street and survival mode kicked in again, so I downshifted and floored it with four hundred horsepower in four-wheel drive blazing across the first vacant corner lot (a shorter distance) into the front yard, and slid sideways up to the front door.

I jumped out of the truck and ran in the front door hollering, "You got a bad chimney fire, who's in here? The upstairs attic is about to burst into flames; everybody has to get out," as I ran to the back kitchen, where a young lady sat in front of the roaring woodstove fire with its door wide open.

She disturbingly answered, "The three kids I'm babysitting for are all upstairs sleeping."

"Shut the door on the woodstove and turn off the air supply *now*, then grab the kids' coats and shoes!" I tore up the stairs into the smoke-filled hall as the first five-year-old was coming out of his room, crying because his eyes hurt. "Where are the other two kids?" I asked.

He pointed to a room across the hall, where I opened the door and entered a smoke-filled room, waking and telling the kids they had to come downstairs. I took one kid, and right behind me, the babysitter took the other. As the girl bundled up the children, I told them to wait there inside the living room by the front door (the smoke was only upstairs), and to be ready to run outside into her car if the smoke got worse. I raced down to the firehouse two blocks away, where a few guys were having coffee when I got inside. A first response truck got out right away and saved the house.

After receiving back my signed deed, I recorded it with the county clerk and recorder's office and paid the past-due taxes, interest,

penalties, and fees, which totaled about $250. Bingo. This solidi-
fied my ownership position right down the middle of a valuable,
strategically located, multimillion-dollar property. Now it's time to
introduce myself to my new partner. *How exciting!* I thought.

I phoned the adjoining multimillionaire property owner in Texas
and left a message with his secretary, three times over the course
of a week. He would never call me back, probably because I left the
message that his new partner Jimmy was calling, and he just didn't
know that he had a partner named Jimmy yet. I was quite annoyed
at the inconsiderate lack of response, so what's a guy got to do to
get a return call? Call back and say, "That's OK if he doesn't call
me. Just let him know that I'm driving a bulldozer through our
property at 8:00 a.m. Friday morning. He can meet me whenever
he comes back to town. You've got my number; have a nice day,"
and hang up the phone. Twenty minutes later, I had a screaming
maniac call me. I explained everything to him; of course, he wasn't
happy at all to learn that I owned a small strip of land smack down
the middle of his newly proposed $15 million casino site. I told him
to call me when he got back to town so he could buy me a corned
beef sandwich on rye, with spicy mustard, and get to know the fine
hardworking man who was then his new partner.

A couple of weeks later, Mr. MBA came to town, and we had
lunch. Since the property was located one short block from Main
Street, we came to agreement to build a large parking lot that I
ran. I also had a half-dozen other parking lots in town that I had
creatively acquired, built, and ran for several years. I didn't believe
in gambling, though, so I never put any money into a slot machine,
except after three years, I finally broke down and put in a one-dollar
coin while walking out of a casino after having lunch one day. Ding-
ding-ding: $2,500, thank you very much! As the new casinos in town
started making money (obviously not from me), they all bought me
out of my parking lots. I sold my house and moved to Arizona with
my new girlfriend and her two boys, whose natural dad had taken

his own life a couple years prior. I didn't realize at the time the extraordinary challenge that I had undertaken.

A higher authority told me I needed to raise the boys, though, and since I was turning forty at the time, it was a bit late to start with babies of my own. So, poof, instant family! Off we went to Arizona, living the American dream with the boat, motor home, Jet Skis, vacations, monthly trips to Vegas, and all the rest that comes along with a big party lifestyle. Moving into the desert was a major lifetime mistake for me, though, as it was contrary to any style of living that I had previously experienced, nor did I have any desire to adapt to an environment in which I felt no natural connection. It was a way out of the mountains as well, but the culture repulsed me to the bone, even though I thought that maybe I would assimilate. At the time, I didn't realize that keeping busy by building spec houses and playing with all the toys only suppressed my underlying distaste for living in the desert. Party lifestyle as it was, the boys' education was primary though, and today their engineering and finance degrees serve them well. As I look back, I realize the lessons I learned from Lenny and Leo, about life and myself, were among the most profound positive influences to benefit the core of my being, making me a better person for the remainder of my life.

In 2005, when my mom passed away, I flew back to the same cemetery in New York a week later when my uncle died four days after burying my mother, to return home and have my ex tell me three days later, "I found another place, and I'll be moving out the end of the week." Whoa! The party was over. Of course, I went into an emotional tailspin for a while, but I hired the finest professional team of psychiatrists, psychotherapists, and spiritual advisors to properly advise, and help me; I had daily appointments with Dr. Jack Daniels, Dr. Johnnie Walker, Professor Jim Beam, Reverend Don Julio, and, of course, my old friend, Professor Puffsky. But after a few months, I realized they weren't helping me at all, so when they showed up for work at my home office around noon one day, I fired them all and kicked them out of my house. The feeling was familiar and reminded me of a couple of other periods in my life when I was at a complete loss to figure out what to do. Maybe I just needed to relax some more, as I knew this was quite a shock to both my mental and physical body. Little did I know at the time, that series of events would cause me to be reborn by the most incredibly powerful change to benefit my life, that I could ever imagine in my wildest dreams!

CHAPTER 3

TURN OFF
THE TELEVISION

I thought maybe that traveling for a while would give me some relaxed time to figure out what I wanted to do when I grew up, so having an interest in ancient Mayan culture for many years, I began reading maps and travel magazines. While kicked back on the couch studying a map of the Baja and Mexico mainland, I decided to go fishing for a few weeks. I packed up some gear, hopped in my pickup with a fistful of fifties, and took off to visit a friend that had permanently rented a vacation house in a small village on the Sea of Cortez. Life for that short time was a grand party with great fishing, good food, and many new acquaintances who, like us, didn't work, and some of the scenery was out of a storybook. One problem was that a few local acquaintances were later learned to be a retired government assassin, a cartel boss, and the Las Vegas shooter of several years ago, whom I had lunch with in a beach bar one day while shooting a couple of games of billiards, along with many other similar characters. I must admit in all truthfulness, though, Tony was a true friend.

On a relaxed afternoon driving out in the countryside, I made a wrong turn and ended up at a cliffside radio tower, where I asked one of the men there for directions and then quickly left. By the surprised and uncomfortable reaction of the three men there, I suspected the small radio tower was being used to unload the "unknown" cargo of two small fishing trawlers waiting a half mile offshore. After escaping a late afternoon hijacking attempt by several coordinated unknown men a few days later, I went straight back to the house, loaded my truck, and got out of Mexico as fast as I could. Almost to the border with only ten or fifteen miles to go, flashing red and blue lights appeared on the car behind me. I pulled over, and two half-uniformed men got out of their '63 Chevy with machine guns pointed at the ground. They asked for my ID, looked me over, and let me go. I haven't been back there since.

Back home from a wild adventure, I mostly kicked back on the couch for a week at a time, which definitely was contrary to my style, but after what had just occurred, I was drawn to becoming a couch potato. More and more relaxed, I slowly returned to myself again and could actually feel the energy being replenished in my body and brain. Until one evening I turned on the six o'clock news and immediately heard something say, "Turn it off, turn off the television!" I thought there was someone in my house, so I muted the remote, got up and looked around checking all rooms, closets, and the bathrooms. There was no one other than me, so I wondered how this was possible. Returning bewildered to my chair, I increased the volume again to watch the news.

Two minutes later: "Are you going to turn off the television or not?" I heard again, loud and clear. I thought, *OK, voices in my head, I must need a shrink again,* so I ignored the repeated directive a couple of more times, hoping that the voice would go away, until I firmly thought, "No, make me."

"We can, but we won't, because we already know you'll turn it off for the reason that you want to hear what else we have to say," was the response.

Deeply worried in suspense and slightly confused, I wanted to laugh, but I hit the "off" button on the remote and asked, "Who are you? Do I know you?"

"We are a group of spiritually aligned energies that work for God. We help humans that help us help other humans." Again, thinking that I really should make an appointment with a psychiatrist to get this problem fixed, I got the reply: "Go ahead and see your psychiatrist if you want; you'll be wasting your time and money though. It won't change anything, and you will eventually end up working with us anyway. It's just a matter of time because your so-called shrink is only going to delay you, take your money, and cannot help you. *We* can help you, Jimmy, and you can help *us*."

Help you? I thought. *You don't have a body, and I can help you? You can do anything you want and make things happen from the ether; how can I possibly help you?*

"No, we can't do many things, Jimmy, that's just it. You have a body and we don't; we need you, and that's what we want to talk to you about. We have been with you a very long time and have worked together in the past, having accomplished many things; you just didn't know that it was us, and you don't remember. Working together, we can accomplish great things, and you will have an incredible (as perceived from the human dimension), wonderful, adventurous life, one that you desire, and by the way, to which you have previously agreed. In the past, we've done many things together in a subtler way, but now it's time, as you say, to go full bore."

I agreed to this?

"Yes, but save that subject for another time. We have a great life planned for you. You've been prepared for this your entire life, and now you are ready."

But I'm having a hard time with this. Can anything bad happen to me? Why should I believe you?

"We have never let you down before, nor anyone else, that is not in our nature. Of course, you have a lot of questions for us, and we will accommodate everything you need to know, and more, because you having the confidence and trust in us is absolutely crucial for our combined success of working together. But for now, we need your help."

Why me? I asked.

"Because there aren't enough humans doing this work, and everyone else is busy right now. That's why we're asking you. There is an old lady whose *palapa* caved in during a hurricane, and she needs your help. She is extra special and has always given everything of herself in her community to help other people all her life, even her own food when others had none. She would go hungry herself because she has nothing. She has no money, and there is no one else to help her."

Where does this lady live? I asked.

"Mexico," was the response.

No way! A few weeks ago I almost got killed in Mexico!

"That's because you weren't listening. Just don't go back there, and you'll be fine. Go someplace different, far away from there to the opposite side of the country; you'll get to make new friends, go fishing, and enjoy a nice beach."

I thought, *How am I supposed to find a lady in Mexico? I don't even speak Spanish!*

"We told you we will help you, so just go to the other side of the country, and you'll find her. Will you do it?"

This is hands-down just nuts, the most insane, craziest, off-the-wall thing ever, I thought. But I finally answered, *Yes, OK, I'll do it.*

"Good, we will leave you now to absorb this, and we will return when we think you are ready to move forward. You have a lot of learning to do, but know that we love you. We'll protect you; we've been with you a long time, since before you were born, and have thoroughly prepared you for this. You are ready, and we are going to be a great team and a force to be reckoned with," my Boss replied. "Don't let that last thought be misinterpreted since it will only be used when necessary." I had the feeling it was meant primarily for defense. "We will talk again soon," they said.

OK, good night, I thought.

OK, so now what? I had the superficial thought to continue as planned, seeking professional help, but then recalled my previous experience as a teenager. I realized that if I made an appointment with a shrink, there would be no fishing trip to Mexico for me. Besides, they'll probably just give me some new drugs after a really hard-sell story of disbelief to another professional nutjob with a shingle and a desk. Who the hell needs that when I can smoke a joint? With a couple shots of Jack Daniels, I can put my brain in the same place at home on my own couch! *Maybe I'll just go take a couple of aspirin, go to bed, and I'll feel better in the morning*, I thought.

Upon my awakening the next morning, I felt and heard strong confirmation and validity of my experience the previous night. After allowing the new thought-communication incident to settle in, I knew it was the real deal, so I started planning. What's the drawback if I don't find this lady in Mexico? I get to go on a neat vacation, have a few beers on a nice beach, go fishing, and also if I don't locate this particular lady, I'll have a great story to tell a shrink when I get back! Two days later, I received confirmation, again from my Guides, to continue as planned. It's time and it's a *go*, so I made my plane reservation, began tying up loose ends, and prepared to take off for a few weeks. A week later, I was on a plane with $5,000 in my pocket, headed to a place I had previously been to once before: Cancun. Hearing twice "the opposite side of the country" determined my direction.

After arriving at the airport with no idea where to go, I went outside and slowly walked past a line of twenty parked buses. I spotted one with a sign displaying "Playa del Carmen," and thought that would be a good place to start, so when the driver, standing in front of the bus door, asked, "Playa?"

I said, "Sure, how much?" I paid ten dollars, got a ticket, and boarded the bus. An hour later, we arrived at the bus station in the middle of town, and I began my walk down main street in search of my new temporary home. After a dozen blocks, I thought, *Neat, this will work!* A block from the beach with lots of bars, restaurants, and tourist shops. *Looks like as good of a place as any to be stuck*, I thought. There was a sign, Rooms for Rent, right there over a restaurant, with a hip open-air bar and good music across the street. *I'm home.* So

I rented a room and went upstairs, sat on the end of the bed, and looked in the mirror. That's when it all set in. This is the craziest thing I've ever done, and I couldn't even talk to myself, so I changed my shirt and shoes and went downstairs to the bar across the street.

Hanging around, having typical tourist chat while watching a soccer game, I met Christina, who could see dead people and read energy signatures, especially those of murderers. We had lots to talk about. My first new friend in my kind of place! (Over the following several months, we occasionally walked in the evening down the main street, among multiple thousands of other strolling tourists, identifying the aura signatures of killers and assassins. When one of us said to the other, "Cross," that just meant there was one coming our direction on our side of the street). She said the proportion of bad people to good was normal, as compared to most other cities.

Waking up the following morning, I realized it was time to go to work. I had to find this old lady. Where did I even begin? I took a local bus to the outskirts of town at the edge of jungle and started walking and asking people if they spoke English, and if they knew this lady I was looking for. Of course, when they asked me her name or where she lived and I said I didn't know, they just thought I was one more totally wacky tourist. This made things extremely difficult, but I knew I had to persist and just figure it out. I walked about fifteen miles that hot day, and returned to my hotel completely exhausted. After a short rest, I went back downstairs across the street for a burger and a beer. I saw Christina again, and later that evening we enjoyed a glass of wine together while I told her about my day.

Her parting words to me that early evening were, "You need to rent a motor scooter tomorrow, that will probably help you find her."

"I will do that. Thank you, Christina. Good night."

"Rent a scooter!" she hollered as I walked away.

Since I couldn't bear a second brutal day of walking for ten hours in the hot sun, the following morning, I rented a scooter from a rental agency around the corner from my hotel. Stopping on the outskirts of town at various places of access to outlying villages, I asked, and asked, and asked at cafés, tiendas, and bus stops, over and over. Nobody knew anything. All day I persisted, trusting and knowing that as time wore on, eventually I would find my target. By late afternoon, I was really depressed, and I returned to the busy city center around 4:00 p.m., thinking that I needed to reformulate my plan because things weren't working out too well. Driving my scooter in traffic with only three blocks more to reach my hotel, a sudden flash of energy penetrated my body and brain. My Guides began hollering to me, "There she is!"

"Where?" I asked. Immediately I thought, *How is this possible here in the city? So something is very wrong.*

"*Stop!* It's that blond lady across the street on the opposite corner with her back toward you! Yes, she's the one talking to that police lady; she knows the lady you are looking for! Go talk to her *now!*"

So I stopped quickly, parked my scooter, and ran across the three lanes of taxis that were aiming to run me over. Tapping the woman's shoulder from behind, I hurriedly asked, "Do you know a woman whose palapa caved in during the last hurricane? She has no money, no one will help her, she has always helped other people in the community, and now she needs help herself?"

I was expecting a yes, no, or "Screw off, buster," but she turned around and surprised me with "Who the hell are you!" with a look and demeanor of total amazement.

"I'm sorry. I thought you were someone else, an old friend; you look just like her, I apologize. *Please* forgive me," I replied.

"No! I do know someone like that! Do you want coffee or a beer? Because we have to talk," was her reply.

"Well, I've been looking for you all day, and I could really use a beer."

"Good, I was hoping you'd say that. Across the street there's a bar. Let's go!" she said. We dodged a few taxis and quickly relaxed in the air-conditioned bar.

Joanna and I visited for about a half hour, where the most important thing to her was understanding how I knew to find and talk with her. Calmly, I told her it was intuition and refrained from revealing any of the details; otherwise, she may have turned me away. She was volunteering at a small medical clinic on the edge of the jungle in a typical poor area. After revealing that I was ready to begin immediately, she wrote an address on a piece of paper and said, "Give this to a taxi driver, and come here tomorrow morning around ten, and I will introduce you to the woman you are looking for. Allow about twenty minutes to get there."

"OK, great, see you tomorrow," I answered.

Later that evening I visited with Christina, and she asked, "So did you get a scooter?"

"Yes, and I met a lady that will introduce me tomorrow morning to the lady I am looking for," I replied.

"Told ya!" She smiled and laughed at me with a big grin.

The following day, I proceeded as planned, and Joanna took me to a caved-in palapa, with an older lady named Maria sleeping in a torn hammock strung across the back corner of what was still standing of her original thatch-roof hut. The women spoke in Spanish for a couple of minutes, and then Maria got mad and started to cry. She at first thought this was a cruel joke because nobody drops out of the sky from a foreign country and appears, just to build her a new house. While discreetly showing the women my pocket's cash wad, I asked Joanna which one Maria would prefer, a new palapa or a new small cement house. "*Cemento*," was her reply. We walked off the corners, approximately five meters by eight meters, and I asked if she knew anyone looking for work. "Yes, there are two contractors down the street, and one speaks a little English." Excellent. We were introduced, and construction started the next day. After a month or two had passed, Maria told me that she communicated daily with God, Jesus, Mother Mary, and other angelic Beings. Upon completion of her new house, she disclosed meeting my mother in Spirit, and has thanked her dearly for raising me to become the person I am.

After initiating my new project, I immediately found and rented a furnished penthouse apartment on the north end of town, a block from the beach, overlooking the ocean. An awesome rooftop place it was, to recover in a hot tub with lady friends under the stars, after an overdose of recent brain damage!

Finally, my first project in a foreign country was underway in fewer than three weeks from "Turn the television off" to breaking ground. Supervising three men working daily, construction made good progress, and I was learning to speak Spanish at the same time. Dating the bookkeeper of the medical clinic not only helped me get things done at a fair price but also gave me some insight as to the inner workings of the community and their systems—certainly, nothing to be proud of.

Three months to completion and under my anticipated budget, I broke ground on a second house, rather than an extension on the existing structure, because I did not listen. Margarita was raising her two adorable grandkids whose mother, I was told, tried to sell them a couple of years prior. Also having dedicated her life in service to other people and the community as well, I realized more how blessed and special Margarita is, and that we both work for the same angelic entities. When the house was almost completed, her two adult children showed up, when I originally thought she was raising her two grandkids by herself. Although it was only a few months' detour for me, the lasting rewards made it well worthwhile, as the happiness and joy of her family will always hold a dear place in my heart, as I do in theirs.

Occasionally returning briefly to the States to pay bills and put my house up for sale, I also printed out reams of PhD thesis on string theory that I brought back to study in my rooftop hot tub in paradise. I took a strong interest in mentally correlating string theory science with Spirit, contemplating distances and nonphysical dimensions in other realities as to how they relate, and where we humans fit in to the big picture. I was determined to learn and understand who

God is, and where He and His helpers live. In the beginning of my studies, comprehension was in the 10 to 15 percent range.

After six months, my comprehension was up around 65 to 70 percent of the verbiage. Forget the math; what's the point? The equations just back up the theory of the author, and there are boards of professors to verify that stuff, so to me, the rocket-science and quantum-theory math was irrelevant. The scientific understanding helped accelerate my opening of deeper awareness and realization of the ether, directly leading to a firmer foundation of identifying and accepting higher vibration energies and alternate realities. Several highly advanced theoretical scientific concepts, places, and objects have since been shown to me while awake, and also in both meditative and dream states. Those personal experiences and disclosures have been among the most fascinating and profound occurrences in my life.

Meeting Charlie

Several months after my arrival in Playa del Carmen, I decided to take a taxi home from the supermarket one day, after I bought quite a few things that were a bit too heavy to carry for the six blocks' walk back to the penthouse. For some reason, all of a sudden, while descending the escalator with my groceries, my choosing the correct taxi became extremely important to me. Initially, when I was about to take the first one in line, I felt, "No, not this one," so I walked slowly to the second one. "No" again, and I continued to the fourth or fifth one, until I finally chose a driver that expressed a seemingly pleasant disposition; his name was Sergio.

After I loaded my groceries and gave him directions, we drove off and chatted briefly until he asked, "Would you like to meet a nice young lady?"

I annoyingly answered (foul language redacted), "All you taxi drivers are the same, selling drugs and prostitutes. I don't want anything to do with you."

He pulled the car over to the side of the road and came to an abrupt stop. While turning to me in the back seat he responded, "Jimmy, I am the Father of the Catholic church in [name of a local barrio], I am an honest man aligned with God and only said that to you because you seem to be a different kind of man."

I then took notice of the cross and beads hanging from the mirror and a Bible on the dashboard, as he took out his wallet and showed me his Catholic Priest identification card. This was really funny to me, as I would never have used the language that I did if I had known prior to opening my mouth that he was a priest. I asked why he was driving a taxi if he was a preacher. His response was, "The church congregation where I minister are very poor people, and I drive a taxi to supplement my income." I felt terrible and sincerely apologized, and I then asked why he was asking me. Sergio answered that Marcy didn't know many people because she was there visiting her father from Guatemala, who was working nearby. He said he was friends with her father, Roberto, and he would only allow her to date someone from church who was single.

So, after asking a few more questions, even though I learned my lesson with blind dates a long time ago, I agreed. Sergio said he would have her in the car when he came to pick me up at 7:00 p.m., take us to a restaurant, and then return two hours later to pick us up, and first drop me off back home before taking her home. If we wanted to exchange phone numbers, then we could, which is all exactly what occurred. We got along well. I wanted to learn better Spanish, she wanted to speak better English, and she was really cute, so I agreed to exchange phone numbers, and she called me back the next day. Over the next few weeks and months, we dated and began to see each other frequently as our relationship developed.

After two months, Marcy said to me one day, "My son likes you and wants to meet you."

"What, you have a son? How come you never told me? When I asked you, you told me that you had no kids!"

"Because I was afraid that you wouldn't like me anymore," she replied.

"How can he like me if he doesn't know me?"

She went on to explain that her son Charlie was nine years old, telepathic and quadriplegic, and he followed her in an alternate dimension when she went out, and had been pestering her multiple times a day for several weeks to allow him to meet me.

"Do you tell him everything about me?" I asked.

"No, nothing, only your name," she said. "But he knows everything about you."

"Oh no!" I laughed, while thinking that was kind of wild, so I agreed to come to their house the next day and meet him and her father, Roberto. Sergio picked me up and took me to their house the next day.

Marcy introduced us, and although we were unable to verbally communicate clearly, because Charlie slurs his words in Spanish, we had a pleasant visit, and I felt some type of inexplicable connection with him. After a half hour or so, I realized he was reading my mind, and he knew I was thinking about an outing somewhere for our next visit. I saw a vision in my mind's eye of dolphins playing in the ocean, so I asked him, "Would you like to go to the beach, Charlie?"

"No," he answered.

Again, I saw dolphins. "You just want to visit with the dolphins?" I asked.

His emotional response was a resounding yes, although at the time I wasn't entirely sure of exactly what had just happened. That was my first experience of recognizing IPP, or "Inter-Personal Projection" as I have created the term for use here, and more extensively define in a subsequent chapter.

We made plans for a few days later to travel twenty miles south to the dolphin pens in the marina harbor at Puerto Aventuras. Sergio picked us up early one morning, we went to McDonald's drive-through (Charlie's preferred five-star restaurant), and then we arrived at the harbor's dolphin pens about an hour before the tourists began their daily distraction. From the seawall at the water's edge, it was clearly obvious the dolphins were aware of Charlie's presence by their jostling each other for priority position in front of him the moment we got to the water's edge. We sat there at a picnic table for an hour, knowing he was at total peace physically visiting and telepathically communicating with his friends.

After enjoying the breeze and walking around the yachts and fishing boats for a few hours while watching the dolphins and tourists, we took a table at a dockside restaurant to have a snack. While sitting there chatting with Marcy, all of a sudden, Charlie became quite disturbed, and by his facial expression, we knew he mentally went "off" somewhere for a minute or so. After coming back to himself, he explained there had been an earthquake where people got hurt back in Guatemala. He said that all his family members and neighbors ran out of the house into the street, but everyone was OK in their neighborhood, with no damage to their house. Later that evening, the television news showed what happened, everything exactly at the time and place Charlie told us, seven hundred miles away. Marcy also confirmed that, after a phone call home that night to her family, everything occurred just as Charlie said.

Visiting the dolphins became a common outing for us, but the last time we were there, we all got kicked out because Charlie kept asking the dolphins to jump for us, and the trainers were freaked out. He thought it was extra funny that we got in trouble when a security officer told us to leave, because he really hates some of the police. Thank goodness no one else understands him when he curses at law enforcement people that he intuitively knows perpetrate injustice on society. We had a good laugh, too, when I told the security guard that he should probably go ahead and call the police because Charlie was being disorderly, causing a disturbance, and should be arrested.

The more time that Charlie and I spent together, the more I realized that I was constantly receiving telepathic messages and information from him. Whenever I had the opportunity, we practiced sending and receiving messages with each other, although we had limited time together. He would answer all kinds of questions for me to which no one else whom I knew had the answer or any knowledge of. The easiest way for him to communicate is telepathically since it is the most efficient in speed and energy. The second-easiest method is to ask him a yes or no question, because his response is quick, definite, and easy.

He told me of time-travel visits with family ancestors two to three hundred years ago, with specific names and years, later verified by the great-grandmother's book of the family tree containing hundreds of names and dates, which Charlie had never previously seen. He has the ability to transcend dimensions, both near and far, traveling in the ether between worlds, at will. Many of Charlie's friends are Spirit children living and playing in the astral on the other side of the veil. He spends much time with them and interacts more easily with Spirits, because he thinks that humans are stupid, difficult, time consuming, archaic, and frustrating for verbal communication.

The short time we spent together exponentially increased my understanding of God, interdimensional reality, and our human role within it. He explained to me many, many things, but most importantly that he works with exceptionally powerful Archangels, and that he also is a Soldier for Jesus. Charlie has been the most fascinating gift and experience in my life, since being taught by a most loving boy living in another dimension more than 50 percent of the time, is incomprehensible to most. One day he asked me if he could have my television from Florida. I answered, "So you like my TV on top of the dresser in the bedroom because it plays DVDs?"

"No, I want the big one in your living room," he said.

"Charlie, what's in my second dresser drawer underneath my bedroom television?"

"Ha ha, your underwear." That's true.

Whenever Charlie and I were out in public together, whether at the mall, marina, or beach, or strolling down a street in a tourist area, numerous people approached me to express their appreciation and sincere gratitude. Many times I was told various compliments by complete strangers: "Thank you," "You are a very special man," "God has a very special place reserved for you," "You are an angelic Being in a human body," "I can't even begin to express in words what you do," and a continued stream of compliments spoken to me from unknown people everywhere we went. Several times when our paths crossed, while near one another, older intuitive Spanish women sent me inter-personal telepathic projection (IPP) messages, explaining that they are like me, and I am like them, working for Jesus and Mother Mary. I kind of felt like those old ladies were my supervisors, and I better be on my best behavior, or I'd get a swift kick in the rear end! Most compliments came from Spanish speaking people, and very few from North Americans or Europeans.

My second construction project was nearing completion, and my lease was expiring at the same time Roberto, Marcy, and Charlie were preparing to return to Guatemala. We all sadly said goodbye, and I returned to the States feeling an empty void left by parting from Charlie. Marcy and I kept in touch via email, and Charlie frequently visited me at night in the ether. He would come to "pick me up" so we could travel and play together flying around the planet, while riding dolphins in the aqua blue green waters of open ocean along pristine, white, sandy beaches, and toured vast expanses of our planet from high above the atmosphere. They were some of the most blessed experiences of my life.

One evening he came to me in the ether and said he wanted me to join him fighting evil, on a mission for God. "Are you sure we're safe? Can we get hurt, killed, or separated from our soul somehow and then unable to get back to ourselves?" I asked.

"No, none of that. We'll be helping very powerful forces; we're just kind of like backup, but we need to help them, so come on." I didn't think I was ready, but he reassured me, and he also suggested we bring my empath buddy Jim, who lives near my condo in Florida.

We went and picked up Jim, and the three of us all fought together with many other Soldiers for Jesus. With Archangel Michael leading the charge, we fought a long battle, which seemed like all night, and destroyed much evil until we returned safely to our human bodies —I still don't totally understand it. I awoke the following morning completely wiped out and exhausted for most of the day, and since then, I continue referring to myself as a Soldier for Jesus. Receiving clear, concise, clairsentient confirmation, I know that I have fought many times since then, and I continue to do so.

Spending time with Charlie permanently expanded my personal being-awareness, and I have looked at the world through a very different lens since he has come into my life. He further propelled me into the ether, resulting in expansion of my dream state and improved understanding of spiritual concepts, telepathy, and projection, which also complemented and enhanced my interest of space science and metaphysics.

CHAPTER 4
INTO THE COSMOS

I n November 2011, I awoke one morning in a motel in Durango, Colorado, and felt the call to visit a local metaphysical bookstore. After breakfast, I drove a few miles to the store, and while I was moseying around inside wondering what I was looking for, another customer came in, and we started to chat. She told me of a planned, huge assemblage of crystal skulls in Crestone, Colorado, the next day for a special 11/11/2011 ceremony. We chatted a little before I thanked her for the information, and not giving it much thought, within a minute, I felt a powerful internal force deeply urging me to attend. I continued about my business that day, returned to the hotel, and went to bed early since I had decided to leave at 3:00 a.m. the following morning in order to arrive for the opening meditation, two hundred miles away through the mountains on the other side of the continental divide.

On my way to visit the skulls, I stopped at around 4:00 a.m. on top of Wolf Creek Pass to freeze my butt off (it was 7°F that morning) while gazing at the crisp, starlit, clear night sky. Speaking and pointing to a constellation in a region of the western sky (which I no longer recall the name of), I called and gave a command to my friends to transport and accompany me to the crystal skull ceremony later that morning. At the extension of my arm pointing up to the western sky, and moving it rapidly west to east with a firm finger pointing while hollering out my command, a brilliant star shot across the sky from horizon to horizon, rapidly following the path as if it was a direct extension of my finger. The bright shooter disappeared in the eastern sky above the San Luis Valley, where the skull ceremony was to occur later that morning. Wow, that rocked my brain! What a wild experience *that* was!

I hopped back in the car and then arrived in Crestone about three hours later with no recollection of driving for more than ten to fifteen minutes, half that time through the mountains at night. Thanks for that time-slip, guys! I got to the Dharma Ocean conference center for the opening ceremony and powerful morning meditation as planned, with the skulls. Around five hundred people were gathered in the conference hall, with dozens of large stone, glass, and crystal skulls displayed by their guardians on tables alongside the huge ceremonial drums on the center floor. It was a great day of meetings, presentations, ceremonies, and lectures, where an intense, powerful energy permeated the entire conference center all day long. The energy felt powerful enough to levitate the entire building with everyone in it, but it remained stationary the entire time I was there. Darn!

That evening, I checked in to a room nearby at the White Eagle Inn (that displayed, by the way, some of the finest metaphysical art I have ever seen) where I met Julie, Bryan, David, Donna, and Rhonda. Underneath the star-filled, clear, crisp Colorado night sky, we all shared fireside stories of extraordinary personal experiences. Dave had been to, and thoroughly described, the undersea stargate accessible through the Bermuda Triangle, and he also shared stories of other star systems. Several months prior, I had seen two massive underground explosions in the far-off distance, yet on this planet, having thought that vision might have applied to the destruction of the underground bases in Virginia and Colorado. Donna confirmed that was true, having said she felt the recent "earthquakes" were ultra-high-level destruction of the problems underground in those same places, and now just the "cleanup" will continue. We have won a long and important battle, and passing through the December 2012 shift would solidify and secure humans' dominance of the planet. The entire weekend experience was educational and spiritually fulfilling, to say the least.

Back in western Colorado several nights later, I had a brief dream of a head-on collision. The next night, I again had the same dream but more defined, having clearly seen a truck, small car, two-lane mountain road, and that the lady driver will die. In my dream state, I suggested a plan to save her life: replace the other truck with my Tahoe, she can hit me broadside in the curve, go under me (she had a low-profile car); I would flip and roll, destroying my Tahoe, but I would crawl out and walk away. Thinking that I was in no hurry, I could save her life without getting hurt, and insurance would replace my truck. Motion denied.

The following morning, I was delayed a few minutes leaving the hotel before heading up to my camp in the mountains (I was already in my truck and went back inside to the breakfast bar to get a cup of coffee for the drive). Arriving at a state patrol roadblock on the two-lane mountain road ten miles from the main highway, I asked, "What's up?"

"There's been a real bad head-on with a car and a logging truck, and there's a lady compressed in her vehicle," said the policewoman.

"How long ago did this happen?" I asked.

"About five minutes. Why?" she replied.

I then explained and took a detour. The lady, of course, died. Later that day, on my way back, I stopped at the side of the road in the same curve where the accident occurred. I meditated on it and saw that the lady was trying to pick up her cell phone off the floor from a difficult spot. There was also a dog in the car.

I returned to Arizona, where I spent much of my time cleaning and sprucing up my house, which I then put on the market for sale. After selling my house there, my Guides suggested it was time to travel farther south in the Caribbean in order to fulfill my request of assisting more people, rather than just one at a time. I packed a couple of bags, and off to Honduras I went.

HONDURAS

Finding a seemingly peaceful tourist island in the southern Caribbean, accessible off the mainland coast by air or ferryboat, I settled in and rented a condo with a pool on a nice beach. I was initially attracted by strong energy there; I just didn't know what kind of energy. After exploring the island meeting locals and ex-pats, I soon realized that all was other than what initially appeared. Much dark energy emanated from the island, partly due to mass deaths and burials from previous plagues and hurricanes. Many of the dead were buried in the yards of various houses around the island, generating many stories, sightings, lights, and apparitions of unexplained phenomena. Holding an internal light of protection of oneself was important and necessary for spiritual people living on the island, as darker energies, of course, are attracted to light.

With lots of free time, I studied Spanish daily to more thoroughly increase my linguistic ability to communicate with locals and non-English-speaking tourists. Meeting like-minded spiritual people became a near-daily occurrence. Speaking a second language, I learned that new international friends all held unique spiritual wisdom of a common denominator, for which we all exchanged information. Discussions of sprites, animal Spirits, Angels, Ascended Masters, ocean and jungle Spirits, alien entities, and Beings from other star systems, to the local dog whisperer and certain preachers—we all elevated each other's wisdom and awareness. We occasionally held small group meditations on a dark beach at night where I was shown by friends how to open an energy portal of connection to other energies and dimensions. The most powerful connections then introduced and confirmed to us a wide range of God-centered Spirit entities, including Jesus, Mother Mary, Archangels, and Ascended Masters, with whom I conversed regularly. My personal Guides would still avoid disclosure of their names, though, and just reminded me that many Masters hold substantial influence within their collective group. They go by energy signatures, so I continue to call them "my Bosses," "Master Controllers," "my personal Spirit Guides," or simply, "my Guides."

Marcy came to Honduras to visit me from Guatemala for a few days, and we had a great time. There was strong emotional attachment between us, just as it was the day we parted almost a year prior. It was a difficult situation for both of us knowing that I can't live where she does, for safety reasons, and Charlie needs to live near his large family since they all help with his daily maintenance, care, and social support. Unfortunately, Charlie was unable to come because it is too difficult to travel with him; however, his presence is always with me, both with and without messages attached. His most frequent message is, of course, "When are you coming to see me?"

I enjoyed being on the water, so I frequently took the ferryboats around the local islands, and also to a few outlying islands. There were some great local restaurants that served nutritious and tasty lobster and seafood dishes for low cost, which made the boat trip worthwhile. I definitely spoiled myself with lobster and scrambled eggs for breakfast a few times a week! With just a little hot sauce please? And there was nothing like a side of rice and beans cooked with local spices in coconut oil to go with it! Yum! I get hungry just thinking about it!

Almost every morning just before sunrise, I made my morning coffee and took it out onto the beach, where I sat to watch the main event. A few dolphins would occasionally come by, with Charlie and Carolina, to say hello (I will introduce you to Carolina in a later chapter). I have always had a powerful energy connection to the ocean, and my morning meditations there provided a direct channel to Source, which allowed informational downloads and upgrades of a higher order. It was from there that I experienced off-planet travel, where many basic answers of all that *is* were presented to me as a gift, or reward, since I was then sensing a shift in my learning cycle.

During one morning meditation, a tiny golden speck, light years away, was presented in my mind's eye, which slowly grew in size, taking mental form. It opened into a clear, brightly lit, full color, suspended form of precise detail: a beautiful Calabi-Yau Space (a theoretical form of string-theory fame). Little did I realize that my morning sunrise meditation was a superhighway to elevating my core vibration, leading to a more powerful connection with Spirit each day.

It was there on the beach at morning meditation that "we" often planned the day for my highest and best good of whom to meet and where. I was told to rent a golf cart in order to access people and places at a farther distance, so I did that. After getting the cart, almost every day I was sent on a mission to do something for my Guides that helped other people, or to meet someone who would substantially contribute to elevating my personal awareness. Many new spiritual experiences expanded my conscious horizon, including seeing firsthand how an uncontrolled Spirit can take over someone's body with their permission, known as "talking in tongues." Creepy stuff. There, was my first introduction to inter-spiritual occupation (ISO), which I will describe in a later chapter.

Floating in the pool one afternoon, I felt, "Go to the local supermarket right now."

Why? I thought.

"It doesn't matter; you'll find out when you get there. Are you going or not?"

They don't like it when I argue, so I just headed off to the market, thinking, *What should I buy?*

"A bottle of water, or a soda if you want," was the response.

Oh, this should be a good one. I felt as if I was off on a wild-goose chase with no purpose other than to buy a drink at a market when there were a half dozen at home in my refrigerator. I got my bottle of water and got on line at the checkout, as the poor local lady in front of me realized at the last moment that she had no money to pay for her and her two kids' box of cornflakes (their meal of the day). They all appeared as though they wanted to cry. I just said to the cashier, "Hey, I got that; put this all together," as I pushed my water bottle forward on the conveyor. They sincerely thanked me.

I paid, said "Have a nice day," and got back on my golf cart. While driving away, I looked into my mind's eye at my Guides, and no one said a word. Then, after a brief silence, they lovingly smiled, and I said, "Sorry" (for questioning them before I left), and I headed off to the beach.

On the way back home from town one day, I got, "Turn right at the corner." I knew better as to ask why, so I followed intuitive directions a mile or so through the fairly rough neighborhood until I reached a small, old church. It was quite impressive but unfortunately had lacked maintenance and was deteriorating rapidly in the salt air with large wall cracks, faded and stained paint, and broken or missing cement chunks. After parking my cart and walking around it, I realized that it would be a great opportunity for a personal, spiritually aligned restoration project for the community. It appeared as something that I would very much enjoy doing, working with concrete, patch, tile, and paint. Guides said that was "offered to me as an option," but I had more recently been aligning my thought with finding a project to directly help a group of people, like twenty or thirty; I just didn't know who, what, or where. I kept the little old church in mind, though, and went back to see it occasionally, but I never took on the project.

There was a nice little yoga retreat place a few miles up the beach that I heard would have full moon drumming one Saturday night on the beach after dark. There often seemed to be a robust energy under the palms there at the water's edge, with an intriguing ambiance. Since it was just an hour or so before sundown, I headed up to the restaurant/bar on the beach for supper, and recall having a great two-tail lobster dinner for about eight dollars. There was a good mix of visitors that night, as more spiritually aligned conversation seemed to permeate through the group of twenty or so. After trading stories, and having a couple of beers to wash down a tasty supper, fourteen of us went over to the nearby water's edge and settled in to drum. The enormous orange full moon was rising directly out of the ocean, with a rich, colorful hue that enhanced its size and beauty, reminding each of us that the best things in life are free.

After about an hour, we decided to end the drumming and have a ten-minute prayer circle, all standing and joining hands, completing one big circle, with my back to the moon and my feet barely touching the calm water. We agreed to each say something in turn, and I was asked to be last to say the final words. Most everybody spoke a spiritually significant and powerful sentence or two, so being last, I knew I had to let out something strong. Feeling that a powerful portal of energy had already been opened by our group, I decided to call a collective group of Archangels to open us all and guard us in that safe space, and also in our future travels. I then called and requested Jesus, Kuthumi, and Metatron to come meet and introduce themselves to that special group of humans gathered there at that place and time for our benefit of knowledge, wisdom, and elevation of vibration of all mankind.

"We all gather here to exchange energy and appreciation with each other, and also with You. We give thanks for Your guidance and protection, Lord, and we all here choose to go forth in life according to God's plan. We desire to take with us from here, off into our individual lives, back home with us to our families and friends, collective energy particles of which You have infused into us, and this space."

Ending with all of us reciting aloud the Lord's Prayer, an electrical/energy charge with increasing intensity circulated through our connected hands of everyone in the entire circle. It was powerful enough to vibrate every last cell in our bodies and brains, and I felt as if I was being electrocuted with my feet in the water. Two girls let out short screams; one lady tried to speak but couldn't. Another lady cried, three other girls all freaked out and hugged each other, and one guy exclaimed, "Oh my God!" There were a few comments from several other people, and a guy and girl came together and threw their arms around me while wiping tears from their eyes, saying, "Thank you, just thank you!" Quite the moving experience!

I vibrate just writing this, and even when I reread it. Thank You, God! Now you've got to admit, that was some *Real* Powerful Stuff! Woo hooo! We be rockin'! Yeah, Jimmy! Ha!

When I woke up the next day, I went straight out to the beach to talk with my Spirit Guides, who laughed at me in love, at my full moon experience, and I thought, *Now that's the kind of work I like!*

"We enjoy that too," I heard. It was not only powerful for me, but also an extremely important experience for the others, and more than could be explained to me at the time, I was told. Although I was still vibrating from the night before, my early morning sunrise meditation brought a lot of clarification, confirmation, and new insight as to where I needed to go with my Kriya teachings when I returned to the mainland.

Completely relaxed one lazy afternoon, floating on my raft in the pool while having cocktails with friends, I got "Go drive north up the beach."

Yeah, OK, later, I thought.

"No, go now."

Is it important?

"We wouldn't bother you if it wasn't."

Bummer, but I got out of the pool; put on my T-shirt, hat, sandals, and shades; grabbed my keys; hopped in the golf cart; and headed out. After first driving about one mile on the road, I turned out onto the beach and continued driving along the water. I then saw a gray-haired older gent trudging along in the hot sun and drove up next to him from behind. "Hey, gringo, you want a ride?" I asked.

"Sure, where are you going?" he asked, as he got on board and sat next to me.

"Wherever you're going," I replied.

"I was just going for a cold beer up to the Jimbo bar."

"Well I guess that's where I'm going too," I answered, as he looked at me weird.

We bounced along the beach chatting and continued conversation when we got to the beach bar. He was a retired professor from an American university who was planning his twenty-seventh expedition to Turkey a month later to locate Noah's Ark. I asked him why he thought he could find it this time, since every other search he was thinking the same thing but returned home empty-handed.

"This time I've got satellite photographs with some help from NASA. I have the GPS coordinates where it is sitting at 16,300 feet on Mount Ararat," he said.

"Well, I wish you the very best with that, Mr. Richard, but no matter how much help you've got, I'll tell you exactly what's going to happen. When you locate it, if you don't have a local Shaman and preacher bless the site, bless the Ark, pray to Jesus, and do the right thing with the Ark spiritually, you'll be planning your twenty-eighth mission because you won't be coming home with anything."

By the look on his face, he couldn't believe his ears. He asked several more in-depth questions about spirituality and religion, for which he expressed sincere appreciation for my responses. I wished him well with blessings and went back to my pool. Several months later while watching the CNN ticker-tape news, I read, "Noah's Ark has finally been discovered and located by a team of researchers at an elevation of around sixteen thousand feet on Mount Ararat."

There were several small local organizations on the island, besides a few churches, that promoted goodwill work among the expats. I also met a local woman with a legally registered nonprofit name desiring to establish a new local orphanage. Intuitively I knew she was a scammer, and the other organizations were more for show, promoting their ego, so I didn't get involved with any of them.

I then learned of a local, popular church that was interested in cosponsoring a new safe-house orphanage for women and children on the island, since physical abuse in their society is rampant, uncontrolled, and has been an accepted way of life for generations. After I met with the preacher and heard the plan, he said a local donor had promised to contribute $5,000 once the new account was opened, so I donated $1,000 to open the new account and begin the fundraising effort. I also had a commitment from business acquaintances to contribute $25,000 once the new account balance reached $25,000, as the estimated budget to get the first shelter open was $50,000. Several weeks had passed while I went back to the States, and then I returned to meet with the preacher for an update on project finances.

"The first $1,000 went to legal fees, so you need to donate at least $5,000 more now to open the account."

I just looked at him in disbelief and said, "See ya," turned around and walked away. Welcome to Honduras.

I talked to my spiritual lady friend, Maya, about it, and she suggested that for Christmas, we should just do a toy distribution ourselves. I thought it was a great idea, so the following week, we took a ferryboat to the mainland, where we walked a few blocks to a supply warehouse whose huge store stocked enormous amounts of toys. We bought three hundred toy trucks and three hundred Barbie doll look-alikes, the warehouse porter hauled them on a handcart from the store back to the dock, and we took them back to the island on the boat. For Christmas, we wore Santa Claus hats and drove around on the golf cart into the poorest neighborhoods, and gave out the toys we had stashed in big white pillowcases. Since most of those kids usually got nothing for Christmas, seeing their excitement of receiving a toy was worth its weight in gold.

I will always remember many of those kids, but the best was when we found three cute little girls while they played with a few sticks and rocks in the dirt street next to their house. After we gave each kid a new doll with a different color dress, they had smiles on their faces from ear to ear. Within moments, a big African lady came running out of their tiny house with a bloodcurdling scream you could've heard a mile away. Maya and I looked at each other and instantly thought the same thing—get the hell out of there fast, before we get shot, so I floored the gas pedal, and we were off. A few seconds later, the lady began hollering, "Thank you" multiple times, so I made a quick U-turn and went back, as we all laughed and said Merry Christmas to each other. When she beckoned us to come over while blessing us and crying profusely, she said, "I'm sorry I scared you, but nobody ever, ever, has given my babies a Christmas present as long as they been alive, because I just don't have the money. In Jesus's name, God bless both of you!" As shivers shot through our bodies, we wished her and the kids well, while Maya waved and hollered to them all, "We love you!" as we drove off straight to the nearest bar for a double shot of tequila, and then went back to work! Powerful stuff.

After the New Year, I heard about some nonprofits on the mainland, so I decided to go investigate. I packed my backpack, got on the ferry, and then took a bus on the mainland to the country's interior. Spending a few days traveling by bus, exploring small villages here and there, I located an old folks' home in a peaceful, rural setting, where I introduced myself to the director and began volunteering there by sweeping the floor, emptying the trash, taking down Christmas decorations, and talking to residents. It was a good spot to get in touch with nature and some of the local Spirit energies. After I met some locals, it seemed that everyone had a story about some type of unexplained phenomena. I heard many tales of orbs, lights, apparitions, persons who mysteriously vanished, and strange jungle creatures. It seemed to be a high-intensity place.

Talking with the residents, many of whom had lived in the area for almost one hundred years (and a few a little longer), and hearing their stories, was a most often a rich and rewarding experience. Their stories of life before electricity, jungle animals, farming, and general ways of life gave deep insight into living in a third-world country a century ago.

While walking past a half-dozen residents relaxing on the balcony in their wheelchairs, I said hello to them, and one lady hollered loudly at me, "Give me my sweater! Give it back; I know you stole it!" I felt terrible and went straight to the kitchen to talk with the ladies who had worked there a long time. They all laughed and told me the woman's daughter gave her a new sweater for Christmas twenty years ago and threw the old raggedy one in the trash!

One nice, ninety-nine-year-old man said to me one day, "Jimmy, do you know why people say I have lived so long?"

"No, Mr. Lawrence. Why is that; how do you get to be almost one hundred years old?" I asked.

"Well, I'm not sure myself, but other people say it's because I am such a nice man."

"As nice as you are, Mr. Lawrence, you're going to live to be a hundred and fifty!" I said, as we both laughed.

For a week or two, I did odd jobs there until I felt that it was time to move on, as I felt my service could be utilized more efficiently by Spirit. I then learned of an orphanage with a few dozen kids in another small nearby village that could, of course, use some help, so after saying goodbye at the old folks' home, I decided to go make their acquaintance.

CHAPTER 5
CULTURE OF THE JUNGLE

After locating the children's home in a five-block-long village far off the beaten path, with unpaved pothole streets, of course, I introduced myself to the director and offered to plant a fruit and vegetable orchard so the kids could go outside to pick fruit to put on their morning cereal. She thought it was a great idea, since nutritious food, of course, was always scarce, but first I had to clear the dense jungle land nearby to make space for the orchard. We agreed that I should clear an area in size of about a few acres. I figured that they could grow extra food for the surrounding local villagers nearby and also sell the extra fruits and vegetables at the weekly market. That would assist with needed income to help provide for the children, while also substantially oversizing the orchard in order to create needed jobs nearby.

The first evening after meeting the director of the orphanage, Spirit confirmed to me that it was my next, progressively larger mission that I had been asking for. As I relaxed with my head on the pillow before falling asleep, my Guides not only reaffirmed my great new project, but imparted to me that it was much deeper in significance than what they could then currently disclose. When I asked for more in-depth explanation, I was diverted to other insights of current interest, in particular, focusing on my more immediate needs and consequences of actions. Being refused additional information at first caused me to question taking on the new project, but my spiritual path was quickly affirmed and solidified.

Now with my intent and direction to locate the manpower for this mission, I hiked the next day through the peaceful village, delivering rice, beans, and chicken by backpack to the elderly, women, and children with malnutrition living in severely deteriorated, clapboard, moldy houses. While I was walking down a quiet, deserted street that afternoon, I ran into a guy whom I casually knew from the islands—what a coincidence! Ha! He was a pleasant younger guy in his twenties or so and seemed to be a God-centered family man. I asked him if he knew anyone who might want to work for a month or two chopping bush (jungle) because I wanted to start clearing land for an orchard.

"Sure, I know lots of guys around here that need work, Mr. Jimmy. I can bring you all the workers you need," he replied.

I was instantly hesitant, since I hadn't seen an able-bodied man anywhere around the neighborhood all day, other than him.

"Are you sure, because I don't see anybody around here other than kids and old people?" I asked.

He laughed while answering, "Don't you worry. There's lots of guys around here right now at this very second; you just don't see them."

I would later find out that a half-dozen or more guys were watching me have that conversation out in the middle of the street from behind the cracked boards of their small houses in between the fields of vacant lots. After I filled him in on all the details, he said he was ready to start the next day, and the going rate of pay to chop bush was about USD$15 per day.

"How many guys do you need, Mr. Jimmy?"

I told him four altogether, including him.

"OK. I know a lot of guys that need work, so I will have you three other guys and me, with our machetes, at eight o'clock tomorrow morning."

"Well, that sounds great. Excellent! See you tomorrow!"

The following morning at five minutes before eight, there came four tough guys walking up the dirt road toward me with machetes in hand, two big black African guys and two medium-size brown-skinned Mestizo guys. I could only imagine what they were thinking while approaching this big white guy with their machetes. We briefly introduced ourselves, confirmed the hours and pay, and then they went to work. They worked methodically, chopping jungle nonstop until 10:00 a.m., when they all sat down to smoke some pot for a break.

"We break at ten for ten minutes, Mr. Jimmy," one of them hollered.

"No worries." I waved.

They went back to work and at noon hollered, "We take one-hour lunch, Mr. Jimmy," and they all walked off.

"No worries." I waved. I wondered whether they'd return after lunch.

They went back to work at 1:00 p.m. and chopped until 3:00 p.m. "We take ten minutes at 3:00 o'clock, Mr. Jimmy."

"No worries." I waved.

They smoked some more pot and went back to work, chopping methodically until 4:00 p.m. "It's a long day, Mr. Jimmy." They smoked some more pot.

"No worries." I waved.

At 5:00 p.m. they waved and walked off, saying, "See you in the morning."

"Thank you." I waved.

The next day, repeat day one, next day, repeat day two, and so on...until Friday. After I paid them at five o'clock, they said, "Thanks, see ya, have a nice weekend," and they walked off smoking some more pot. Jungle pot is very mild, with little THC content, and smoked regularly by many just to take the edge off, since they have no money to buy cigarettes, and it's free, as many of them maintain a few plants for themselves by growing it wild in the bush.

I left the island early enough on Monday morning to be on the job at 8:00 a.m. As long as I showed the workers that I was diligent, I thought they would feel that I showed some respect and

appreciation for their work as well, and continue to consistently produce without me being there every day. I would get them started on
Mondays and then return to the island, going back to the mainland
on Wednesdays or Thursdays for Friday payroll. They watched over
themselves as to the fairness of each man working equally, and I
was able to easily see how much work was done in my absence by
the amount of jungle that was cleared from the time of my last visit.
I enjoyed walking through the freshly chopped open areas (always
on the lookout for snakes) to check out the newly exposed large
trees (which they left standing), of which there were a couple dozen.

You had to be especially cautious walking around there because
there were a lot of poisonous snakes, especially the fer-de-lance, one
of the most venomous snakes on the planet. They are overly aggressive and when encountering humans, tend to display an attitude
similar to that of a pissed-off pit bull when you're taking their food
away. It's also jokingly referred to as the "two-step terror" because
of the distance you walk before you die after getting bit.

All throughout Central America, I had seen many guys in villages with one arm or one leg missing, and I was told that's because
they got bit in the jungle and had to cut off their limb in order to
survive. Most often, a hospital with antidote is too far away to reach
in time, so then it becomes a life-or-death choice. After losing a
limb, it's necessary for them to live in town, since it isn't possible
to live long in the bush with only three limbs. The guys working
for me had seen and killed many of them in the area, and one the
first week on the job.

One Thursday afternoon I bought my ticket at the airstrip for
the next day's afternoon flight back to the island. I paid the guys
at the orchard, and a half hour before my flight, I was still in town
at the local outdoor market where they sold wholesale fruits and
vegetables, and I bought a ninety-pound bag of oranges to take back
to the island with me in the four-seat Cessna. I quickly grabbed a
burrito from one of the food vendors near the taxis, and when a taxi
driver asked me where I was going, I told him *"Aeropuerto, rapido,"*

while first throwing the bag of oranges onto the back seat and then jumping in with my backpack. We quickly left for the short drive out of town to the airstrip, located off a dirt-road turnoff with its driveway entrance obscured by three-foot-tall roadside weeds.

Flying down the highway at sixty miles per hour, the driver slammed on the brakes at the last second and cut the wheel a sharp right. We skidded, missed the driveway, flipped, and rolled down the twenty-foot roadside embankment, and came to a stop, nose down and half upside down with me stuck on the back floor and the bag of oranges wedged up under the back window. The top of the bag slightly opened in the roll, and from directly above me, out of reach, the oranges began one by one falling out of the bag, hitting me in the face. The driver was stuck on the floor wedged under the steering wheel, and we both confirmed we were relatively OK. While waiting for other passersby to help get us out, I was able to grab some of the oranges that fell out of the bag, and while cursing at the driver, threw each one at him on the front floor below me, hard. After I got him a good half-dozen times or so, help arrived and got us out. I gathered my oranges and backpack and walked the remaining short distance to the tiny terminal, where the plane showed up five minutes later. At least I didn't miss the plane. Good thing, because I sat with Miss Mexico, who was on her way to a photo shoot—in her award-winning miniskirt, I might add.

Back in the bush for Friday payroll, I was pleasantly surprised with the amount of work completed while I was away, so I went into town and bought two chickens and a case of beer, returning around two o'clock. I told the four guys, "Today you stop work in another hour, at three o'clock, but you get paid until five o'clock. We are going to have some chicken and a few cold beers to celebrate good progress this week on your new orchard." They all just looked at me, smoked some more pot, and went back to work. I started a fire in the shade and got the chickens cookin'. At around 2:30 p.m., I passed out cold beers and told them they only had a half hour more and needed to quit at 3:00 p.m. because the chicken would be ready. They drank the beer, smoked some more pot, and went back to work.

At three o'clock, they came over and said they wanted to keep working. I asked why, and the response was because they needed the money. I repeated, "Do you understand that you are getting paid until five o'clock anyway, whether you work or not?" They all looked at each other in disbelief because they had never heard of such a thing; getting paid without working for it was incomprehensible. I paid them on the spot and told them the chicken was ready, or they could just grab a couple of beers and go, no worries. They decided to stay, so then we all sat down on our own log around the fire for some chicken and drank a few beers, smoked some pot, and then all said thank you and have a nice weekend, before going our separate ways. We hardly had spoken ten words each since they started the job a couple of weeks earlier, but I sensed things were changing. I caught the next bus back to the dock and the last ferry out to the island. Party weekend.

Weekends on the island would find a dozen teenagers kayaking a mile out to the reef for fish and lobster. Their parents would kick them out of the house in the morning, and they weren't allowed home until they brought sufficient food for the entire family. Watching them with binoculars from my condo beach chair, I saw them fighting with each other all day long, beating each other up and trying to drown each other out on the reef. When they got back to shore in early afternoon, their canoes and kayak buckets were filled with lobster and fish. They sold most of it because if they brought home a bounty this week, their parents would expect it every week, so they kept just enough for their family's needs and generated extra cash (which they hid from their parents) for video games. They usually sold me an extra five or ten lobster tails for about USD$1.50 each.

After almost a month of Friday afternoon chicken, Dranoel said to me one Friday afternoon as I was starting the fire, "We've all been talking about you, Mr. Jimmy, and we all want to talk with you today. It's kind of serious."

I quickly responded, "I told you that if I ever insulted you in any way, you needed to tell me right away because I don't understand everything about your culture, so you need to explain it to me, and I can apologize right away!"

"No, no, it's nothing like that." He chuckled. "Remember out on the island, we used to talk a lot about Spirit stuff? Well, it's like that."

I said "Oh, OK, sure."

At three o'clock, they quit work for the day. I paid them, and the chicken was almost done. I thought we might then have a nice conversation between us about jungle Spirits, because they were all thoroughly aware and well versed in local spiritual beliefs, customs, and nature. Since I sensed that they had become more amicable in acceptance of working for a white guy, I looked forward with anticipation as to what I could ask and learn from them. Talk about being blindsided! Whoa! Hold on, we're gonna do a cerebral readjustment here and go for a wild ride in another world!

Eyeing the feast on the grill under a huge shade tree, we set our individual seats of logs around the fire and cracked a few beers. The guys prepared a few sticks for themselves with their machetes to use for utensils since I only had a couple of forks. With no one saying a word, and only a few quick glances between them, each of us eyed and turned with sticks individual pieces of chicken on the grill in front of us that we were mentally claiming as our own. The social atmosphere was quiet and reserved while we filled our bellies, until...(names have been changed to protect the not-so-innocent: Worker 1, W2, W3, and W4).

Worker 1 started the conversation with: "Well, like I said, Mr. Jimmy, we've all been talking, and I told these guys about when you used to tell us about hearing messages in your head, out on the island. Remember the nights out on the dock with Maya, Jeannie, and David? You helped me a lot, and these guys would like to hear some of that stuff too."

ME. But you agreed to never say anything to anyone because so many people are superstitious and have weird beliefs; they'll think I'm a crazy, evil white man, and they'll kill me. Just like a couple of years ago, remember when those two hundred village people showed up with machetes to kill that crocodile guy and his wife because a local shaman said they were evil? After I met them, I thought he and his wife were really nice people. They were like me—just doing good. At least they escaped with their lives, though, before the villagers burned down their house.

W2. Yeah, I heard about that. What was that all about?

ME. Well, some of the local people thought that those two little kids that disappeared were used as food to feed the crocs, but even though it wasn't true, the local shaman said that it was true, and that's why half the village turned out to kill them.

W2. Uh-huh, I heard that too.

W1. (*Laughing loudly*) Then a week later, they found the real guy that kidnapped those kids was from some other village a half hour away. He was getting ready to sell the kids on the black market, but he got caught, and the kids returned home. Then they almost killed the shaman, so he had to move away too! (*There was a pause.*)

W1. No, what we talk about stays right here; don't worry. And besides, everybody around here knows that you're OK because there's some other people heard about you from their family working out on the island. You used to buy chicken once in a while from the guy across the street from church, right? We got friends living out there on the backstreets too. Besides, if you weren't OK, I would be dead by now just for being friends with you. So don't worry; you're safe here because we protect you.

ME. (*Chuckling*) Wow, you guys have a pretty good reporting system around here!

W1. We have to, Mr. Jimmy. We gotta stick together, or half the village would be in prison. (*He chuckled.*)

W3. Not half, but three quarters, 'cause it's not only the men!

ME. Got it.

W1. See, you said that you work for Jesus, right? And we think you can help us.

ME. Sure, I'd be happy to tell you whatever you think could help you. Like what? Just promise not to say anything to anyone, please.

W2. The same with you, because we could all end up in prison for what we're going to talk about.

ME. Well, you in prison and me dead—we're no good to each other, so you have my word.

W1. See, what it is, Mr. Jimmy, is that we hear messages, too, except we hear messages tellin' us to go kill somebody.

(At that moment they all looked up at me to see my reaction, but I never missed a beat, continuing with another bite of chicken and a huge guzzle of beer, with an impressive, healthy belch to follow it up so I wouldn't choke on what I just heard.)

ME. That's some heavy shit. You ever talk to a priest?

(W1, 2, 3, and 4 were amused; they all laughed at me and said no, because the priest would go straight to the police.)

W1. Mr. Jimmy, did you ever kill anybody?

ME. No, almost though. A long time ago, I wanted to, after a guy cheated me out of a million dollars in a business deal, but I didn't.

W2. But how come you didn't?

ME. Because I felt and heard something very powerful inside my head tell me, "Don't do it. That's not the answer; it's someone else's job, not yours, and it's not the right thing to do." Something said to me, "It will be dealt with, guaranteed, just not by you."

W3. Well, that's the problem. We get told to go ahead and do it.

ME. So you guys killed somebody? What, like last night or something?

W4. No, nobody here has killed in, what? *(He looked around at his friends.)* A few months?

W3. About six months for me.

W2. Me too. (*I picked up that somebody killed just one to two months earlier, though*).

Mᴇ. You mean all you guys killed different people?

W1. Yeah. C'mon, guys, we all agreed. We're gonna fess up. Let's tell him now. I did, but just once. W2, how many you kill? (*He held up four fingers.*) W3, how many you kill? (*He held up three fingers.*) W4, how many you kill?

W4. I ain't sayin'. (*They all got on his case for not fessin' up.*) OK. (*And he held up five fingers. Then they all started raggin' on him because they all knew he wasn't telling the truth since it was more.*)

W3. No way, W4, it ain't five, because that doesn't include those last two girls!

W4. All right. (*He held up seven fingers, as he continued eating a dark meat chicken leg.*)

W1. This is why we need help, Mr. Jimmy. We don't want to do this anymore because it's getting to us in our head. It's making us crazier as time goes on. That's just part of the problem; there's more.

Mᴇ. What do you mean? How is that?

W2. Well, see, uh (*a couple of them started to laugh and giggle*), no, I can't say it. You say it.

W3. No, I ain't sayin' it.

(There was a pause in conversation while we all readjusted and replenished our empty beers.)

MULTIPLE W's *(each taking turns)*. After killin' some-body, you gotta take off into the bush for a couple of months. Some guys stay even longer because the regular police don't go far into the jungle lookin' for no one, 'cause they know they just end up gettin' killed themselves. See, sometimes there's just no food, no animals to trap, no berries, fruit trees, roots, nothin'. It's just a matter of whether you live or die from starvation, so you do what you gotta do.

(I had a sneaky suspicion of what was about to be disclosed, so it took the edge off a little bit.)

W1. OK, see, it's not as bad as it sounds, though, you gotta understand, see, two of us ate our kill. Not me, though. *(He stated this seriously.)*

I had a temporary brain freeze from information overload, so I just responded with "Uh-huh" and "I gotta think about that for a minute." Looking back, I now realize my initial overload occurred due to the voluminous number of Spirit entities that wanted in-put with me at that moment. After a minute of silence to allow my Guides' influence, I told the guys that it was going to take me several hours of talking with them in order to explain, because we were dealing with two different, very complex issues: killing and consumption. I said that our conversation should continue the fol-lowing week so I could get into details of how evil Spirit tempts and controls people, but first I briefly initiated discussion of Spirit occupation in order to determine where each of them was coming from. By participating in conversation at their level and subject matter, my confirmation of understanding their problem solidified their commitment to continue their discussions with me.

> W4. (*Holding up a piece of chicken after taking a bite, he talked with a straight face.*) I like my meat cooked like this piece here. (*He finished it off and threw the bone to the side.*) Hey, can I use that fork you got over there?

> ME. Sure, here you go. (*I handed it to him, thinking,* Oh, this should be interesting: a cannibal with a fork!)

> W3. We thought you liked sushi! (*He was making fun of his friend.*)

> W2. Hey W4, we heard you were with that guy so-and-so when he ambushed and killed that bush soldier-of-fortune dude that was huntin' him down a few months ago. Did that really happen?

> (*Everybody became quiet while readjusting and turning the chicken on the grill, waiting for his response.*)

> W4: Yeah, and we cooked his ass too. (*He paused while eating a dark meat chicken leg.*) As a matter of fact, this piece here reminds me of that guy. His name was Henry.

As everybody busted out laughing, I couldn't believe what I was hearing. Trying to process this was a whole new territory for me, and I didn't even know where to begin, but I knew my Guides would help me get through this. *This is some incredible stuff,* I thought, and couldn't imagine how my Guides would let me end up in a situation like this in the first place. "You've been prepared for this, Jimmy, and your talks here will extend through them far and wide, to impact many of their friends and families, and people living in villages far away from here as well. This is an *extremely* important mission," I heard.

> W1. And you gotta tell us W4, how did that blonde taste? Was the titty meat sweet? (*Everybody chuckled.*) What parts of her did you eat, and did you eat any of that raw meat? We heard you had sex with her too. Did you do her? (*Everybody started laughing, squirming, and hollering in dismay.*) Was the body still warm?

> W4. Half the women you have sex with act like they're dead anyway, and with the body still warm, it was hard to tell the difference!

Everyone was laughing their asses off with comments, snickering and cringing at the same time, totally out of control, while I momentarily felt as if I was about to pass out (from the information, not the beer). If I mentally processed with judgment and envisioned the physical acts, I probably would have thrown up. But removing emotion, the mental/visual connection, and personality from the conversation maintains separation, and the subject matter is then only words, with no personal emotional processing or feeling of the dysfunctional reality of their actions. While the guys spoke, I continually asked my Guides to help me.

> ME (*to W4*). Yeah, so how long can you survive in the bush on one body? Like, how many days will it last?

> W4. Well, usually the best I could get was just two or three days before the animals sniff it out and come for it, 'cause I ain't about to fight no hungry jaguar over a piece of meat. Even if you wrap it in palm leaves and bury it and cover it, the animals find it.

(The conversation continued for a minute or two longer, with more in-depth, insane details than is necessary to repeat here, with commentary of particular body parts, and then there was silence.)

Me. Well, I guess it's my turn now to fess up too. (*They all looked up in disbelief and remained quiet while I told them three times in my life, two of which were in different restaurants in Mexico, where I was served cooked human meat on my dinner plate because they probably thought I was a CIA, DEA agent, or another local restaurant owner.*) Maybe they think I'm with the government because nobody else does what I do by themselves. They serve the meat as a message to certain people, as an example of what happens when a restaurant owner doesn't pay their tax, or when somebody interferes with their business. One place I was in at suppertime, there were four tables of men, each seated with their families in a nice local restaurant, all served the same as me. The families all got served their meals first by their waiters, and then we men got our plates from a different guy in a suit and tie. "This is the house special, just for you," the boss said, as he set the plate in front of me. I looked at the other guys as they casually looked around the restaurant at me and the others, immediately after receiving their plates, all with a small serving of various types of meats and vegetables. Then, after close examination of the pork, beef, and chicken, we all instantly knew. There were a couple of bad-lookin' goons at each exit door watching to see that everyone ate their supper like good little boys. I thought about leaving my money on the table and walking out, but I knew something really bad would have happened to me later that night, so I had no choice but to stay and eat most of my dinner. I agree with you, W3 and W4, you know right away when you see it and chew it, but it's not too bad when cooked the right way, especially with some hot sauce and seasoning. (*I was joking.*) You just can't think about it.

This was through no choice of my own, and it took a while for me to spiritually address that issue, but after it was fully explained that no energy or Spirit matter remains after departing a previously living instrument of matter, Spirit and I are totally fine with it. It is no different than consuming any other cooked, dead animal. I just happened to walk in the wrong restaurant at the wrong time, so I got served like the other guys.

W4. Yeah, it ain't too bad after you get used to it.

W3. Where was another time?

ME. Yeah, well, the first time was when I was a teen-ager back in New York one day, there was this friend of mine, Ralph, that owned a local delicatessen, and he gave me a small chunk of the same grayish colored meat and told me to eat it. He said, later in life, I would thank him for it. So I guess now is good a time as any. Thanks for educating me, Ralph! (*I raised and tipped my beer while we all laughed.*) It's true that once you eat it, you'll never forget the taste. There's nothing else like it. (*The guys all agreed.*)

W4. It's really not that bad, and sometimes it actually tastes pretty good. Depends on how hungry you are.

W2. Why did Ralph have it?

Mᴇ. Because a business associate friend of his gave
him some to give to another guy. They have networks,
just as you guys do. I think he was friends with the
men that once in a while put guys in a hydraulic car
crusher in a junk yard, but I don't know for sure.

They chuckled and continued to talked about which body parts
were the best cut to cook and eat, while we all threw in a few more
sick comments and jokes. I was mentally processing a lot of stuff,
and after a moment of silence I asked, "Holy shit. How come you
haven't killed me yet?"

They all just sat there, looked at each other, then looked at me,
started laughing, and said, "Because we like you, Mr. Jimmy!"

W3. Besides, you got a little too much fat on you.
Makes for extra work to cook.

Mᴇ. Thanks, I appreciate that, so I better eat some
more ice cream!

W1. But, seriously, we want you to tell us what you
think, like what makes us do this stuff.

Gazing into the hot coals of our dwindling fire (while realizing
one or more of them had already thought about killing me), I asked
my Guides to come, and please help me *now!* "This is your work,
and you have been prepared for this Jimmy, so don't worry, and just
continue talking."

Mᴇ. First, we better have another beer, while I get in
my head what I've got to tell you because you guys
ambushed me with this shit. In general, I'll give a
short answer to start with, and that's because there's so
many evil Spirits around the jungle, and they are just

using you to do their dirty work for them. You're a tool
for them, just as you use your machete as a work tool.

I continued talking briefly about different types of human
Spirits, jungle Spirits, walk-ins, ocean energies and Spirit entities,
plasma entities, projection, cosmic stuff, evil temptation, and the
battle between God, Jesus, Archangels, Ascended Masters, and the
devil. I reduced it all to the two most powerful energies that influence all of reality and mankind: those of light where God lives, and
darkness, where evil lives. What's light is right because darkness
cannot exist in the light. And equally, there is no light in the dark;
otherwise, it wouldn't be dark.

I scientifically spoke about how other dimensions exist and explained how it's possible that many types of Spirits can access their
mind without them knowing, through subliminal channels. I told
them how dark forces of evil disguise themselves to trick you into
working for them with promises of unrealistic rewards. Evil forces
feed and thrive on your and others' pain; it's like food for them,
so, of course, they will do anything they can to continue making
you feed them. It knows that in order to access your thinking brain
for consideration of you to do or think something that it wants, it
needs to get inside your processing department. For example, just
as you feel now and feel every day when you wake up, you *know* there
is a little dark force sitting there way in the back of your head. It
sits there in a little "waiting room" just inside the back base of your
brain where it hides, privy to all the information and opportunities
passing through your normal brain's processing center; it just waits
there to ambush you. A couple of them nodded their heads and
acknowledged they were aware of that.

"So, from now on, we're putting up a big, solid door back there
with a giant cross on it. Anything coming through this door is now
entering a house of God, *your* brain, and everything wanting access
to your normal brain processing center has to come through this
door first. The instant that any 'dark energy thought' tries to enter,

that door gets slammed shut in a microsecond flat, so it never even makes it to your processing department, so then it doesn't exist, and can't be considered as a thought. Kicking those darker thoughts out the back door like a football dropkick works too.

"The door is open only for light, and everything else gets slammed out the back without having to waste your processing center's time to even consider it. You will no longer feed the dark force of evil or temptation. From now on, you will *immediately* close the door of darkness and only let in the light. You will follow the light because you know what's right and you are safe there, just as I know that I'm safe here because all of you have decided to work for God, and no more for dark or evil. You will no longer allow the hijacking of your brain. Your brain belongs to *you* and no one else. It does *not* control you; *you* control *It* because *you* have more power. *You are the power in charge.* If a dark thought wants to use you, chop it up with your machete and spit it out. If things get out of control and you need help, call on Archangel Michael, because he works for Jesus, too, and he will help you. He's the dude with the sword that slaughters evil Spirit." I talked nonstop for well over a half hour.

While talking, I knew the presence of my Guides were helping me describe and channel things in a way these guys could relate to. I knew I was channeling and just continued in the flow, without much recall as to what I actually verbalized. The Spirits of many of their victims were also in attendance at this meeting but were held aside to observe and support the more authoritative spiritual entities impart teachings, through me, into their killers to hope-fully raise their God-centeredness and return them to living in the light so they wouldn't kill any more people. During my speaking and teaching, I felt many of the victims express their appreciation to me, as the ones in attendance were appreciative and cooperative. I saw a long line of victims, men and women standing side by side, shoulder to shoulder. One white girl told me to tell her killer that she had forgiven him, but a higher authority instantly suppressed that action for not being in the best interests overall at that time.

Many victims' Spirits were also present in the area days or weeks prior to this discussion, but I didn't know who they were at that time, and now that I think about it, they were there watching me, I think, from day one.

W4 was persistently interested as to what happens after death and wanted to know as much as possible about his victims as to what they felt, where they went, where they are, if he can talk to them to tell them he is sorry, and what they are doing. He wanted to know what he could do to help the ones he had killed because he felt so terrible about it. While we sat there around the fire, he explained that it was the exact moment of death when their souls departed that was getting to him, since the event continued to play over and over in his head. He said that at the exact moment their souls departed their bodies, he felt a powerful energy around him, and also inside him, change and pass through him instantly.

The remorse was eating deeply into these guys' heads, with one of them proclaiming that if he had to kill again, he already told God that it will be himself. They all had thought of suicide to varying degrees, and we discussed it frequently over the course of the remaining few weeks we had of working together. Every day when he woke up, W4 asked himself, "Is today the day?" I avoided disclosure that I sensed, or saw, any of the victims because that would have caused more of a mental disturbance than benefit to them.

> W1. Well, Mr. Jimmy that really does help. Thanks, because we don't know that stuff. There's one more thing we really want to know if you could tell us. And that is, What can we all do right now to start making a change in our lives for good? We want to make a change right now, like start on something even if it's just little by little.
>
> Me. *Start?* It's too late to ask that question. (*I laughed.*)

W2. What do you mean? (*The others' undivided attention prevailed.*)

Me. Y'all already started when you began working here a month ago. I told you I work for Jesus and his friends, right? I'm here trying to grow food for this bunch of kids that don't have parents and no family to feed them. I can't do this myself; I need help. So you guys aren't working *for* me; you are doing the same thing *as* me, so you already started working for Jesus a month ago when you got here. Now you're settin' it up to feed all these kids for a long time, and there's gonna be plenty extra for you and your families too. The money you get paid with isn't mine; I just bring it here from other people who earned it working for Jesus also, mostly by working their whole lives helping, cooking, providing, and serving food to other people in restaurants and a bakery. They just can't come here because some of them are too old, and some are dead, but it's their money. I only pay my own rent, food, and beer. So now the good people's money is going back to other people doing good for other people, *you*, because you're working, and working hard, to provide food for orphans that really need it. Get it?

They all looked at each other in amazement and felt really good after hearing that, because it brought some relief to them knowing they have already begun to make right choices to follow the right spiritual path in life.

"So now you want to continue doing something else, and that's prayer," I said.

W2 said, "That's something else we all want to talk about too, 'cause we don't really know how to pray, so could you teach us?"

"Absolutely." For ten minutes, I summed it up for the afternoon by briefly teaching them how to pray, cowboy style (or bushmen, in their case) and resumed more in-depth prayer lessons the following week. We all agreed that conversation never occurred, and we would continue talking in confidence the next week. See you Monday! Everybody was feeling good and we parted ways.

Back at work Monday morning, the guys showed up at work with their new attitudes and outlook on life just where we left off on Friday. It was great seeing these guys as if they had a new lease on life breathed into them. I continued feeding them spiritual information multiple times a day, and most importantly, I explained that Jesus will only interfere with them if they ask Him. Unlike the dark evil force that enters you to take advantage and use you without asking, Jesus has great love and respect for your soul and will never take advantage of you or interfere unless you ask. As reinforcement, we continued daily spiritual discussions and lessons, enabling their understanding of their own reformation, ending with a jungle prayer on almost every day thereafter until the end of the job.

To get around on the mainland, I had rented an older pickup truck from a local businessman a month earlier, since bus service was difficult in some farther-off places. When I was ready to start acquiring trees and plants while the men continued to chop bush, I got directions to a Mennonite community that sold trees and plants, about ten miles off a paved highway down a narrow, bumpy dirt road back in a jungle valley.

Off I went to a beautiful community without electricity or mechanization, where men worked in the fields as if they were dressed for church, and also the women worked in what appeared to be their Sunday dresses, washing laundry by hand on their front porch. I passed a sign upon entering the community: "Welcome to Jeremiah Town. Appropriate Attire Required. Women in Shorts, *KEEP OUT!*" Whoa! I continued driving slowly past the two enormous oxen pulling a loaded logging wagon until I came to a little storybook house along the road with a sign reading Flowering Plants. Responding to my inquiry for fruit and vegetable plants, the woman directed me down the road to seek out Mr. Leroy, who had fruit trees. After visiting under a shade tree for almost an hour, he and his son took me to their orchard and proceeded to cut, prepare, and load me up with about thirty to forty banana, plantain, papaya, and mango trees.

When I offered him one hundred dollars, he just looked at me and said, "What am I going to do with that? We have no use for money here, so you can just keep it."

"Well, Leroy, that's very nice of you, but maybe you could use the money to buy something when you go to town."

"We don't go to town, so next time if you ever come back this way, maybe you could just bring us some fish from that island you live on."

"Of course, I'd be happy to do that. I'll see you in about a week or two. Thank you very much," I answered, and then drove out on my way back to the orchard to plant our new fruit trees.

Returning just before lunchtime, a half mile from the worksite, I saw a guy walking and asked if he wanted a ride. "No, I'm trying to sell this," he said. He opened the bag so I could see it.

"What is it?"

"A skinned and cleaned armadillo. I would like seven dollars for it," he said.

"If I give you ten dollars, would you cook it for me?" He jumped in the back of the truck without another word, and I drove back to the work site. When we arrived back at the orchard, W1, W2, W3, and W4 all hollered, "W5, what's happenin', bro? Wow, it's good to see you. Are you just comin' out?"

"Yeah, I came out this morning," he replied. They were buddies, and he was just like them, coming out of the jungle after months of lying low. He cooked the critter for lunch for us, but it was a bit too chewy for me. He had been in the deep jungle (hiding out, as many others do) on the run from the law. It was like old home week for them.

After almost two months, 120 new trees and plants had been planted, and this particular job was over. We had our last chicken-and-beer afternoon with a parting prayer in jungle church, and since we would be parting ways, as a send-off, they invited me to their small village block party they had planned for that Friday evening, to celebrate a few local residents' birthdays. But I had to agree to leave no later than 9:00 p.m., because after that, there would be more than a hundred of their friends coming from hours away on the bus, and they were unable to guarantee my safety.

"We've got about thirty-five killers live here, Mr. Jimmy, and more than half of them is your private army. We just can't promise anything about the other half; plus a lot of their friends are coming here, too, and they are just like the rest of us."

"How is it that you say half will protect me?"

"Because they're all our friends, and we stick together. Actually, most of them like you, Mr. Jimmy, because they all were the ones peeking out from the inside of their houses during the days when you were bringing rice and beans to their families and teaching their kids about Angels. If they didn't like you, you would have been dead a long time ago." They laughed.

"Wow, I had no idea!" I thought that was kind of funny.

Even after my Guides' reassurance, with a great deal of apprehension, I showed up to the block party around 7:00 p.m. with a case of beer, a bottle of whiskey, and a few bags of chips. There were already fifty or so bad dudes milling about in the street, none of whom appeared real happy with my presence. My first stop was the house of three brothers in the middle of the block, where I set my peace offerings on their community table set up in the front yard of their house. With a couple of dozen notches on those three brothers' belts, they were among the heavyweights of who made the rules in the community, so I figured it was best to report in to headquarters and tell them I would be leaving in an hour. W4 was there, and we briefly said hello. I cracked open the whiskey, took a slug, and passed him the bottle, while saying thank you very much for all his help, and then I reminded a few of them that the orchard's bounty was for their kids and parents as well. Collectively, local residents had killed over one hundred people during the course of the previous six to seven years.

Casually visiting and strolling through the crowd of killers along the dirt street was a phenomenal experience, and it is unlikely I will ever repeat it. The dark energy was so dense among the crowd, I felt as though I could almost walk *on* it, instead of walk *through* it. Lots of kids said hi. I visited with some of the older residents whom I had become acquainted with, had some laughs, said good night, and went my merry way around 8:30 p.m.

The next day I went back to the village to deliver a few large bags of produce to several elderly women. There was yellow police tape blocking off the street in front of the house with the community table where I had placed my peace offering the night before. I saw W1 walking.

"Hey, buddy," I yelled. "Did you have a good party last night?"

"Good morning, Mr. Jimmy," hollered W1. "Yeah, for a little while. See, these two guys came here from the city around ten o'clock last night and said one of the guys owed somebody some money. They got into a tussle in the street right in the middle of the party, and some other guy came from behind with a machete and split his head in half, clean down the middle! Even split his nose in half from the back!" he exclaimed. "We got our own rules here, and those guys were just askin' for what they got. Funny thing is, when the police came, they asked a bunch of people about what happened, but nobody saw anything, so they put the guy's headless body in a bag and left. They shoveled up most of the brains from the street, but there's still some over there if you want to see."

"No, thanks, I'll pass! Good thing I left early." Incredible. We said goodbye and wished each other well.

I returned my pickup and went back to the island a few days later. My beachfront sunrise meditations were calling because I needed answers! Although the island was a slightly safer place, there was still one really bad guy who had been occasionally stalking me. My buddy who was "in the know" told me the guy had killed his brother, went to a different part of the country and killed another guy, and then he was there on the island, stalking me. I inquired about him to a local politically connected businessman acquaintance as to whom I needed to donate to, and how much it would cost me to have the official government tourist protection squad get him off the island. Having realized the security and safety situation was totally out of control, I decided it was time to start planning to move on. Several days later, my friend told me the bad guy had been removed from the island, and while chuckling, said that he probably wouldn't be coming back, but I knew my mission there was finished.

Years later, in meditation, I recalled the series of events that led me to work in the jungle with really bad guys. I wanted to revisit the whole anthropophagy thing, since many years ago I at first had deep concerns as to spiritual ramifications and consequences. I clearly understood that Spirit planned my experience; it was set out for me by design, it was essential to prepare me, and it was no big deal. A practice that has been ingrained in our species since time immemorial was deemed necessary for my experience to effectively enable my interaction with the killers and cannibals that I met, and also for other counseling discussions evading mention herein.

To better understand the functionality of my choosing which projects to participate in, I was analyzing the interface of spiritual influence on my mental thoughts and subsequent follow-through of my physical actions. At the time of assignment to plant the new orchard, I was told and knew that it was huge, much bigger than face value. When I asked why it was so much bigger than face value, I encountered a deep, dark, impenetrable wall of space that blocked me from obtaining additional insight. Now it all makes complete sense, though, because if the extensive details were known by me in advance, as to working with killers and cannibals, I most likely would have moved on elsewhere and found a different project.

CHAPTER 6
INTO THE MAYA

Previously, while living on the beach in Mexico, I also traveled around the Yucatán to Chichen Itza, Tulum, Coba, Mérida, and many other smaller, lesser-known archaeological sites, following my interest of study in Mayan culture and origin. Feeling that I had unfinished business there, I wanted to continue to further investigate other ruins in the ancient heart of their kingdom. My monthly rent was quickly coming due, so I gave away many personal belongings, said goodbye, packed up what remained, and headed to the mainland bus terminal. I then took an uncomfortable overnight northbound bus, and a couple of days later, I made a temporary home base in western Belize near the Guatemala border.

First, I traveled into the lowland jungle up to Lamanai, which was out of the way and a little difficult to get to, similar to most ancient ruin sites. Hiking through the dense jungle for the day absorbing the intriguing architecture, carvings, and symbols impacted my mental vision memory board of many similar ancient stone carvings that I had seen at other sites. It was intuitively made clear to me that they were carved in respect of their ancestor gods, that all originated in the cosmos, and that I'll find them almost everywhere I visit in this part of the world. The giant German guy I walked with for several miles around the site was into photography, which was great, because he would go off for pictures while I had time to peacefully meditate and connect with the energy there. There were few other tourists at the site that particular day, so my sensitivity of dense Spirit entities was enhanced. It definitely felt more powerful in presence than I had recognized in other places, but I had no explanation as to why.

While my new travel acquaintance and I walked together shoulder to shoulder along the narrow jungle trail returning from the intricately carved, detailed temple in the farthest reaches of the dense jungle site, Mr. German said, "Whatever you do, don't stop walking because we are being followed by two big snakes." I slowed my pace gradually just enough to look behind him on the other side of the trail and saw two fat, eight- to nine-foot-long black snakes, side by side, slithering really fast at our equal speed of about four miles an hour. I prepared to run, but thankfully they slowed down and turned into the bush. I understand the black mambas are just as deadly as the worst of them, although I was uncertain as to what they were. We continued exploring a couple of hours longer, encountering several other smaller structures hidden in various isolated places throughout the site, but no more giant snakes. It was a fruitful day, and I returned to my home base around dark.

Several days later, I took a tour to Caracol, which is located on the border of Belize and Guatemala, with parts of the site lying in both countries. For unexplained reasons, the place just felt creepy to me. There was something about the feel, smell, and atmosphere that caused my uneasiness and discomfort just being there. The jungle was too quiet, so I made my rounds quickly through the smaller site of a few excavated temples, snapped a few photos, and headed back to the waiting area near the armed soldiers under a palapa with a few picnic tables. I didn't know until then that just a couple of weeks prior, a couple of guys from the Guatemala jungle ambushed and killed a guard working at the site. This was in retaliation for the local police previously confiscating their horses, chainsaws, and other timber-cutting equipment, because the two countries have been fighting over logging this particular stretch of borderland for generations. The British army also maintains a jungle training base nearby, but when I was there, I only saw a few guards walking around with rifles.

From my temporary base in San Ignacio, I also visited the impressive temple ruins of Xunantunich and Cahal Pech, among many other smaller and undeveloped sites in the region. To access Xunantunich, I crossed a swiftly flowing river about one hundred yards wide, on a hand-crank barge operated with a cable-and-pulley system stretched across the river. Besides walkers, it could also carry two cars, or one truck, and the trip took around ten minutes. The local township paid a powerful handicapped man to operate the crank, but you could get your exercise and do it for him if you wanted. His genetics qualified him for that job, since his arms were the size of a world champion weight lifter, weighed approximately 325 pounds, had the stature and facial features of a Neanderthal, and an IQ probably around eighty, and he was genuinely a very nice man. It is my understanding that humans with similar physical qualities were bred here on our planet many thousands of years ago by ETs to perform general labor for the more intelligent human/ alien hybrids. They were known at that time as "things." I was quite amazed to actually meet that guy, knowing his similar DNA code has been preserved, but suppressed for who knows how long.

The hike from the river up the road to the impressive site took me about a half hour, but it would have been ten minutes less had I passed up a stop to view the nearby clan of howler monkeys. Their intimidating howls and groans commonly echo for miles throughout the jungle, and there were about twenty of them high in the trees just a hundred yards from the road, where they were well aware of my presence. They knew that I was not a threat, so they allowed me to view them in their natural state, just "hanging out" with their family and friends. Continuing on my way, I arrived at the Xunantunich ruins site and immediately sensed more of an authoritative posture of the embedded energy in the area. A half-dozen large, stately structures occupied the central core of the site, surrounded by many other smaller, overgrown, and unexcavated ruins. Imparted throughout the inspiring site by the very present, nonphysical entities, gave me the impression that this local king was most authoritative throughout the expansive surrounding territory in his day. I enjoyed my lunch from an elevated perch sporting a commanding view of the surrounding jungle and experienced an uneventful but worthwhile day's visit there.

Cahal Pech is also a large ancient ruin site, geographically located in between Tikal and Caracol, about ten miles from Xunantunich, and is a part of San Ignacio town. Many residential houses were built on the ruin site grounds, encompassing the estimated one-square-kilometer perimeter base of the once massive prehistoric complex, and also up the forested hillsides of the approximate three-hundred-foot-tall mound. Many foundations of the houses were built using original stone blocks of the disassembled temples, and most locals whom I spoke with claimed that age-old energy remains embedded within the stone blocks. After thousands of years, many descendants of original families still live there and have powerful stories of Spirit occupation, time-slips, disappearances, orbs, and energy entrapment in the nearby land and hillsides. Now, except for the remaining stone temples of the old central square, most of the site is covered under trees and houses, and it appears that 90 percent of the once-enormous complex remains buried.

At a sidewalk café in town, I met a guy who began telling me local stories and legends that he heard over many years, since he was born and lived there all of his life. Many of his stories put mine to shame! We got along well, and Lenny invited me up to his house, a garage apartment alongside his relative's house situated on a cliff near the mountaintop of the ruin site. After stopping at a local market, we brought a couple of chickens to barbecue with his cousins, along with some other provisions, beer, and soda. Arriving at the mountaintop, we pulled into the dirt trail driveway leading to the rear of the property, which opened up through the trees to an awe-inspiring, spectacular 180-degree view of the surrounding countryside fifty to sixty miles distant.

While visiting, they told me several good stories, with one in particular that I recall occurred about ten years prior. About three blocks from where we were, four middle-aged men of their family began digging a foundation one morning for a new house. When the men never returned for supper, a woman went to get them, and she found all four men sound asleep on the ground, but the work completed was no more than twenty minutes' worth. None of the men drank, or remembered as to why they fell asleep, and therefore had no explanation as to what happened to them. Other people in the area also experienced something similar and then reported seeing many colorful orbs near there that night. Although it was a safe place overall, several people have mysteriously disappeared over the years without explanation.

The following day I explored the main temple square of Cahal Pech, which was about a fifteen-minute walk from the tourist parking area, and the visitor center with exhibits indicating occupation of the site around 3400 BPE. There were no spectacular features out of the ordinary that caught my attention, other than appearing to be a more formal kind of place in its day. After meditating a while, I felt an intense energy at one of the temples entice me to return at night. So, a few nights later with a half moon shining, I returned to the parking lot around midnight. I was unable locate my flashlight, and it was very dark under the jungle canopy, which the moonlight failed to completely penetrate. Of course, there were jaguars and huge deadly snakes (Lenny told me an eleven-meter boa was killed just five miles from there last year, and another of equal size a few years before that), but I headed off to the main temple square with my gold cross chain and ten-inch blue-ceramic replica Mayan mask, as my talismans of protection.

I ceremonially commissioned the mask to guide and protect me on my midnight journey through the jungle, and since I had been in touch with my Archangel friends on a daily basis, I also asked that they all come to accompany and protect me. Down through a gulch and up over a ridge on a dark narrow trail, I eventually arrived at the entrance to a beautiful, open, moonlit courtyard, with the light reflecting off the white stone structures, creating a surreal environment. It was a fascinating moment to view, as I stood there gazing into the courtyard while identifying a strong presence "in the air" all around me. After introducing myself and speaking to the gods, I slowly entered as my energy balanced in harmony with that heavy space and walked to the center of the court, equidistant from all four structures about one hundred yards apart on each side. I stood frozen, center court, for an unknown length of time, mentally processing the power and energy presence from the concentrated reunion of untold hundreds or thousands of Spirits. Unprepared for this overwhelming reception, I called my Ascended Masters for guidance and balance. It was disclosed to me there that I also am an ambassador of Spirit in human form. Little did I realize the significance this evening would hold in my life's future events until after the following powerful and important powwow:

While remaining in the center of the court, I knew to remain motionless at that spot until further notice, so I sat down. A meeting of the highest order, involving me, got underway between my highest Spirit Guides of Jesus, Archangels, Ascended Masters, and a dozen or so Spirit gods of the highest Mayan order. It was there that part of my future course of human life was being discussed and determined. The hundreds or thousands of Spirits initially in attendance were all cut off and "walled away" from this meeting, disallowed from speaking or interfering in any way. Without knowing the specifics of the meeting, I just knew that everything would be OK, although unsettling, and I was to go forth and continue following the natural order of my being.

Returning to my physical senses, I stood up and looked around, knowing that I was being watched, but uncertain as to by whom. I had just one more thing to do: bless this mask on the altar of the steps on the main temple. As I walked forward to the steps, I felt the extremely dense energy presence in the air of the many Spirits in the courtyard. Placing the mask about eye level on the steps, I backed up fifty feet or so and addressed the controlling gods of the site, speaking with appreciation and gratitude. I then verbally asked them to impregnate the mask with the vibration of Spirit in that space, in the name of God. This short ceremony lasted only a few minutes, and then I was told it was time to leave. I took a drink of water and headed out under the dark jungle canopy back to the parking lot, where I returned almost two hours after I started out.

Clearly, I had time-slipped a good half hour or slightly more, since recapitulating, the timing just didn't add up. When I woke up the next day, I knew to leave for Tikal in Guatemala, so later that afternoon, I signed up for a day tour just to get the transportation. After packing my backpack with enough clothes for a few days, I got on the bus and left San Ignacio at 7:00 a.m. the following morning. Throughout the following days, I realized that I had received an extraordinary amount of "downloaded" (or infused) informational energy, which was changing my current course.

We crossed the border early, changed buses and drivers, and drove off in our twenty-eight passenger Coaster bus for Tikal. I had been meditating for five or ten minutes and just didn't feel as though I would reach the ruins that day, because I had the intuition that "something" was going to happen that would change my plans later that morning. I forgot all about it until a couple of hours later; a strong sensation came over me, which continued to become more powerful moment by moment, with increased clairsentient influence. *This is strange*, I thought, but as I was looking out the window at a beautiful lake, passing through a small, pretty village, my Guides said, "Get off the bus; get off the bus *now*." I couldn't believe what I was hearing until it kept getting stronger. I finally grabbed my backpack and walked up to the front of the bus, telling the driver to stop and let me off the bus.

"No, amigo, this is not Tikal. We will be there in thirty minutes more."

"I'm not going to Tikal!"

"Yes, you are!" he demanded.

"No, I'm not! *Stop the freakin' bus now!*" I hollered at my noncompliant driver.

He finally stopped, shook his head while opening the door, and mumbled, "Crazy gringo."

I said, "Thank you," and got off the bus in a little lakeside village in Guatemala. The bus drove off. I walked across the street to a small park and sat there on a bench, looking at a serene lake, wondering what in the hell I was doing there.

TATIANA

I looked around and saw a restaurant nearby, so I went and had breakfast with really good coffee. Clairsentiently, I understood that I needed to stay there for a while, so I went back to the park and sat to absorb the space and confirm what I was sensing. Then I went for a walk a few blocks down the main road. I rented a motel room, kicked off my boots, and relaxed a bit, still trying to figure out what the heck I was doing there. Back out for a walk an hour later, I met Susanna with her three kids: Tatiana (eight), Melanie (five), and baby Junior (one). I bought them some cookies and Coca-Cola in a nearby tienda (small store), for which they were appreciative and grateful. As the kids ran around playing for just a few minutes, Tati sat down, crying in obvious pain. I asked what was wrong, and, disturbingly, Susanna became mad and hollered that Tati was just crazy, as she took the other two kids and started walking away. Tati was unable to walk and continued crying until Susanna came back, hollering some more while handing pretty little Tati to me and demanding, "Here, take her. I don't want her; she's yours." She then turned around and quickly walked away while Tati cried profusely.

While I was mentally freaking out, Melanie asked me to carry her sister, to which I agreed. I gave her a hug and kiss, lifted her up on my shoulder, and we walked off in the hot afternoon sun following her mother up the road. After a half mile, we turned off the asphalt onto a jungle trail leading up the face of a long hill, down the other side, around the bend in the valley, back up another hillside, and down again. Susanna was far ahead and out of sight. Although I did my best to keep up, I had to stop and rest a few times. Thank goodness, Melanie waited at the turns so I wouldn't get lost. An hour later, we came to a small, crude one-room house with a ragged hammock strung in the shade, into which I collapsed and fell asleep.

A half hour later, I woke up to a guy standing over me with a machete. *Holy crap,* I thought, *this woman really is nuts, and this guy is now going to kill me.* After seeing the look on my face while raising my head from his hammock, he laughed and said, "Don't worry; it's OK." With a sigh of relief, I got up and introduced myself. He already had heard the entire story while I was sleeping. The house was that of Susanna's only distant living relatives, since all the others were executed in a nearby village by the government's extermination squads thirty years prior. There were then a few other kids around, and I asked the ten-year-old boy if he knew where we could buy cold Coca-Cola. He nodded his head and replied "*Sí.*" Everybody got really happy when I gave him Q40 (about $5), and then he and a few other kids ran off into the jungle. Twenty minutes later, they came back with two big bottles of cold Coke and Fanta. After visiting with Susanna's cousin for a while, I learned of Tati's seriously painful condition of malnutrition. Susanna was single and had no money, and the kids got very, very little food.

I insisted on taking Tati to a hospital the next day, which I then learned was over fifty miles away. Susanna agreed and said there also was an older lady friend of hers nearby who was dying of ovarian cancer, and asked if she could bring her along with us to the doctor.

"Absolutely, and tell your friend to bring along any other woman that may have ovarian cancer. All of you meet me at the park in the village square at nine o'clock tomorrow morning, and I will take all of you."

I got directions back to the village and headed out through the bush, all the while trying to figure out how the heck I was going to transport these people to a hospital in some far-off unknown place. In the village, I went straight to the first place I could find to buy a cold bottle of water, and there, I met a guy with a large van who was available and agreed to drive for me the next day. What a coincidence!

When I arrived at the park the following morning, there was Susanna with her kids and seven other older women waiting next to the van. I greeted them all, we loaded up, and the van load of us drove off to the hospital an hour and a half away. Thank goodness there was an American doctor at the hospital who spoke English. He became familiar with the local people and their problems after working there for about a year. Explaining that Tati and I established a strong bond in the jungle the day before, I asked him to do anything and everything possible in his power to help her, as if she was his daughter, and I showed him my cash so he knew I could pay for everyone I had brought for help that day. Then I clearly explained that if I lacked sufficient funds with me to pay him to do everything he could to help Tati, I promised to deliver to him whatever amount of cash necessary to pay the bill, at any address, at any time, in the United States. He responded that he understood me clearly, told me to put my money away, and said to come back later that afternoon when all the patients would be finished.

My driver and I went to town for lunch, walked around, and just passed time until we returned to the hospital around 3:00 p.m. The doctor took me into his office, closed the door, and began to explain that all the women had ovarian cancer at varying stages of progression. He gave them medicine and prescriptions, and released all except one of them, who was admitted to stay.

The doctor's office was connected through a doorway, which was open to the pediatric doctor's office. She was a big, forceful Spanish lady who didn't speak English. I understood her when she told my doctor to leave the door open and sit me down so as to be invisible from her office, as she wanted me to hear what she was about to say. She called in Susanna, sat her down in front of her desk, and ripped into her like a drill sergeant on a new recruit that had gotten picked up AWOL. The doctor was so mad that the walls vibrated when she lectured Susanna. They had previous experience together with Tati, and the doctor said if she hears that Tati dies, Susanna will be lucky to go to prison because the doctor will personally hunt her down and kill her. And if she does go to prison, the doctor will just wait and then kill her when she gets out. And if she runs or moves away, she had people that could find her. Powerful stuff. I was flabbergasted, since I had never heard a doctor say things like she did. My doctor confirmed what I thought I just heard, and shook my hand while saying, "Congratulations Jimmy, because you got Tatiana here just in time to save her life." *Really* powerful stuff. He explained to me that sometimes, people only understand that without making necessary change, death will come to them, one way or the other.

He continued to explain to me the abnormally high incidence of ovarian cancer throughout the country, and particularly in the outlying villages. My mom also had died of ovarian cancer, but she never lived in the jungle. It's my belief the underlying cause of her death was due to her lifelong use of talcum powder. With the money she left me after passing over, I do these types of things for others' benefit, just as she would be doing if she was still here. The total hospital bill for the day, including blood work, was a little over $120 for all of them, and the pharmacy was an additional $200 for everyone. We loaded into the van and headed back home after a long day. It was September of 2012, and I remember that I could feel my life was making a radical shift.

MY NEW VILLAGE

I woke up the following morning knowing I should rent a house. After this thought settled in over breakfast, I started asking around if there were any houses for rent in the village. Later that day, I signed a lease and put a deposit on a nice furnished two-story house, situated along a rugged hillside trail three blocks from the main road, which I moved into the next day. Two days later, I went back to Belize to retrieve the rest of my belongings and brought them back to my new hillside house in the jungle, which sported a beautiful view of the lake from my hammock strung across the upstairs deck. It was a supercool pad! Then, about a week after settling in, I went back to the States for a few days, and then to Guatemala City to see Charlie and Marcy.

We had a great visit as always, and Marcy returned with me to my new place near Tikal. We had fun and traveled around for a week, but after she had grown up and lived in a small jungle village, her preference was to live in the city, where it was best for Charlie as well, surrounded by his many family members for daily care, entertainment, and support.

Making new acquaintances in the village, I met a shaman guide who was on the board of directors and worked in Tikal. Together, we took a day trip there for my first introduction, and then I continued to visit several times over the following couple of months. We frequently spent quiet evenings over a few beers in front of the general store, sharing in-depth knowledge and wisdom with other local villagers. Their stories, beliefs, and way of life also opened my eyes to see humans in a whole new context, as their daily existence incorporated time-worn ways of the historic Maya lifestyle.

The Mayan empire at one time grew to control vast portions of this hemisphere due to their aggressive warrior and natural survival attributes embedded in their genetic makeup (i.e., connections to Earth, animal, and cosmic frequencies). Knowing that, generated my desire for more in-depth insight and understanding of the Maya relationship within our cosmic space. I wanted to experience the jungle's natural awakening at astronomical twilight two hours before sunrise, so I hired my local shaman friend Gorgonio, who was the same age as me, and three bushmen as my guides to enter the ruins at 3:00 a.m. one morning. Aware that it is home to many jaguars (it has the highest concentration per square mile of anywhere in Central America), and giant deadly snakes (thirty-five-foot boa constrictors, with some giant anaconda occasionally mixed in), I felt it wise to hire two extra bushmen.

Machetes and flashlights in hand, we headed out on a trail into the dark jungle night with two bushmen in front of us and one behind, walking backward. Reaching our destination behind Mundo Perdido ("Lost World"), the bushmen stood guard while Gorgonio and I sat quietly and meditated, with much information and awareness downloaded in a short period of time. Living in, and learning, the cosmic awakening cycle to which all jungle life is connected was a fascinating experience. It was there that I received more in-depth knowledge and awareness of all that *is*, by understanding and knowing that we all originate from various branches of the unified collective God-Source in the heavens. Afterward, I returned to the village with a more thorough personal understanding of the Mayan connection within nature and their origin from a particular group of God-Sourced entities in the cosmos.

With Gorgonio having grown up in that village, he had natural jungle-survival skills and also had vast knowledge of plants, animals, Spirits, and herbal remedies and natural medicines, which he frequently shared. Relaxing in the hammocks of his jungle palapa, I asked him about cannibalism on several occasions, since in that region of Central America, all bushmen know of the concept, especially those on the run from a neighboring country. He said the same thing as the other bushmen: that when it's necessary as a matter of survival, and the action of last resort, that's what it comes to, although he never had experienced it. Most bushmen seem to survive OK without having to find and kill a human for food, because the jungle usually provides a natural abundance of nutritious plants and animal protein, but sometimes a local area of jungle may just be completely barren of food source. Bushmen on the run and in search of food sometimes cross the borders without even knowing it, since a country's jungle borders can run a hundred miles without even a barbwire fence. Several times, men on the run showed up in the village asking, "What country is this?" and then it could be assumed the guy probably killed someone far away and took off, and then was hiding out in the jungle. Those are the guys you have to be careful of because it is known that bushmen on the run kill each other for consumption purposes when necessary.

Gorgonio then said, "You have to meet my brother. He lives out in the bush a couple miles from here; let me call him."

"OK, sure," I confirmed, waiting to see how it was possible to have cell phone service there. He got up out of his hammock and grabbed a big conch shell off the floor of the palapa. As I watched in amazement, he walked out to the clearing and blew his brother Andrew's conch code into the side of a nearby hillside of rock, short honks, something like 2-1-2. He came back and stretched out in the hammock again while I just looked at him grinning ear to ear, thinking, *What the heck was that?*

Gorgonio laughed and said, "He'll be here in about fifteen or twenty minutes. That was his number, and I told him to bring George too."

I just busted out laughing and said, "Neat."

The hillside face echoed to another rock cliff down the valley, hit another hillside rock face on the other side of that valley, and then reached his brother's palapa on the back side of the mountain. Twenty minutes later, two guys appeared out of the jungle swinging machetes, trimming their trail along the way. They had a small farm on the other side of the mountain and were self-sufficient, except for an occasional beer, which I provided that afternoon while we all had a nice visit.

My daily routine began to take shape as I filled my backpack in the morning with bags of rice, beans, moringa leaf, moringa seeds, Angel cards, Angel pictures, and a large bottle of water. I would initially choose a different trail each day that led out of town into outlying areas of jungle around the village and then quickly paid more attention to intuition in order to locate the people most in need of my generosity. Many elderly people who were unable to walk to the village for food live in remote places, and I was able to intuitively find many of them by hiking directly to their house. They all know about moringa and were most grateful for anything I left with them, whether it was moringa leaves or seeds, rice, beans, or fruit. I learned of and met many people familiar with moringa, who were cured of diabetes, Parkinson's disease, and other neurological conditions, so almost daily, I continued to promote and teach about moringa along with teaching kids about Angels.

Another priority was locating parents with young children to teach them how to teach their kids to avoid nightmares and bad Spirits from entering their mind space and bodies while they slept. There is an overabundance of dark entities in the jungle, and most women find this out when they or their daughters turn eleven, twelve, or thirteen years old. I distributed small Angel cards of Mother Mary, Archangels, and Saints as well, with a prayer on the reverse side, which was much appreciated by all. By showing pictures of Angels to babies at a slow, consistent rate of one every three to five seconds or so, it would generate an uplifting emotional response when a particular Angel was observed that the baby had recognized. Mother Mary was popular, as were Metatron and several others. This made the mothers happy, too, and gave them sufficient proof and confirmation so they would continue talking about Angels with their babies in the future. Many women had an interest in learning more about how to communicate with their Spirit Guides, and although challenging to describe with my limited Spanish-speaking ability, teaching was a lot of fun, fulfilling, and rewarding.

A HUMAN ANGEL

One morning, with my backpack loaded up and ready to head out for a typical delivery day, I felt, "Just leave your things here and go down to the lake; you can come back for them later because you'll be going the opposite direction."

The lake? I thought. *No, I'm not going to the lake now because all the kids are in school, so I will go like usual, when it's hot in the afternoon and lots of people go for a swim. I have work to do.*

"Your work can start at the lake today," I was told.

No, I don't have time to play. I have work to do. It gets too hot after lunch, so I want to get going now, I thought.

More firmly, again, I heard, "Go to the lake."

Slightly confused, I gave in and then walked about a half mile to the swim dock down at the lake. No one was there, absolutely no one, so I sat under a big tree gazing out across the lake, wondering what the heck was going on. Was I being invaded by an impostor?

After ten minutes, as I stood up from under the tree, a tall woman appeared out of nowhere, thirtyish with a camera, and slowly walked toward me. We began talking and exchanged brief information with each other as to where each of us was from. I started first, and after a minute or two of my explanation of how I recently came from Belize, I said, "I know it might sound a little strange, but I have a strong connection with Spirit, and I have a great life working for Spirit."

She looked at me with a big smile and said, "Oh, good, me too. I'm glad I found you because I work for them also. I was sent here, just like you."

"Do you mean here to the village, or here to the lake?" I asked.

"Both," she said. "I got sent here to the village two days ago from where I was in Belize, and just now I was sent here to meet you—well, I didn't know it was you, just that I had to meet someone that works for the same group as me. I help people a little differently than you, though, I help souls from the other side initiate occupation of newborn babies' bodies. I work with expectant mothers who are getting ready to give birth in a week or two."

"Wow, that's really interesting," I replied.

We talked a short while about whom we each work with that assist in our earthly mission, and although we had a few common Masters, we had different groups of "specialists" that help us along our path. Then, having a brain fart, I asked her, "Can I help you find anyone, because I've been here in the village for a few weeks and I know a lot of people?"

At first, she had a big grin, and then smilingly, she responded, "Do you need any help finding the people that you're looking for?"

"Oh, no, that was so human!" I joked. We both laughed (no, we don't need any human interference, unless asked for, thank you), and then after a little more chat, we each said that we were running late because our lake meeting was a last-minute detour assignment. We hugged each other, wished each other well, and parted ways. I returned home, loaded up, and headed out to the bush for another great day of adventure.

GREEN LEAVES IN THE AIRPORT

A week later, I went to Guatemala City to see Charlie and Marcy, who had just returned to their house with thirty pounds of moringa leaf for me from a rural farm near her grandmother's house. It was freshly picked, nice green leaves in four big bags. For ease of transport back to Tikal, we compressed all of it into thirty one-pound Ziploc bags and then put them all in a duffel bag. (I know that a few of you are already thinking that something unfavorable is coming, but don't worry; Spirit Guides enjoy humor, too, and have the power to instantly turn a really bad situation into something very funny!)

After another spiritually enlightening weeklong visit with Charlie and repacking the moringa, I had a morning flight back to Tikal (Flores). Halfway to the airport, my regular taxi driver, Tomas, looked at me and just busted out laughing and said, "I can't hold it in anymore, Jimmy. What the hell are you thinking? Your duffel bag, you are taking that into the airport. Have you lost your mind?"

I never thought about it until then—holy crap, the International Airport in Guatemala City, of all places, with compressed bags of small green leaves! I told him not to worry and everything would be OK, while at the same time, I began to mentally freak out. I thought, *Just be cool, don't act suspicious, and just check in as usual... everything will be fine.*

All of a sudden, my Guides busted up laughing as well, but I didn't think there was anything funny about it. "We were wondering when this was going to hit you; tell all of them that it's just marijuana! It will be funny!"

I still didn't think that possibly getting arrested for drug smuggling in Central America was the slightest bit funny at all. It was highly unlikely the airport police could discern the difference between moringa leaves and marijuana leaves being transported through the international airport. I thought about leaving them with my driver so he could return the bag to Charlie's house.

"Do it!" I firmly heard. "Many people are waiting for you and counting on you to bring this medicine, Jimmy."

So I figured, *Well, what do I have to lose? A few years in prison?* I reminded my Guides that I would be of absolutely no use to them if I was put in jail. We got to the airport. I said goodbye to Tomas, took a deep breath, and stepped out of the taxi directly in front of an armed soldier with a machine gun, staring at me and my duffel bag.

Looking at him straight in the eye, I smiled and said, "Marijuana."

He maintained his stone face, gave me a dirty look, turned away his rifle, and walked the other way.

Ten seconds later, I was stopped by a guard at the front entry door of the airport terminal like everyone else. "Passport," he demanded, while eyeing my duffel.

I held up my passport and smiled, and while pointing to my duffel bag, I said, "Marijuana." He gave me a dirty look and told me to go, and I kept walking.

I got to the check-in counter, and I said the same thing to the gate agent, as she then gave me a dirty look while she put the bag tag on the handle. I figured that would be the last time I would see my bag, until I was handcuffed to a chair in a backroom somewhere. I got off the plane an hour later, went to baggage claim, retrieved the bag, and walked out past another armed guard with a machine gun, smiled at him and said, "Marijuana," when he gave me a dirty look and shook his head. Apparently, I pissed off enough people, and they just didn't want to deal with me. (I could probably write a whole life-story book about all of those people too.) I returned to the village and distributed the moringa over the course of the following month along with about one hundred pounds each of rice, beans, and chicken to many poor, needy people.

SMALL JUNGLE PROJECTS

When I returned to my village on the bus from the airport in Flores, a lady in her late thirties sat down next to me, as it was one of the last seats available. We had no conversation, and I only gave her a small mint piece of candy during the boring one-hour ride. She got off the bus a few blocks before me, where I smiled and said adios. The following morning at eight o'clock, my chain-link gate was rattling when I heard a woman calling, "Senor Jimmy?" I went downstairs and saw the same woman from the bus the day before, so I opened the gate while she said her name was Jeena, and she would like to talk to me.

"Sure, come on into the living room and sit down," I replied.

She told me that my neighbor, a friend of hers, told her that I would like someone to clean and do my laundry once a week. We agreed on the day, hours, and pay, so she started the next day. She showed up after taking her kids to school and left in time to pick them up in the afternoon. She did a good job, including sweeping the leaves off the large stone patio outside.

While eating lunch together a few weeks later, she told me that she lived with a one-hundred-year-old lady, whose family had owned the quarter-acre parcel of land they lived on forever. I asked to meet the elderly woman, and the next day I went to Jeena's house, where she introduced me to Vicenta. To further clarify the length of time after Jeena told me how long her family had been there, I asked, "Do you mean like four thousand or five thousand years?" At a loss to understand why, Vicenta then became instantly annoyed with me. I asked Jeena, "Why is she mad?"

Her response was, "She told you forever, and you said five thousand years. She meant what she said." Holy crap!

She didn't have any other family now because all thirty-seven of them were also executed, while she watched, by the government extermination squads thirty years prior. (I later found out that Susanna also watched her entire family get executed by the army in a small village when she was a little girl.) The small jungle palapa they lived in barely accommodated their most basic needs, and with it being so tiny, I thought about adding on a separate room for Vicenta. After I thought about it for a day and presented the idea to Jeena, I returned and asked Vicenta if she would like me to build her a small cement house (as the cost would be just slightly more than a palapa), just big enough for her. In the jungle, an old woman with a cement house is a queen. She, of course, agreed, and their previous agreement between them was that Jeena was to inherit the land after she passed away, in return for taking care of her. I hired Gorgonio, and he supervised construction of the basic, small casita, about four meters by five meters. On Christmas Eve, we held a move-in party for Vicenta and fifty of her friends and neighbors, with lots of colorful lights strung through the trees, nice music, and excellent food. She was happy, content, and got to live in the house for two and a half years before passing over just before turning 103.

During various adventure travels of my rural works program, I came across several small palapa-style church structures with dirt floors, and some without walls. Whenever I met a preacher, of course I asked what religious denomination they were affiliated with. Regardless of their response, I explained that it was important to me only that they all pray to only one God and believe in Jesus, because I work for God as a Soldier for Jesus.

Often during rainy season, many parishioners attending bush services sit on benches while praying under the palm-frond roofs of their tiny jungle church, with their feet in the mud when heavy rain blew inside. On several occasions, when the preacher or other members of the congregation agreed, I arranged for the delivery of cement, sand, and block for them to construct and install a floor and/or new walls. Many of them felt as God had answered their prayers by dropping an Angel out of the sky to help them. I always remind them that I am only the bus driver.

Several times over the years, as occurred half jokingly, women touched or squeezed my arm to see if I truly was a real person. On one occasion, I was walking down the street of a quaint small village when two elderly women were walking in the opposite direction on the other side of the street. One noble-spirited lady crossed over and came up to me grinning from ear to ear, and asked if I was really a human being, while quickly touching my arm with one finger and then running away giggling. Wildly funny stuff!

CHAPTER 7

DECEMBER 21, 2012

I arose at daylight, and my day began as usual. I made myself a little breakfast and then walked the fifteen minutes to Vicenta's and Jeena's casita to start the men off on their day's work. They were completing the bathroom plumbing and would then finish pouring the remainder of the cement floor. We briefly discussed the remaining work to be completed prior to Christmas Eve, knowing that the official move-in party was quickly approaching, and I left.

That afternoon following lunch, without a sound other than a distant barking dog, I relaxed in my oversized hammock strung across the second-floor balcony, contemplating the arrival of Christmas several days later. While I was thinking about the provisions that I needed to purchase for Vicenta's party, and the logistics of such, I fell asleep for a while, swaying in the tranquil jungle breeze. After a nice snooze, I began to return from a deep sleep when I subconsciously knew that intentionally I was slowly and methodically being awakened by a powerful force, while concurrently being told *do not* open my eyes yet. I strongly sensed, and then *knew*, that I was being watched and that my awakening was being effectuated by a higher power. There was strong influence to be receptive and maintain a calm and docile demeanor, but also to continue interaction with my environment. Having been mentally forewarned and prepared for this, I finally opened my eyes slowly, bit by bit, at first allowing only a slit of light to penetrate without moving my head or any other muscles other than my eyelids.

Then with my eyes progressively opening, I began moving only my eyes all around, and saw that I was being watched by thousands and thousands of Spirits for miles around. They had manifested their facial forms large and small, in the trees, leaves, clouds, open airspace, outdoor wall surfaces of my house, over the lake, in the broken clouds, on the side of a mountain next to the lake, near and far, knowing they were all there to talk or say hello to *me*. Initially I was overwhelmed, until I sensed a few of the many familiar Spirits that previously worked with me impart an unworried, comfortable disposition into my being. Almost all were new-to-me entities seemingly solidified under one cooperative invisible power and control, with a defined energy of authority whom all willingly obeyed, which I understood to be God. I thought and deeply felt, in wonder of that incomprehensible experience, "Wow, this is the most phenomenal experience of my life" and at the same time I received a powerful, brain-implanted reminder message that it was the day long-awaited for: December 21, 2012.

For the first several minutes, I just looked around, feeling as though they were waiting for me to speak first, until I then asked if they were all real. Seemingly, several hundred of them excitedly responded instantly, all wanting to communicate with me at the same time, until order was established by the five or six highest authorities and their assistants that quickly put them all under control. After a moment or two, while the half-dozen Masters laid down the rules to all attendees of that engagement, the Masters among themselves determined the order of it all and who would be my primary contact.

"Yes, Jimmy, we, the ones speaking to you, are the Ancient Ones of God-Source that have helped create your race, and we have been waiting an exceedingly long time for this transition date to come. This is quite an achievement for not only you [humans], but a milestone, as you say, for us as well. It was tremendously difficult for us during the time that humans' continued evolution and survival was threatened and in question due to certain unfavorable developments, dark forces, and outside influences. There were many problems, which caused an altered path from your original design, which we continually correct, and which also would have led to the ultimate destruction of your race and planet, without intervention. We have worked incredibly hard for a *very* long time with vast resources of God's assistance, and have a vested interest in your outcome, so we continue to monitor and oversee your development.

"You have worked other lifetimes with many of us here before you today, Jimmy, although you don't remember us, and you will be working with some of us in the future that are here now, but with whom you have yet to become acquainted." I then sensed that a powerful, quiet group had been introduced to me in the distant "background" by the Masters, but I only became aware of the collective group and not each of them individually. At that time, I became more aware of the vast depth and concentration of the number of Spirit entities (and souls) present for participation, and others infinitely distant solely observing the entire planetary event. I believe they numbered well over one hundred thousand, or possibly a million.

Dozens of them again started talking, and somehow waved to get my attention at the same time, but were walled off and instantly quieted by the Masters. While one Master then directed Kuthumi (presumably because we had prior interaction several years earlier) to arrange my connection with Paramahansa Yogananda, the great prophet Kuthumi took precedent with a cordial welcome and brief introduction and called Yogananda forward. Yogananda greeted me and expressed his pleasure to be assigned to me, stated that we would become acquainted in the near future, and then moved back into the collective. The Masters included Jesus and several of his invisible/unknown to me friends, among other powerful Beings answering to God. Little did I realize at the time that their brief order of entities' contact with me would be directly proportionate to my future spiritual path with them.

Max the crystal skull then sneaked in a message to me that his Spirit was at the 11/11/11 Crestone, Colorado, crystal skull ceremony with me, as was Yogananda. They told Max that he would have ample time and also encouraged him to visit with me back at my permanent home in the United States. For a quick confirmation, Yogananda smiled and said that I looked handsome that day in my white shirt and gold cross! An unknown-to-me high-level Master reiterated to all that in general, they were to refrain from interfering because the outcome of humans' free will is necessary for our independent development, leading to our highest potential according to God's plan, and only critical adjustments would be handled by them.

"This is true that humans now will shift to higher consciousness at an accelerated rate. All this means is that natural development and understanding of more complex scientific concepts and materials, technology, interdimensional Beings, realities, and, most importantly God, will now be absorbed into the human dynamic more quickly. You are a lower vibration race of material matter, and therefore your advancement has been slower but will accelerate now due to many changing factors. We appreciate your work, Jimmy, and many more like you are now coming into the fold to assist. You have affected, in a constructive and positive way, many more humans than you know, and there will be more and more like you as time goes on. The full extent of your work will be known by you after your ascension."

Lacking continuity of time or awareness of my physical being, I continued to look around, and then after much intuitive interaction had subsided, I stood up and took a few steps over to the balcony railing in order to more physically interact with their reality. Looking out over the lake and off to the side in other directions confirmed my privileged experience was as real as the day was long.

"Remember that we are all here for you, collectively as a group, or individually as you choose. Call on us anytime. It has been an honor to visit with you today, Jimmy. We will meet again. Go forth in God." The all-encompassing presence of God-Source energy throughout my body was then amplified greatly for a microsecond, as if to cleanse me, before I felt a physical return to myself.

Poof! All forms and images slowly dissipated, but the ten-minute experience rattled me to the core. Wanting to treasure the event for as long as possible, I had no desire to speak with any other human until the following day. I continued to savor the undiluted vibration in my body, blood, and brain in the most uplifting and captivating spiritual experience of my current incarnation. It took me several days to get back to my normal self, and delivering Christmas toys with Angel cards to many poor children in off-the-beaten-path places maintained the primacy of my vibration and helped ground me at the same time.

After the holidays passed, I contemplated but was unsure of where my next mission would take me. As work on the casita was finished, and I had hiked almost every trail within several miles of the village, I slowed down my daily hiking routine and found myself enjoying the porch hammock more often. Intuition inclined me to begin designing a cabin for myself back in Colorado, which I did. I passed time doing more reading than hiking and began planning my departure back to Florida, where I would wait for my next calling.

One late night in mid-January, I was awakened by the sound of my front gate rattling and then a flashlight flickering and flashing on my bedroom window. All I heard then was a motorcycle drive off into the night, and then I went back to sleep. The following morning my neighbor called me over and asked if I saw the guys climbing my gate last night.

"No. I heard a motorcycle, though," I told him.

"There were two guys climbing your fence," he said, "one with a gun in his hand, and when they saw my flashlight, they took off. They were coming to get you, and even though they were scared off tonight, I guarantee they will come back for you."

That was all I needed to hear. I went for breakfast and made the rounds. I said goodbye to friends and gave away my personal belongings to friends in the village, packed my bags, and got an afternoon bus out of town to a hotel near the airport. The next day, I flew to Guatemala City to see Charlie and Marcy for a few days before going back to Florida. Charlie knew everything that had recently occurred with me and was involved with some level of my protection.

Almost one year later, I went back to the village for one day only to visit with friends and learned that one of the guys who came after me was in prison for killing someone else. The other guy got run out of town by residents enforcing jungle justice and was believed to be hiding in another part of the country. Thank you, God, for the batteries in my neighbor's flashlight!

CHAPTER 8
INTEGRATING HIGHER AWARENESS WITH MY LINEAR BODY

Looking forward to spending a few days at the beach, I headed back to Florida, where I gravitated toward my continued participation with spiritually aligned groups, books, and friends. I finally picked up a copy and read *Autobiography of a Yogi*, which for a long time I always wanted to do but never got around to it. Many things in the book clicked with me, and before I knew it, I established a connection with Paramahansa Yogananda (born Mukunda Lal Ghosh, India, 1893) who is a kind, warm, loving, very funny Spirit, whom I realized had been patiently waiting for me since 11/11/11. While I was meditating on the beach one morning, he told me that he was there on the dock that night with my friends in Honduras when we were first introduced by Kuthumi, Babaji, El Morya, and a group of other light-Spirit entities, and was also with Max at the 2012 celebration, under the supervision of the "Highest Authorities." For a short moment, vibrant, detailed pictures of our previous encounter clearly appeared on my mental vision board of the exact time and place of reference, to confirm his authenticity. Momentarily, I thought my brain was just "remembering" the particular incident, until I realized that it was impossible to recall the exact miniscule details of every single thing, as if I was reliving the experience. It was in fact, a quick powerful projection.

I continued to study metaphysics while recuperating from my extended travel and absorbed the phenomenal experiences of my Central America adventure. Many souvenirs that I brought home from my travels adorned the walls and shelves of my condo, including the blue-ceramic mask that I had impregnated with the Spirit of my midnight trek into Cahal Pech, which sat on a small table inside of my south facing balcony glass sliders. When I call on Archangel Michael, I also call from the south, since my balcony is where I meditate and call Spirits of the light to unite and jointly plan my continued missions according to God's plan. Attending classes, different churches, seminars, and fairs; reading dozens of new-to-me metaphysical books; and getting intuitive readings from newly acquainted mediums, I was continually putting it all together, which, of course, is an eternal project.

MAX

After a week settling in back home, I went to a local event at which the human guardian of Max the Crystal Skull had presented him for public viewing one evening at a small metaphysical bookstore. With only about a dozen people in attendance, it was a warm, relaxing space where I sat in the back row with a direct line of sight to Max, situated on a table ten feet in front of me. I began listening to the lady guardian speak, but within three minutes, she was tuned out, and I connected only with Max. It was like a reunion at old home week for us, although we had never before physically met. At first, recalling December 21, 2012, and recapitulating the day's events and who was there, he told me that day in particular was equally exciting for all of them as it was for me. Then he reminded me of the Colorado ceremony on 11/11/2011, certain prior astronomical events viewed by me, the island in the Caribbean, and a few other circumstances when we'd had prior direct interaction. Conversation with him was so real that I was waiting for him to get up and start shaking hands with people! I even looked around at others in the room to see if they could hear him too! I guess not, because they were all intently listening to his human guardian's story. I felt sad that his guardian lacked the depth of understanding of myself and two others in the room, although she did take her job assignment respectfully and with gratitude.

He told me also that he has worked with the collective group for an extraordinarily long period of time, and was assigned to this particular part of the planet, although he is accessible anywhere, similar to other crystal skulls like him. Then he explained to me some interesting things, such as his group consists of thousands of assistants, including several Archangels, one among them being Metatron, whom I have had interaction with through Charlie. (Excuse me—I should have stated *which* instead of *whom*, since Metatron is a geometric nonphysical entity of energy.) Also, the group supports him with information to primarily promote a scientific agenda, he loves my scientific inquisitiveness, he knew a long time ago that we would be connecting, and he is available for me anytime I choose to call on him. He also informed me of my future meeting later that year with a human "that has a very close connection to another powerful Spirit Guide that was at your 2012 reception." I wondered who it could be. "You have some fine friends, Jimmy."

When our visit ended almost two hours later, we all said good night and headed for the door, except for a few people who remained to speak with Max's guardian lady. As I held the door open for a woman following me out of the store, she smiled and said, "Thank you. So did you two have a nice chat?"

With a big grin, I answered, "Yes, and the conversation will continue. How about you?"

She briefly explained to me that her experience was most powerful as well, before we wished each other a good night and went our separate ways.

VOLUNTEERING

I often found time for morning walks over to the beach at sunrise to connect with Source. Of course, looking for direction from my

Guides as always, two of their options presented to me one morning suggested that I volunteer counseling convicted killers on death row, or volunteer at the county food bank warehouse nearby. I sought out the food bank district office (only because it was closer), introduced myself to the director, and offered to work in the warehouse doing whatever was necessary. She gave me a handwritten address and told me to go there any morning and ask for Jerry, which I did a few days later. I introduced myself to him, and we talked for a while. I explained that I had a few mornings available during the week and would like to use volunteer work at the food bank as a personal exercise program. We got along well, and he told me, "Sure, come back and start Monday for a couple days a week." I returned a few days later, and with three or four other guys, I moved a few pallets of food around, rotating them so that the older, dated stock went out first to the seven county-sponsored distribution facilities. Several weeks later, the USDA food inspector came in, and a half hour later, she gave the boss a copy of our performance report.

Everything was just fine she said, except that "you're not giving the food away fast enough, so we're going to hold back delivery of your next two truckloads, until you get rid of some of this excess inventory." Each of the counties' food pantries were open most every day, all day, for anyone that wanted food, needy or not, no proof required. While making a delivery to resupply one of the food bank pantries one day, I walked past a van in the parking lot and saw through the window about fifteen bags of groceries in the back of a van, while the two women whose van it was were inside getting more handouts. I was told that once a week they, akin to many others, drive around to all seven county-sponsored food banks. Two women, two to four bags each, times seven food pantries, four times a month, at, say, fifty dollars per bag. That's over $7,000 a month. They reportedly sold most of their haul to their neighbors for half price. After learning the rules and requirements for food assistance and finding out that massive food bank fraud was common all through south Florida, I quit the next day. I should volunteer to justify work to maintain the jobs of incompetent government employees that piss away our tax money? I don't think so.

Later that week, I met a local lady who sponsored and organized a volunteer food program for homeless people. Each Monday, she and a half-dozen helpers serve lunch to people in need at a local park. I thought maybe that would be a great opportunity to volunteer, so to check it out, I brought a couple of hundred granola and energy bars from Costco down to the park one day before lunch. We talked briefly, and she explained to me that most of her food is donated by a few local restaurants that contribute their leftovers, because they cook and bake fresh every day. I helped her carry from her car to the table under a large shade tree, pans of lasagna, pasta salads, eggplant parmigiana, bowls of salad, and trays of top-quality tarts and designer pastry deserts. No wonder there were sixty people on line! Lunch was excellent, thanks to the generosity of a few local five-star chefs. Although my offering was slightly appreciated, it was insignificant to the local homeless population there.

I then found out, that daily, in a different local park, many other organizations provide free lunch, with some of them providing hundreds of meals in the same day by providing both breakfast and lunch. Depending on what you want is where you go: County Park A for scrambled eggs or Town Park B for biscuits and gravy and then a hot lunch, or local park C for sandwiches to go, with awesome cakes and cookies. Other individual donors also showed up with cases of juice, sodas, and snacks. Between all distribution and serving facilities combined, I saw so much food dumped into the trash that was left over after serving everyone, it would have been enough to keep five hundred people alive for a full month where I had just come from in South America. No wonder there are so many homeless people in south Florida who come from all over the country; the beaches and parks are great, and the food is excellent! The way I see it, the massive scam is exacerbated by several reasons, partially due to the multiple government agencies involved that have an insane amount of your money at their disposal to indiscriminately waste on unnecessary product, salaries, transportation, benefits, and office expense, without accountability to anyone who is paying for it.

Since I still had a few small boxes with about one hundred energy and granola bars left over from the park, I stopped on my way home one night from my weekly drum circle to distribute the snacks to a couple of dozen homeless people sleeping on a sidewalk. I remember many years ago, sleeping on the sidewalk all night in Arizona waiting for the food stamp office to open, and thought it would be a nice gesture, since sleeping on the sidewalk definitely sucks, trust me. Halfway down the line, while I was handing out two to three bars each, saying, "God bless you," one guy sat up and hollered at me, "I don't want that! Go get me a goddamn hamburger!" I've been eating energy bars lately.

Then I met the director-preacher in charge of a large new-thought church, that supports homeless with meals, clothes, shoes, haircuts, showers, and personal supplies. After our five-minute personal conversation, during which he also attempted to ascertain how much money I may eventually benefit his organization, I realized he was a fanatical Bible thumper ("Unless you believe what I do, y'all are goin' straight to hell!"). There is a place for people with those beliefs, and it's nowhere around me. I know how I live according to Jesus's intent—not perfect, but I sure know I'm not going to rot in hell. There was a man with seriously narrow-minded, immature psychological issues reshaping spiritual beliefs of hundreds of parishioners in a congregation, and quickly realized I wanted absolutely nothing to do with him. He was severely brainwashed and lacked common sense as far as I'm concerned, even though I did feel empathy for him. I was reminded there that brainwashing is still alive and well in many churches, regardless of their religious affiliation, and I felt uncomfortable that radical religious beliefs were also being proposed into the heads of susceptible street people who were in search of a thread of hope. The preacher said he would pray for me to repent so I could be saved. I pray he wakes up.

The Florida government/private support system also provides too much incentive to remain homeless without showing them a way out. It is way too easy to live off the system, and that is partly why the entire homeless situation is so screwed up. I want nothing to do with reinforcing or supporting the many able-bodied, intelligent, lazy freeloaders who know how to work the system. However, working with them is a great way to get in the trenches to find the people in advanced stages of contemplating suicide. I continue my occasional walk in the park in search of them, and most often, I find the person sitting there waiting for me. I appreciate their punctuality, not knowing that I'm coming! Cool!

BACK TO CHARLIE'S HOUSE

Prior to heading out West to spend the summer building my new cabin in the forest, I went back to visit Charlie and his family for Easter. Marcy and her family frequently return to their grandmother's compound for holiday fiestas because it has the physical space to accommodate the large number of family members, with two cement houses situated in a lush, green rural area on several hectares. From Charlie's house, we all loaded into a large van with our backpacks, suitcases, lots of boxes and bags of provisions, and left the city, headed out for a week to a town in southern Guatemala. I preferred to stay in a small motel in town, while some family members stayed at Marcy's mother's house a few blocks away, and others stayed at Grandma's compound several miles out in the jungle.

While relaxing with Charlie under a shade tree at his grandma's house, he told me that about twenty years prior, two young girls were playing along the riverbank behind his grandma's house, until late one afternoon they were found dead, lying in the bushes nearby. I asked his grandmother about the incident, who was at the time talking with a longtime neighbor friend, and they both confirmed that, yes, indeed, that had occurred. Charlie was friends with, and played with the Spirits of, those girls for many years, until last month, when he and a half-dozen family members went to visit, the Spirit girls were no longer there. Charlie said that he was unaware of what happened to them, but many Spirits of dark souls from the jungle continue to congregate in a group nearby, and it was they who caused a human to kill those young girls.

We had a great party, which included family, friends, and neighbors from the surrounding rural area. The women ensured that we ate well, since their cooking many natural, chemical-free home-grown organic foods was nothing short of superb! We went to church with Charlie, took him to the carnival on Friday night, and shared our resources of extra food with many poor neighbors. Each night around sundown, a half-dozen family members escorted me back to my gated motel, we said good night out front, and then they left.

After almost a week of typical early evenings, my escorts said good night and left me near the motel gate as usual, while the night watchman unlocked the gate to let me in and then locked it behind me. He quickly gave me a really strange look that something wasn't right and then ran inside the nearby office, diving over the counter into the back room, and turned off the light. I knew then, obviously, something was seriously wrong and figured it was time to leave the next day, one day earlier than planned.

I went upstairs to my second-floor room and went to sleep until 4:00 a.m., when I was awakened by three shooters from the adjoining, dark schoolyard next door, with two full auto machine guns and a .45 caliber or .357 Magnum pistol, that opened up firing on the exterior wall of my motel room, with a burst of rounds into my window. With glass and bullets flying around the room, I was under the bed in two seconds flat, until the 150 rounds or so subsided. Figuring that they would be upstairs, kicking the door in at any moment to finish me off, I, of course, began calling Jesus and my Guides to assist me to prepare for my imminent crossing over. Many Spirits were there watching and answered me, but I couldn't hear them because I was too freaked out. I just waited, waited, and continued to wait, until a half hour passed while I expected my door to be kicked in, and finally I realized they weren't coming. What a privilege to have them waste 150 rounds on me, considering that for most people, they usually only use two!

I packed my backpack and headed out at the first crack of daylight and walked to Charlie's grandmother's house. I went inside, sat down in the kitchen, and waited for the first person to wake up to make me coffee. Charlie's grandma, Lisa, was naturally surprised to see me sitting in the kitchen when she came in to light the stove. Others quickly began to awaken, and while having breakfast, I explained what had just occurred. After breakfast, I said goodbye to everyone before Marcy and I walked to the bus station, where we took a three-hour bus ride back to Guatemala City.

As we sat on the bus before leaving, I pointed out to Marcy a lookout guy who was watching me to make sure this big gringo was leaving town. Marcy said, "Give me twenty dollars, quick."

"For what?" I asked.

"I'll tell you in a minute. Just hurry."

OK. She took my twenty bucks, ran off the bus, and with her rural roots kicking in, on her tippy-toes, with her finger pointing directly into the tattooed face of the big, bad-looking dude, she sternly gave him an order and handed him the twenty dollars, after which he nodded his head in agreement with her order. When she got back on the bus, everyone else knew exactly what happened except me. After a few minutes she told me, "You're safe now" and that I would be able to come back and visit in the future, but to wait for her email in a few weeks and she would let me know for certain. I didn't ask her why in the world she thought I would ever want to go back there.

After we arrived in Guatemala City, we hugged our goodbyes. She put me on another bus, and ten hours later, I was back to my old village again. With some food, a case of beer, and a gallon of water, I headed off on an old jungle trail and a short time later passed out in Gorgonio's hammock. I was awakened by him standing over me with his machete, while sporting a big smile on his face, laughing at me. We then both laughed. Of course ,I told him what happened, and after a couple of days of calming down, I headed back to Florida.

Three weeks later Marcy sent me an email stating, "The big boss said you can come back anytime you want to visit, but you can't stay longer than three days. For the seventy-two hours you are there, you will have the cartel boss's personal, private army protect you twenty-four hours a day, even from the police, but after that, they won't promise you anything." I guess paying for the bullets was a nice gesture, but I have never been back to Grandma's house. Charlie was really mad at those guys.

When I returned home to the condo, of course, I went straight to my enclosed sacred balcony space to check on my beautiful two-mile view of the Intracoastal Waterway with a peek out to the ocean, which never gets old. Before leaving the condo a week prior, I had securely repositioned my blue ceramic Mayan mask on a small, level end table, checked, and locked all doors securely within the hurricane-proof enclosure. As I opened the curtains to the balcony, there on the floor I saw the mask in one thousand small pieces. No one else had entered the house and all windows and doors were completely closed and airtight. The mask had exploded. I knew instantly, but messages received later that day confirmed to me when I inquired, was that the Spirit occupying the "object" was of lower vibration and was unwelcome there. The next day, I swept up the pieces, put them in a bag, and scattered them into the ocean.

When I drive long distances, I'm often able to consolidate messages into decisive and effective plans, and the following month while driving to Colorado to begin supervising construction of my new cabin was no different. I felt everything in order and commenced my new project according to plan. Things went well and allowed downtime for me in between contractors' work schedules so that I could take off for a few days in my camper out to Utah. I enjoy viewing the dark night sky from various National Parks; my favorite is Canyonlands, and I was fortunate to again witness a few more "night clicks" of time-slip. Gazing up to Arcturus, the Pleiades,

Orion, and the Sirius star systems continually attracted more of my interest, since I have always known there exists some type of intelligent information waiting there for me to access. Grandpa told me so.

Getting away from a toxic environment of massive numbers of freeloaders on society, some government employees included, was a relief. Connecting to Source through core energy continued my in-depth reception of teachings while both awake and asleep. I recalled a slow regression of my personal attributes and makeup, which offered more insight as to previous lives and how everything all fits together. Kind of like a giant puzzle—slow and steady finishes the race. Many fascinating (to me) details were revealed, repeated, and explained to me in a way that I was afforded comprehension and absorption of the extreme depths and complexity to which everything and all life is intertwined, as has been previously presented to me. Multiple experiences of clear perception are necessary just to begin one's conception of the whole. Meditations continued to reaffirm that "south" was most important for me to continue my knowledge and search of origin, since the past few years had accelerated my desire to follow both the spiritual and physical path to Source.

SANTA LIBRADA

After several months of working on my mountain retreat, I decided to take a quick trip to experience a great annual fiesta that I heard about in Panama, called the Festival of Santa Librada, so "south" it was, and I ended up in Panama City, Panama. I checked in to my hotel, walked around to explore the city for a while and, of course, found my way to the fish market, one of the best! The next day I made my way to Las Tablas on the Azuero Peninsula. The annual festival of Santa Librada has continued there for hundreds of years and maintains many original traditions in music, dress, dancing, food, rodeos, and drinking. It was my first experience of a street party that went on twenty-four seven for a week that was safe, and their Atlas beer was excellent. What a concept, as this was a new Central America that I previously had been unaware of! Various events each day were entertaining, with nightly fireworks, a grand parade, rodeo, music, lots of friendly people dancing in the streets, and many food vendors, and at the end of the festival, the grand prize winner with the most beautiful pollera (their customary exquisite dresses that sometimes take a year to create) was crowned the Festival Queen. Several parade floats were intricately decorated with extraordinary symbols and reproductions of ancient heads with goggle eyes, hybrid animals, and religious artifacts, indicating their recognition of our potential origin.

In the early 1500s, three Catholic nuns "brought" the Spirits of Santa Librada and her sisters from a European village back to Panama to protect the country from the pirates of centuries ago who robbed, raped, and slaughtered the residents of Panama City. The Spirit apparition of this Saint is frequently reported to appear throughout the region, often in Las Tablas late at night hovering above a residential intersection to make sure the walking person gets home safely, and also, she has been seen many times out on the ocean watching over fishermen. After five hundred years, Santa Librada and her sisters remain to this day the patron Saints of Las Tablas and the Azuero peninsula.

In the village park one night, across the street from the church, I zoomed in my digital camera to the open attic window above the front doors and clicked away. The next day when I examined the photo chip in my laptop, I had an amazingly clear picture of her Spirit apparition. Try taking a photo with your digital camera sometime at night, with no flash in a dark church or cemetery. Then put the chip in, or send the picture to your computer. Those small circles of light, rounded colorful orbs, or powerful radiant light beams jutting out from Earth into the atmosphere are extraordinary treats of nature exposing little-known phenomena, and there is nothing wrong with your camera. Try this also if you vacation in western US national parks at night, by clicking away in total darkness. Whoa! Surprise!

While driving back to Panama City to return my rental car and then fly home the next day, on a rural stretch of highway, I sensed my Guides wanted me to take the next left. *No way*, I thought, because I still had a long way to go and it was getting late, so I passed the corner and kept driving and instantly sensed, "You've got one more chance, so turn left at the next corner!" OK, the curiosity was killing me. I thought, *What's up?* I turned left at the next corner about a half mile farther down the highway and drove slowly through a sparsely populated neighborhood of older houses while looking for someone, but uncertain as to whom. After a quarter mile, the road then began to circle around in a big loop back to the highway to the street I passed up the first time.

A hundred yards up the street, there was a guy slowly walking along the road, where I stopped to talk to him. He had a ten-inch-long stub extending out of his shoulder with two fingers and no arms. I told him I was just traveling through because I thought that his neighborhood was very nice and asked him what it was like to live there. You can imagine his answers describing living in a country with little or no government assistance for the disabled, and him being unable to provide food for himself. We spiritually chatted for a few minutes before I offered him a little financial assistance and then continued on my way back to the highway, when I heard, "That meant more than you know. Thank you for doing that, Jimmy." I drove back to the city, returned my rental car, and flew back to Colorado the next day.

RETURN TO CAMP

After a few weeks back in the mountains doing my typical daily work chores, I became aware of, and familiar with, a new group of associated energies of various vibration, neither good nor bad; they were another aspect of a conscious group operating in an alternate dimension. Primarily, I connected to the Ancient Ones, who that summer I learned have been with me "since the beginning," and were also the same as the Ancient Ones in my previous travels to

Central America. I was told that we will communicate more frequently since I have a desire to know truth, but their presence with me would remain unchanged. With more time spent under the western night sky, my interest became more pronounced in studying human origin, especially since I have always felt that much of our mainstream textbook teachings have frequently professed a big load of bull manure. And people actually get paid to teach and sell it! What a concept…getting paid to sell bullshit! Wow, there's a productive contribution to society for ya! Sounds not unlike some of the real estate agents I met.

Continuing meditation and communication in the forest with a large group of various Spirit entities, while kicking back next to my daily campfire, we agreed to hold and maintain the land and new cabin for only those of light vibration. Certain information and responsibilities were imparted to me at the time, primarily focusing on attention, although I didn't entirely understand it at the time. I sensed that area had become a sacred space for central meeting and planning by light energies, to invite other lower earthbound energies to also participate, plan, and teach according to God's plan.

After finishing my supper next to the campfire one late summer afternoon, I hopped in my old beater F-250 pickup truck and headed up the mountain on a narrow one-lane dirt road about ten miles, to view the sunset from an expansive viewpoint. Halfway up the mountain, I pulled over and stopped in the dense, heavily wooded forest on the left-hand side of the road to take a leak next to a big bush under the tall pines. I opened the door and stepped out, just a few feet from my truck, when instantly on the other side of the straggly bush a giant bear stood up on two hind legs on the other side of the bush, just fifteen feet in front of me. While we stared each other down, eye to eye without a blink, my heart stopped, and I froze, and then began my mental prayer to Jesus thanking Him for my life, and told Him to get ready, "'Cause I'm coming." Something deep inside my brain told me to then intensely send telepathic energy to my potential opponent, which I did for the better part of a whole minute.

I tried to send a sense of peace, love, and calmness in a nonthreatening manner for what seemed like eternity, but actually it was less than a full minute. The enormous bear, with beautiful cinnamon-colored fur, then slowly turned away and lumbered off into the forest on all fours, with her baby cub sniffing at her butt following behind. I continued to stand motionless, in awe and shock, watching them walk away through the trees until they were out of sight. Although I was in shock and didn't feel as though I was occupying my body, I got back in my truck, turned around, and drove back to camp. The experience shook me to the bone, and I continued for the rest of the evening trying to wrap my brain around what had just occurred. The indescribable experience impacted me enough to keep me awake for two days straight and also permanently changed me, as to how I view life, death, and the perception and connectedness of thought consciousness by animals.

As the cabin shell neared completion and the half-dozen subcontractors were then finished, all of a sudden, within a week of their finishing work for me, bad things started happening to most of them. One guy ended up losing visitation rights to his kids; another guy got really sick; another guy had a high-speed motorcycle crash and was in the hospital for three months; another guy lost his house; the electrician flipped head over heels walking off the front porch; and the last guy, a roofer with only three screws remaining to install, fell off the roof and broke his back. What did they all have in common? The only thing I recall is that while I sat meditating in front of my campfire every day, they were the ones that made fun of and spoke derogatory words about me, Jesus, and Spirit. Do *you* believe karmic law prevails? Ask them.

With my laidback lifestyle in camp for the summer, meditations continually unveiled stronger connections to Source with clarity. It was strongly suggested by Source that I needed to complete an important "diversification" project in the Caribbean. Where should

I go? I have no idea, and it doesn't matter, because where I end up will be exactly where I am supposed to be. It was to be for a larger group of people, but I wasn't able to clearly see or feel what I was supposed to do. I have learned by now that details are unimportant to know—just go.

After winterizing the cabin and cleaning up camp in preparation for winter, I returned to Florida in the fall and bought my ticket to the Dominican Republic for eighteen days. A few days prior to my departure, I visited with one of several intuitive friends at Cassadaga Spiritualist Camp (in north Florida), where I occasionally seek advice. We chatted for a while, and one of the things Claire said was that I would be doing something in Haiti. Well, of course, I figured that was probably "bleed through" because the two countries share the same island, and I had no intention of going to Haiti.

DOMINICAN REPUBLIC

I packed my bags and headed to the airport a few days later and ended up in a hotel on an other-than-great tourist beach. While walking around the main tourist area that afternoon, chatting with expats and experiencing their local culinary specialties, I learned of an exceptionally poor neighborhood about five miles away named Barrio Hai-ti. I felt that was *the* place, so the following day around noon I hailed a taxi and told the driver to take me to Barrio Hai-ti. He told me that it was a really bad idea for me to go there due to safety concerns, as it was known as an exceedingly dangerous area. He said, "No, let me take you to a nicer place."

I firmly told him, "Just go. Don't worry; nobody bothers me, or else just let me out of the car right here." So after one more attempt to convince me otherwise, he finally agreed to drive me where I asked to go. Upon arrival to the middle of the barrio, I saw a small vacant block of land about the size of a football field turned into a local park with some swings, a basketball court, and a few things for little kids to play on. The neighborhood park was surrounded on three sides by short blocks of small, run-down houses side by side, where I noticed several people closely watched me as I departed the taxi to sit under a shade tree for cover from the intense afternoon sun.

It was obviously a rough place in an economically distressed area, where only a few kids and women were out and about, although several more of them watched me from their second-floor balconies while calling on their cell phones asking each other who the heck is this big white guy sitting in their little black park. I sat peacefully contemplating, and within twenty minutes, a well-dressed man carrying a Bible walked past me and sat beneath the next tree about thirty feet over.

After a few minutes passed, I said hello and asked him, "Sir, would you like a cold Coca-Cola from the tienda (small store) over there?"

"Well, yes, I would like that very much, thank you," he smilingly replied.

I went to the little store across the street and came back under the tree where we visited with our cold sodas. He explained that he was the preacher of the local congregation and told me of the religious hardships they experienced while living there because Dominicans don't like Haitians in their churches, and that Dominicans have been killing Haitians for hundreds of years, just because they are Haitian and for no other reason. I asked him where his church was, and he told me they only pray in some of the church members' houses, twenty to twenty-five at a time, because their houses were too small for all of them to pray together at the same time. I thought that maybe this could be my project, building a small church. I asked him a few questions regarding his religious beliefs, and after his response, I felt the Masters smiling at me, with a warm euphoric feeling flowing through me, in complete silence. That was all I needed to know.

"Do you have any land to build on?" I asked.

"No, but we have approval to build a prayer center on the second floor of that community center down there on the corner," he replied, while pointing to a newly constructed cement-block building about thirty feet wide by eighty feet long. "An international volunteer group built that building for the children in our community. You see that brown car parked across the street from the center?" he asked while pointing at it.

"Yes, I do."

"Well, in the back of that car, there are approved plans stamped by the architect and the building department, ready to go; we just don't have any money," he said.

I proceeded to explain that I maintain a strong line of communication with powerful forces of the universe, in particular God, Jesus, and the Archangels. I then explained that I am a Soldier for Jesus and do small independent missionary projects such as installing cement floors in jungle churches and assisting quadriplegics, kids with malnutrition, and rural women with ovarian cancer, among other things. I told him that his project fell within the guidelines of my work and then asked if he knew a general contractor, and if so, I would like to talk to him.

He made a phone call, and ten minutes later, a parishioner contractor showed up in his pickup truck. He said he was a general contractor (GC) familiar with the plans and was looking for work. For a half hour, we discussed the cost of materials, the cost and availability of labor, and his fee, and shortly thereafter, the three of us drove to the construction materials supply center, where I bought $5,000 worth of materials on my American Express card. The GC said there were more men available than we needed, ready, willing, and able to start work immediately. I suggested fifteen men, and he agreed, but he thought it was best to hire eighteen so that he could fire three of them after a day or two, ensuring that the other workers put in an honest day's work for the remainder of the project or get canned themselves.

The following morning when I returned to the barrio after breakfast, seventeen men, more than half appearing to be overly tattooed "bad dudes," and I mean *really bad dudes*, were shoveling a truckload of sand up onto the roof. Others were cutting rebar and wire, along with putting up bags of cement and block, with a few guys already mixing cement and laying out the first course of block. I walked around the site, accounting for the delivered materials, and said good morning to everyone, and thought the whole situation was fairly impressive, since I had left my condo in Florida only forty-eight hours prior and already had a full-blown project in gear. I was a bit taken back, though, because I sensed a *lot* of those guys, too many, were ruthless, merciless, immoral animals. Throughout my travels, I have learned to identify also ones stalking me in preparation for robbery, or worse, and almost every one of them fit the energy signatures of the worst of all. I place my full faith and security in Jesus, AA Michael, and many other Spirits for undeterred focus on completion of our mission. I am a Soldier for Jesus at the core of my being, and I march forward with unparalleled security to effectuate completion of a project.

Visiting with the preacher while watching the men work, as we sat under the shade tree across the street in the park, my Guides gave me confirmation: "Just like old home week, brother, a bunch of them are killers, and most of the others have done some really wicked stuff." Their message caught me by complete surprise, as I began mentally cracking up laughing at them, while I felt equally amazed by the scope of the project at the same time, and the entire situation that had been manifested by Spirit. *Unbelievable*, I thought. *You're throwing me into a massive lion's den!* I hollered at my Guides. *Why are you doing this to me!* I internally hollered. Then there were a few moments of silence while I mentally recomposed myself.

Which ones? Who are they? Tell me; I want to know which ones! I firmly thought.

"You've been prepared for this; it would be best for you to find out for yourself, so *you* can do that," was their unexpected response. "You can do that." It seemed that I was just given permission to screw with these guys' minds! So cool! Of course, I was determined to know who the killers were on my new construction crew, so I had to get creative. Hmmm…I need to spin their brains and unsettle them a little, each one of them, right? I thought about it carefully for a while, to methodically and safely create a plan in the best interests of all concerned. Got it! For only twenty bucks, I get to find out. *This will be awesome,* I thought. How exciting!

So at 2:00 p.m. that hot afternoon, I bought eighteen cold Cokes and brought them up to the work area. I personally handed out the bottles, mostly one by one, which allowed me to look directly into the eyes of each guy. Half would not look at me, and two of them wouldn't come near me and told me, "Just set it over there; I'll get it in a minute." The energy signatures of more than a half dozen of them just reeked of violent death, and many of the others, pure evil. I said to each of them things like, "I don't know if you realize what you got yourself into working here, but you're helping to build a house of *God*!" I chuckled and pissed off the first one, before I turned to the next. "You're workin' for *Jesus* today!" I hollered as I handed over the second soda. "Careful now, you might start workin' for Jesus *every* day!" as I walked over and belted out to the next. As I kept moving slowly around the project, I laughed at the next guy while handing him a bottle, and said, "Did the boss actually tell you that you had a job buildin' a house of God today? You probably never thought a day in your life that you might work for Jesus, didja? Well, things are different today, for *all* of you, whether you like it or not, 'cause you're buildin' a church!"

After a few moments of silence, I continued, "Each one of you will have a small favor of something good come to you from Spirit, in appreciation of your helping build this prayer house, maybe not today or tomorrow, but within the next few days. Something will happen to you, and you'll know. You'll see. And the more things you do to help Spirit, the more good things will come to you in your life." A minute later, while handing over three more Cokes to three guys together, I loudly and firmly demanded, "Now, you're gonna teach your kids about Angels before they go to sleep tonight! Jesus told me to tell *you* to *do it!*" Then, after a comment to almost every one of them, after the last guy there was silence; no one said a word. Before descending the ladder, I turned around and spoke to all of them: "Who are you really building this place for? Not *me*! It's for your mother, your grandmother, your wife, girlfriend, and kids." I belted out, "So when it's done, they can come here and pray for your ass, and *mine* too, 'cause the Lord knows, I need it!" I went down the ladder quickly, before anyone of them could get to me and throw me off the roof!

I know it crossed the mind of two or three of them to kill me right there on the spot, but I got through to a bunch of them. Even though they may have wanted to, they wouldn't hurt me because there was too much at risk. If anything happened to me, all of the guys would be out of work, and they were depending on the job to at least provide a good meal for their families' Sunday dinner and new pairs of shoes for their kids. They were not only killers, but rapists, child molesters, extortionists, kidnappers, and an arsonist. Several had killed multiple people, including an old lady. Just like old home week!

I returned across the street back under the shade tree in the park, and after recomposing myself following the soda distribution, although still feeling quite unsettled, I recall laughing when Spirit reminded me again, with the humored dual message of "Turn the TV off; everything is OK." It was extremely comforting to hear that. That particular message caught me by complete surprise, as my previous impression was that Jesus comes from the highest level of core consciousness and ultimate reality, and there, He reconfirmed His and the Masters' direct, hands-on participation with me, and that the Spirit group working with me has been the same all along. Jesus and His friends all work together.

The men were paid weekly with cash that I gave to the general contractor the day before payday, since I was nowhere to be seen around the barrio on Fridays to reduce the risk of me being kidnapped and robbed by one or more of their friends. My invisible Helpers and I accomplish amazing things together and successfully completed another mission even while working in the midst of brutal killers and child molesters. After two weeks, my work was finished. I said goodbye and returned home to Florida. What continued to spin *my* brain, though, is how Jesus and His friends led me to work with some really bad people, yet kept me safe at the same time, even while messing with their screwed-up heads and pissing off the worst of them!

That was a crazy mission! Apparently, just a typical day on the job for my Bosses though. I don't recommend *anyone* antagonize killers, under any circumstances. It will most probably lead to your having a really, really bad day, and most likely your *last* day! That was a unique time, place, and circumstance, of an appropriate lesson given with assistance and guidance channeled under the direction and protection of Spirit, working for Jesus. I pulled out a journal and jotted some notes with extra details about that mission, since I felt it would be a good story for me to entertain a church congregation someday. It never occurred to me the story would end up in a book.

YOGANANDA AND KRIYA

Finishing up with the journal and kicking back on my balcony reading a magazine, I saw that Roy Eugene Davis, a direct disciple of Paramahansa Yogananda, was to give a Kriya Yoga lecture in West Palm Beach the following January. I cut the ad out and laid it on my desk as a reminder to revisit the thought a month or two later. Then, about a month prior to Roy's class on Kriya Yoga, I had a powerful middle-of-the-night spiritual visitation from Yogananda, who told me that my plans were made to attend and meet Roy: "So don't forget." Learning Kriya was important to me because of the similarities in beliefs between Christianity and Hinduism, and I wanted to know the connection.

I showed up to a hotel conference hall and enjoyed the lecture with about two hundred other folks one Sunday, half of whom later that afternoon met the requirements as taught by the lineage of Yogananda and his gurus and became Kriya Initiates, including myself. When Roy gave his introduction, he began by stating that he left his family's farm in Indiana at age eighteen, and that he was intuitively guided to go south, so he went to Miami. A few days after arriving, he knew he was in the wrong place because he then realized that he went southeast and was supposed to go southwest. (This was significant to me because I also have detoured many times due to misinterpretation.) A week later he was on the bus and arrived in California; shortly thereafter, he met Yogananda by "coincidence" and was then accepted by him as a disciple. In the class, I learned the history and dedication of Roy's life, being ordained by Yogananda and promoting Kriya in the traditional lineage as taught by Babaji, Lahiri, Yukteshwar, and Yogananda. Maybe you know that Jesus and Babaji were good friends. It wasn't until the following weeks that I recognized a deeper awareness and connection with all of them. Did Jesus send me there to begin with?

Many of the teachings of Kriya Yoga resonated with not only my thought process, but also in ways I have often lived. When I understood the parallels between Jesus's teachings, Christianity, and the common thread of Oneness that unites science and religion, I decided to purchase several cases of Roy's books on Kriya and meditation for distribution in my travels. Roy published several excellent pamphlets and many authoritative books of qualified instructional information on Kriya, in the interest of following Yogananda's desire to teach millions of people how to find and connect with God. In the springtime while driving back to work on my mountain retreat, I detoured to visit the Center for Spiritual Awareness (CSA) in northeast Georgia, built and maintained by Roy Eugene Davis.

Driving on the interstate in north Florida on my way to the CSA compound, hosted by Yogananda, I had no intention of stopping in a restaurant to eat. When driving longer distances, I usually get gas, buy a snack, and continue down the road eating in the car. This particular day, however, was a bit different in that I was told to get off the next exit and go wait a half hour in a restaurant. Reluctantly, I exited, found a Denny's or Village Inn, and took a booth for coffee and a slice of pie. After checking the weather map and reading and sending an email or two, I had my pie and coffee. Before leaving the restaurant, I checked the traffic map and saw there was a major crash causing a backup fifteen miles north of where I just got off the interstate. Checking the time of occurrence, it was exactly fifteen minutes after I exited the freeway to have coffee. Several people were killed and many injured in a multiple car wreck.

The night before arriving at the CSA, I stayed in a nearby hotel when, at approximately 3:00 a.m., Yogananda personally appeared to me in Spirit apparition, by calmly waking me from my sleep. He expressed his sincere appreciation to me, and while we visited briefly, he thanked me for my interest in continuing his work and teachings of Kriya.

He knows I have a strong personality, so before departing, his last words to me were double-edged humor. "Go easy on ol' Roy," I firmly heard.

"Oh, my gosh!" I exclaimed; I was cracking up! "Oops, my bad (intentional). That's right; when you were a child, you were born into the Ghosh family!"

He was very OK with my comment, as Spirit deeply appreciates lovingly expressed wit and humor. It was also funny because Yogananda knew that I had already predetermined to buy a fifty-pound bag of "Ol' Roy" dog food at Walmart in Colorado, as I have done many times in the past, to take up into the forest for the animals (primarily for the birds), and Roy at that time was already in his eighties.

After arriving at the CSA compound the following morning, I found my way into the meditation hall, since Roy had not yet arrived to his office. I took off my shoes, walked in, and sat down directly in front of the wide altar, where the white marble busts convene of Babaji, Lahiri, Yukteshwar, and Yogananda, and just began to relax. I felt a strong, concentrated energy presence in the room, when after a few minutes I opened my eyes, and while looking at each one, I felt they were readily available and eager to communicate. I mentally asked different questions directed to each of them while looking directly at their eyes, and I gained a wealth of enlightened information, which assisted me to continue on my unique spiritual path. I understood their common theme was that they also work for Jesus. Each one of them thanked me and said they appreciate me greatly, and they will assist me in promoting Kriya Yoga, or any other spiritual or religious practice that draw people to Jesus or Kriya, to whatever extent I choose, anytime, anywhere.

I went back to Roy's office, where we visited for a short while, got the books loaded into my Jeep, and headed out. During the course of the following three years, I distributed over one thousand books and pamphlets to various people in groups, churches, meetings, and organizations where they had an interest in learning to connect. The teaching of meditation straight from the lineage of Babaji has helped my life in so many profound ways; therefore, I continue to distribute the best information that I know how to help others elevate their knowledge, wisdom, and vibration to live a spiritually awakened and rewarding life like myself. It's not about teaching who God is but *is* teaching people to find God themselves. Occasionally practicing Kriya has also opened other areas of my higher self; among them is allowing recall of events before I was born, such as when I was ready to first occupy my new body. I was so excited that I almost came into being too soon, when my Guides held me back for a minute or two so I would circumvent becoming my sister! She is two years older than me.

The year 2015 seemed to pick up the pace for me, as my reception with spiritual events continued to occur more frequently, having become more aware of and in tune with spiritual messages. It was either a combination of my evolving, or a misconception on my part because of then regularly having maintained a journal of my experiences, which enabled my recognition of the frequency of improbable coincidences. Examples are presented here with hope that readers will elevate their listening ability, trust, and understanding of personal God-Sourced Spirit Guides that impart messages to them for their benefit and society as a whole.

MEET CAROLINA

On one of my visits to Guatemala for a week to visit with Charlie and his family, his cousins who also live in the same house, began to talk about occasionally having seen Spirits in the middle of the night when they got up to use the bathroom. Once there was a dark apparition of a man on the rear inside stairway, but most frequently seen was a pretty young girl with long black hair who sat on the stairway landing with a view of the hallway, kitchen, and bathroom entry door. While lying on the bed with Charlie my first night of that particular visit, he explained to me that the Spirit girl was his friend who lived in the house with her family a long time ago. He told me that her name was Carolina, and they have been very dear friends for the past several years, although he has kept that to himself, other than referring to her as "another" Spirit. Knowing that others would make fun of him having a Spirit girlfriend ten years old, he said nothing until I suggested that we have a spiritual prayer gathering and ceremony to officially recognize, welcome, and adopt her into his home and family.

The following evening, we set a place for her at the dinner table. I lit a candle in her name, and I said the Lord's Prayer aloud in English, after which everyone else said it in Spanish. I explained to the family, that Carolina (Carli) was to receive the same respect as everyone else in the house, and they needed to understand that she helps protect them all because she loves them. She never had love in her family while she was alive, so she truly appreciated and longed for being a part of Charlie's family with massive amounts of love that now permeate the walls of his house. She frequently slept on the bed with us, next to Marcy, Charlie, and I, and many times, I physically felt her presence cuddling in between us. Forty years ago, Carli's mother and father had severe familial issues, resulting in her mother causing her death. Both of her parents, and younger brother, are now deceased; however, Carolina's aunt (her mother's sister) was alive and well.

While out for a walk around the neighborhood one evening after supper, Charlie directed us to, and pointed out, the house three blocks away, where Carli's aunt lived. I knocked at the door, but no one was home. I asked one of the neighbors a few questions, and he confirmed that the lady we were asking about had other family members that used to live a few blocks over, a long time ago. "But they are all dead now," he replied. Charlie said that Carli's aunt could have prevented her death but refused to interfere. The visit there was unsettling, and Charlie never wanted to return near that house. Due to her death, Carli's mother was sent to prison and died there. So now, I too, have what many people would refer to as an "imaginary" friend. It is a privilege, no matter what you may think.

The evening before I was to return home, with most of the ten family occupant members present in the living room watching television, Charlie said, "I don't want you to help me anymore, not now." There was deafening silence when his aunt muted the television, while we all looked at each other, unable to process what we just heard. Since I have substantially provided for his well-being for almost fifteen years, that was quite a shock for all of us to hear. His aunt asked him to repeat what he just said, and he did.

"It's time for you to help someone else," he said.

"Who, Charlie?" I asked.

"A boy just like me, with a crazy family like mine," he laughingly replied.

I asked him, "Is this a joke?"

"No!" was his very serious response.

"Where is he?" I asked.

"Mexico," he answered.

Of course, I instantly thought there was no way, been there, done that, almost got killed there, and I'm not going back. "Where in Mexico?" I asked.

"You know. Just go there, and you will find him; I will help you," he said.

With the television muted, total silence continued throughout the room, until Marcy and his aunt Rosa asked him a few questions for clarification. I was to find this boy, help him, and afterward I could continue helping Charlie and his family again. (Doctors, medicine, supplies, medical equipment, daily care, and maintenance for a quadriplegic are substantial costs, even in Guatemala.) I said that I would think about it because Mexico is just too dangerous.

"Just go fishing. You will be safe, and I will help you," he said.

"Tell me where I should go fishing, Charlie."

"Go where you used to live a long time ago."

"Baja, Mexico? Cabo San Lucas?"

"Yes," he replied.

I realized how important this was to him and told him I would think about it. While I returned on the plane to Florida, he sent me numerous, repetitive telepathic (IPP) messages reminding me of my next mission.

ANOTHER WILD MISSION

Day in and day out over the following two weeks, Charlie telepathically reminded me to do what he asked. He has a way of being a persistent pest when he so chooses! I finally gave in and agreed to go fishing, so I booked a ticket to Cabo San Lucas, a place I was familiar with from a three-month-long visit twenty-five or thirty years prior. Two months later, from Colorado, I was on my way after packing my duffel bag and small backpack, my preferred way to travel.

After picking up my rental car at the airport, I drove to my hotel, checked in, and went for a walk around town to stretch my legs after a long flight. I had a bite to eat, and then while continuing my walk past an old apartment that I rented many years ago near the marina, I came across a teenage quadriplegic boy in his wheelchair, along with his grandmother sitting on a piece of cardboard, holding out a cup for donations. Of course, I stopped to talk with them, and after a few minutes, I realized that it was Christian and his family whom I was there to help.

The grandmother's answers to particular questions then led me to know that I was there to install a cement floor in the bathroom so that Christian could be bathed with dignity. Up until then, it was their daily practice to sit Christian on the dirt floor, which then turned to mud while washing him. His basket-case mother, Tina, showed up fifteen minutes later. We introduced each other, and Grandma proceeded to explain to her in Spanish what we had been talking about. Tina agreed to accept my assistance, we walked back to my car, and then I drove us about five miles out of town to her house so that I could see what was going to be involved.

We pulled up to what appeared to be, from the dirt street in front, an enormous pile of trash. It was the saddest situation seeing two rooms inside of filth and trash, but I was determined to follow through and install the cement floor for Christian, where there currently was a dirt floor with a grate over a hole, and a nearby hose for water. I agreed with Tina to meet the following morning when we would go to Home Depot for the cement and drainpipe. When I returned in the morning, I was introduced to Christian's uncle, who was more than willing to go with me for the materials, since he volunteered to put down the floor. We purchased the materials and arranged for delivery, for which he was very thankful, and said he would do the work in the next day or two. I then left Cabo and drove north to the town of Loreto, where I got a local hotel room in town that night. It's a peaceful, scenic place with a few offshore islands, where I went fishing a long time ago, there on the Sea of Cortez.

Out that evening for a beer after a long day's drive, while I was sitting at a crowded bar, a guy asked, "Hey, don't I know you?"

Having little interest to hear vendors hawking and peddling their wares, I quickly replied, "Nope!" and he went his way out the door. As he exited the bar, a gut feeling told me that I *do* know that guy. I jumped up to chase him, but he was gone, as he quickly disappeared into the crowded street fiesta. The following morning, while sitting at a sidewalk café for breakfast, I saw the same man walking on the other side of the street. After I ran over to him, I sincerely apologized for my rude response in the bar. I introduced myself while he did the same, and I invited him back to my table for a coffee. After ten minutes of our back-and-forth rapid questioning, the names of twenty to thirty places we each had lived or traveled to over the past several decades, we were about to give up, having thought that it was a mistake on both of our parts. We were perplexed and just laughed while unable to figure it out, until I slammed the table with my hand and hollered out, "Time-share in Cabo!" and both of us busted out laughing at the same time, while Rudy recalled a few specific details of our working together twenty-seven years ago. The weather was too windy for fishing that day, so we took a day drive up into the mountains of central Baja, reminiscing about parties past, and just explored a few neat places for the day until we returned to town late that afternoon. It was good to see old Rudy.

Over the next couple of days, I slowly headed south and arrived one evening back to my hotel in Cabo San Lucas. The following morning, I had to return my rental car, and then afterward, I took a taxi to see Christian around noon. His uncle was just finishing up the job, so I didn't have much work to do in the sweltering heat. The family was grateful, and Christian was happy about getting a new floor. After we finished up on that late Friday afternoon, I said goodbye since I was getting ready to go home the next day, and then hopped on a bus headed downtown toward the marina.

I got off the bus about five blocks away to enjoy an early dinner at a nontourist restaurant, and thereafter walked in the hot sun the rest of the way while contemplating an ice-cold beer waiting for me somewhere. There are quite a few bars and restaurants located around the expansive perimeter of the marina, so I was just thinking about which one I would go to. Then I heard, "Good job, Jimmy; you can go have your beer now."

Wow, how nice to receive a message from you guys after finishing my assignment, that's so nice of you, I thought, while feeling totally wiped out from the heat.

"Who said you're finished?" I heard. "We said you could go have a beer; we never said you were finished."

I'm exhausted, tired, hungry, beat up, thirsty, my back hurts, and my feet hurt, I'm done, I thought to my Guides.

Then they know how to really get to me, by asking, "Are you quitting?"

Oh, you guys are really funny, why do you even ask me that! You know the answer, I've told you a hundred times before: no, I will never quit!

"OK, then, we have an incredibly serious and important job that won't take long; just continue to the marina and go have your beer. As a matter of fact, that's where your job is, and when you're done, you're going to want to drink two. You can rest afterward."

I knew right away this impending task was very serious because they have never, ever before told me to go drink beer. I asked what it was, and they wouldn't say anything other than, "Just don't worry. We're with you, every moment. You're safe, and everything will be OK because we're *all* with you." Then I knew it was something big, really big, because they have never presented anything to me in that manner in the past.

Continuing downhill to the marina, I arrived shortly thereafter where I walked slowly down the dock, passing each bar-restaurant while viewing the dockside tables, trying to figure out which one was mine. It was early, with hardly any customers around to distract me. The open-front bars all appeared the same, one after the other, but I chose the fourth or fifth establishment that I walked past. "There's your table," I heard, so I stepped up the two front steps, turned left, pulled out the first chair from a table in front of the rail, sat down, and kicked back, overlooking the hundreds of boats in the marina. There were about ten to twelve waiters in yellow shirts hanging around at the bar, waiting for the start of their typically busy Friday night.

Several minutes later, some cocky-ass scumbag punk waiter in his midtwenties swaggered to my table with his pad and pencil, and arrogantly stated, "What do you need?"

I was about to get up and go to the next bar because the waiter's energy made my skin crawl. Instantly I heard from my higher authorities, "Sit down; you're not going anywhere."

"Modelo Especial," I replied, with the same corresponding tone and attitude as his. I then instantly knew—here we go.

He turned around and headed back to the bar without saying a word, while my Guides then said, "OK, get ready. When he comes back, you're giving this guy a message, a *big* message."

"Message!" I exclaimed. "But I don't give messages!"

"You do now, and this is very serious and important, Jimmy. Just do it; we're counting on you."

What do I say? I wondered.

"Just open your mouth wide while looking at him, and we'll do the talking. Don't worry; just let it flow *strong*, and *follow through*."

I thought, *OK, something big is about to go down, so I need to figure out really fast how to do this. When he approaches with my beer, I'll begin to open my mouth while casually raising my finger as if I'm going to ask him a question.* Their preparing me with "OK, here he comes; get ready," was racing through my mind. I went over it many times in my mind while watching the waiter return from the bar. When he was in position at the moment of setting my beer on the table in front of me, all happening within an instant, the old New York Jimmy fired it up with my finger pointing in the guy's face, half raising out of my chair. Aggressively looking him straight in the eyes, loudly I demanded, "Don't you even *think* about following through with what you're going to do! If you do, you will *not* pass go, and you *will* go. Straight. To. Prison! Do you understand me!" My finger and I continued following him while hollering in his face as he backed away. He looked at me in complete shock, didn't say a word, turned around, and walked back to the bar.

I sat down, took a slug of beer, and slowly processed what just occurred. I couldn't believe that I just did that, but was immediately told, "Great job! And if he comes back, we're giving him some more of the same, *strong*, so don't back down. Get ready for round two, take another sip, and relax." He went back to the bar, gave my ticket to a coworker, and although he momentarily appeared to consider a return to my table, he then quickly walked straight out the back door into the parking lot. Everyone around there thought that I knew him, and they were all looking at me like, "What the hell was that all about?" (Don't ask me, I have no idea!) A few minutes later, a new waiter came over and politely asked if I would like another Modelo.

"Sí, *muchas gracias*, amigo" ("Yes, thank you very much") I pleasantly replied.

While relaxing with my second beer (I had permission for two, remember?), an employee who came in to work opened the back door, to where I could see all the way through the restaurant, down the hall, and straight out to the rear parking lot. I saw waiter number one leaning up against a car smoking a cigarette, and the door swung closed. I paid my bill and walked back to my hotel and finished packing my bag, and before going to sleep, I asked my Guides about what the heck had occurred several hours prior. On my mental vision board, I clearly saw my waiter shooting a male clerk in the head behind the counter in a small liquor store. After a good night's rest, I flew back home the next day. A month later, I asked an empath friend about it, and she also clearly saw that waiter was preparing to kill a guy after work later that evening.

That was quite an interesting mission, so I couldn't wait to get back underneath the one-hundred-foot-tall pines at my mountain campsite to relax in the oversized hammock that I brought back from Guatemala several years prior. I spent the next few days absorbing the interesting turn of events that had just occurred in Mexico, while I enjoyed a cold beer next to a nice campfire. Completely relaxed, swaying in the breeze, I heard, "Enjoying that beer? Bringing back old memories?" It was really funny; you should have been there! As they jokingly referred to my last beer in Cabo San Lucas, the Guides explained to me thoroughly that this was no big deal to them. "Just another joint mission for us, or as you say, just another day on the job for us." They appreciate my cooperation greatly. Although they are well aware that lecturing killers is not my favorite pastime, I agreed to perform these types of tasks for them when necessary, only if they guarantee my safety 100 percent. Then I think to myself, *Only if? You're bargaining with God? Are you out of your mind?* Well, now that you mention it, yes, because that's where Jesus lives and where I connect with Him and His friends.

Daily connections with Source under the massive pines strongly influenced my future physical change of direction. They slowly encouraged me more and more to seek out Source and human origin, but suggested that I first follow through with my idea to build a large pyramid structure in the space over and around my campfire pit. After laying it out on paper with my detailed calculations and measurements, it came to be a footprint of approximately twenty feet square. I needed four, 18 foot long, 8" x 8" beams for the main frame and began to think about where I would acquire them, until I clairsentiently got "Just hook up your trailer and drive west. There's a sawmill off a forest road, under an hour away." The following morning, I hooked up my eighteen-foot flatbed trailer and headed out to where I drove directly to meet Woody at his sawmill in the forest, just under one hour away. He didn't have the beams on hand, so he agreed to cut them for me, and I went back a few days later to pick them up. I did buy some rough-cut fence lumber from him while I was there, which kept me busy for a few days, while I also dug the footers for my new pyramid cabana until I went back to pick up the beams. Since I haven't perfected levitation yet, I hoisted the frame in place using ropes, pulleys, chains, and scaffold, where the peak of the capstone would be around twenty-three feet tall when it's installed.

My new pyramid cabana frame has defined enhanced energy in its space in the surrounding forest. It has not only clarified Source messages, but also increased the Spirit volume of many living things (i.e., birds, trees, animals, plants) in a way that makes their energy signature and presence more identifiable. Earthly mountain Spirit entities have also been attracted to the space, with varying degrees of light vibration, since it seems that powerful Spirits of light occupy the space there continuously, and less than favorable energies are run off. Taking an afternoon siesta in the hammock, now strung out and hanging between the beams under the pyramid, had more benefits for me at night as well.

My dream state of the times I am able to remember, frequently offered, took me, or showed me advanced concepts and locations of spiritual and scientific significance. Source information relays the fact that science concepts and technology are clearly the forefront and priority of their participation with the human race. There are armies of other entities assisting us with theory, information, creativity, and influence in support of advancement of our species. Continually seeking a stronger connection, my highest-level Guides suggested that I go farther south in my quest for more in-depth understanding of origin on this planet. If I chose to continue on my path, I needed to head to Peru, and then further south down the continent. "Just go south, all the way," was a frequent message.

CHAPTER 9
EXTENDING MY REACH
IN SEARCH OF ORIGIN

OFF TO SOUTH AMERICA

My first visit to Peru was to Cusco and through the Sacred Valley for a few days, where I absorbed an overwhelming amount of spiritual information as to the Ancient Ones' occupation, culture, connection to the Earth, cosmos, and origin. Hiking around numerous old Inca-claimed sites of massive stone fortresses built by ancient races was also a great exercise and weight-loss program for me. I had no interest to visit Machu Picchu, though, due to the excessive greed of the site's administrators and overcrowded masses of tourists interfering with, and diluting, the embedded energy there. It definitely is a must-see site, however, for those a little short on time who want a culturally impactful immersion experience. There was equally beautiful scenery and more significant pre–Ice Age places of importance to me, as I was informed, so the popular tourist site was unnecessary for me to visit, especially after I realized that many ancient sites were actually built by a pre-Inca civilization.

I spent several days taking both independent and group tours of the many massive and stately abandoned compounds, admiring the meticulous architectural construction, with many of the sites located in spectacularly stunning locations. It was there that I learned with certainty that much of our mainstream history's teachings regarding construction methodologies are deceptive to the bone. The bulk of mining, movement, form, and placement of the enormous stones was accomplished utilizing levitation and natural energy concepts, currently referred to as "unknown phenomena." I understand that it was a process of realigning and focusing a type of geoelectric magnetic energy field to harness the power necessary to perfectly cut, move, and mold the gigantic stone blocks into place on the hillsides and mountaintops. I don't think they had heavy lift helicopters back then!

After almost a week exploring the Sacred Valley, "continue south," was the predominant message. So I headed south on a bus to Puno for a few days to Lake Titicaca, where I made tour arrangements to spend two nights at a homestay on an island with a local Aymara family in their guesthouse. When I showed up on the island with a thirty-five-pound sack of provisions (i.e., fruits and vegetables from a local mainland market), I received a welcome comparable to that of a long-lost brother. Farming as a way of life is difficult at over twelve thousand feet, and any contribution to the kitchen table is much appreciated. My host family were local farmers that worked from sunrise to sunset, as most other six hundred residents did on the island. They were welcoming and accommodating with their extremely limited resources, and I felt like I had stepped back in time while I was there. Because of limited electricity and light bulbs on the island, the night sky was fabulous, lacking distortion by light pollution. Nightly connections were profound, and I was able to connect with localized indigenous Source energies in common with the Maya. *How could this be?* I thought. *Thousands of miles away here in the Southern Hemisphere, having the same Source connection, while at the same time identifying completely different Spirits?* It was all finally beginning to sink in, as the picture-puzzle of life began to form.

One funny thing in common with many places I had visited was that each time I showed up in a new town, there was a parade that started within a half hour of my arrival, except for Puno, where the annual indigenous *sampona* (Andean pan flute) festival had already begun earlier that day. The event consisted of fifty outlying villages' marching bands beating their drums while parading through the streets around the center of town, with each group creating their ancient music with twenty-four sampona and twelve bass drums. The indigenous bands each had between ten and thirty dancing girls, all wearing and spinning in their colorful native polleras, which substantially added to the ambience of the event. Having a free schedule without definitive reservations allowed me to travel intuitively, and the four or five different cities and towns where I visited that week, starting in Cusco, all the way to La Paz, Bolivia, coincidentally greeted my arrival with a parade! Sounds to me as if there's a party goin' on!

ISLA DEL SOL

Before getting back on the bus a few days later to Copacabana and Isla del Sol, at seven o'clock in the morning, I sat waiting in the Puno bus station. I wondered, *Why do so many people say to be careful in this particular bus station? There's hardly anybody here, except an old lady and a few vendors.* Ten seconds later, a guy walked through the waiting area, picked up a cardboard box package off the floor, and took off running toward the back door, until he was chased and tackled by an undercover security guard. Then when I stood up to watch, the old lady came near me and tried to pick my pocket. Go figure!

I boarded my bus and arrived several hours later at the boarding dock for the Island of the Sun, or in Spanish, Isla del Sol, about 150 miles toward the southeastern part of the lake, at the Bolivia border. It is claimed by many indigenous teachings and legends to be the origin of mankind in South America. Located underwater in many areas near there, at varying depths, are numerous remaining stone carvings, steps, and foundations of structures believed by some to be from villages that date from several ice ages past. I bought my five-dollar boat ticket, and twenty of us set out on our relaxed one-hour excursion over to the island. After paying my tourist tax upon arrival, I hired a porter to carry my duffel bag, as many tourists did, and we began our exhausting one-hour ascent of the mountain. Stopping to rest a few times was necessary, since the air was pretty thin at that altitude, and my deaf-mute teenager guide didn't do too well with directions.

While based for several days at a five-cabin motel perched on the mountain side, with a fabulous panoramic view from my picture window, I explored the island daily. I hiked parts of the old Inca trail and waited three nights for the sky to clear so I could spend time under the stars at the top peak of the island. With little light emitted from the surrounding distant villages after dark, the night sky over Lake Titicaca is comparable to a living planetarium on a clear night. Except, the clouds had been solid during my entire stay there, so I went to sleep early the third night, ready to depart the island the following morning. Asleep like a dead horse after hiking around the island all day at 12,500 feet elevation, around midnight I heard, "OK, Jimmy, let's go! It's time to get up, get dressed, *now*, and get your boots on. Get going! Move it." The stronger they speak, the faster I move, so I was up and dressed in no time flat.

As I looked out my window, the sky was partly clearing, and I got, "But you have to hurry; we've got only a short time." After I put on four layers of warm clothes (it gets really cold up there on the Altiplano at night, two and a half miles high), I tied my boots on; grabbed my hat, binoculars, and flashlight; and headed out hiking back up part of the old Inca trail in the pitch darkness where I had been earlier that day. About forty-five minutes later, I arrived exhausted at the mountaintop and lay down on the flat roof of a small concrete lookout tower under a mostly clear sky overhead, gazing into the core of the star systems of some of our galactic neighbors. It was a spectacular show with a few shooting stars, of course, while I also had a clear connection with my Guides, whom I asked for advice on several things, including how we could lead an effective meditation for a group of people.

The Cochiti tribe, related to the Hopi, have been the preferred drum builders to other tribes for thousands of years, because they have reportedly always built some of the best indigenous drums in the Northern Hemisphere, which they used to trade for goods with other tribes. Incorporating the use of my large Cochiti ceremonial drum that I had acquired last year in New Mexico, I contemplated teaching a group of people in Florida how to open their personal connection with Source, Angelic Beings, Ascended Masters, and their higher Spirit Guides. Knowing that I would receive spiritual assistance, input, and support by utilizing that particular drum was confirmed. A thorough and detailed program was provided to me, which is available for me to use at any time. The use of my Native American drum was found particularly interesting, and its use was then reinforced by some of my Guides, due to an insufficient number of humans who function as ambassadors of Spirit, as this one does.

They also reminded me of the previous format that I used at the water's edge in Honduras, noting that my particular presentation that evening was obviously very effective as well. I also asked them a few other personal questions, including, as usual, "Where do I go next?" Although I thought that I was on my way to visit a town named after ancient star people several hundred miles away, Tiwanaku was the resounding response; however, they finished with, "But you will be continuing south." My time window of cloudless sky began to close as clouds moved in and stars disappeared after almost an hour, so I headed back down the mountain to my motel. As I opened the door to enter my room, it began to drizzle, and a minute later, it was pouring hard rain.

BOLIVIA

The next day I continued my journey to La Paz, Bolivia, and walked around the city center tourist area of a couple of hundred shops selling all kinds of pretty, colorful handmade items of fabrics, blankets, clothes, and tourist knickknacks. Of course, the "Witches' Market" was interesting, where two blocks of vendors' shops sell everything from incense and herbs to dozens of dried llama fetuses, strung from a rope for street-side display (used in symbolic ceremonies for sacrifice).

Of all the many blocks of tourist shops promoting their colorful wares, I entered one of them and met the owner, Vicki, an older Aymara lady. She and her husband help support about five hundred homeless kids living on the street at twelve thousand feet, in a brutally rough area of El Alto not recommended for gringos, about fifteen miles from downtown. They work to buy rice, beans, and used clothes for the kids, which they distribute at a church on Sundays. I wrote a small sign in English for Vicki that she could display in her store, to catch the attention of non-Spanish-speaking tourists: "The only reason I run this store is to buy food to feed homeless children."

After one night in the bustling city, I took a local bus to Tiwanaku and Puma Punku the next day, where I checked in to Hotel Akapana and asked for a room on the second floor with a window facing the ruins. I slowly walked around the village my first day to absorb the energy and culture and found that the place vibrates "ancient" to the core. The following few days I spent exploring the ruins' sites and the two local museums.

While gazing out my hotel room window at the Kalasasaya site, meditating at two and three o'clock in the morning, I established a profound connection with Source energy. They sought to inform me with deeper understanding of the culture, society, and the overall development of humans. These spiritual entities were of the most ancient origin that contributed to the establishment of humans on this planet. They also confirmed that it was them I connected with on the top of Isla del Sol; they have watched and guided my travels and connections with other ancient Spirit entities since starting in the western United States and were also the hosts of my 2012 reception. Then I heard, "Turn the TV off," and laughed with a big sigh of relief in amazement and understanding. They really do have a sense of humor (I had no television in the hotel room that I was in), and it was they who started me off on my current journey, although they have been with me all my life and prior lives as well. After this thorough and powerful realization settled in, I felt a serene sense of comfort, laid down, turned my brain off, and floated off into la-la land until I peacefully awoke the following morning.

They had waited for my arrival in Tiwanaku to confirm with me they've been the same ones all along, and to confirm the authority and Source of their Beingness, so as not to be mistaken for lower-vibration Spirits. It was imparted to me that we are all direct descendants of these ancient Beings of interdimensional higher intelligence entities that have descended and assisted God in colonization of this planet. They have been involved with the design of, and have made many adjustments to, humans' development here on this planet and in other worlds as well.

In the village, I found a local tour guide who spoke Aymara and English and asked if she would help me the following day take a taxi out to the surrounding countryside to translate for me, while we distributed three hundred pounds of quinoa to elderly people. After I answered a few of her questions and agreed on her twenty-dollar fee, we set a time to leave the following morning. She and the taxi driver picked me up at my hotel, where I had the three one-hundred-pound sacks sitting by the door ready to go. We loaded up and headed out, and a half hour later, I decided on my first little adobe house up on a hillside in a small grassy field. "OK, that one," I said.

Many houses there lack driveways and have only a narrow footpath leading to their property, since most of them have never owned a vehicle. After I rebagged twenty-five pounds into a smaller sack, we hiked ten minutes up to the one-room crumbling adobe house. Angela began hollering in Aymara, asking if anyone was there, and when she opened the door, we saw an old lady sitting inside on a blanket on the dirt floor. The women talked briefly as Angela explained that I had a gift for her from Jesus and Mother Mary. We prayed, chatted briefly, left her the bag of food, and continued on our way down the hillside and into the taxi, down the rocky dirt road, dodging cows, sheep, dogs, and a few chickens. A few miles later, we found another old person, and continued doing the same thing ten more times throughout the rolling countryside. It was an awakening day for me to say the least, as I was introduced to a whole new way of life.

Nearby life in rural areas and villages at 12,000 to 13,500 feet without mechanized agriculture is brutal. Working daily on their family plot of land, as their ancestors have done for millennia, makes up a good portion of their day, depending on the season, of course. With no money or source of substantive income, growing food to survive is their daily priority of life, along with grazing llama, alpaca, and sheep for protein, and to make thread to weave their clothing. Often, when rural people are too old to work in the fields because they can no longer walk, and they have no food, no money, and no means of support, then it is generally accepted in their society as the cycle of life that it is time for them to prepare to die. Stop work; you die. That's the way it goes. Abandonment of old people is an accepted way of life not only there but also in many places that I visited throughout South America.

The following morning, I saw Angela in front of the ticket office to the archeological site, located in the old train station across the street from the museum. After we greeted each other, she asked me if it might be possible for me to help an old lady whom she had forgotten to tell me about the previous day. Normally, I avoid or refuse help and assistance to people who ask me, except on rare occasions, because I prefer to locate people by myself through intuition. But since I had a free day before leaving town to continue on my journey, I listened.

"Well, see, Mr. Jimmy, there is a lady that lives by herself who had her house blow up, and I was thinking maybe since you like to build things [I had mentioned a couple of jungle projects to her the day before], maybe you could help fix her house," she said. I thought about it for a minute, and after she told me some more details, I agreed, so I hired the taxi driver standing in front of the ticket office. We drove off with Carlos and went a half hour up into the hills of the countryside on a one-lane dirt road with expansive views overlooking Lake Titicaca.

We arrived at the barren hilltop, where I saw a tiny adobe shed near the charred remains of a four meter by five-meter adobe house that had two walls and the roof blown out when it got struck by a lightning bolt. With the busted-out wall blocks strewn all over the rocky, grassy field I asked, "Well, where does the lady live?"

Angela motioned for me to follow her to the two-meter-by-three-meter adobe shed, which I did, and upon her opening the four-foot-tall door, I crouched down to look in and saw a sixty-year-old lady (who looked as if she was ninety) wrapped and curled up under a blanket in the corner on the dirt floor. At first, she appeared to me as a mummy until she and Angela spoke briefly in Aymara. I then learned Juanita's name, and they asked if I could help fix her house. I looked at Juanita without anyone talking for a moment and clairsentiently felt that she was preparing to die.

I firmly responded in English, "No. Why would I fix her house if she is preparing to die? Ask her, Angela!"

In Aymara, I knew Angela asked Juanita exactly what I felt, when Juanita just sadly responded by nodding her head in agreement, saying yes.

I loudly demanded, with the Jimmy finger rising to the occasion, "If you want your house fixed, then you promise God, Jesus, and *me*, right here, right now, that you will live at least thirty more years!" As indicated by her weathered eyelids raising at the precise moment the words "God" and "Jesus" came from my mouth, I knew she had an idea that something positive was coming, because the instantaneous energy of hope that was emitted from her facial expression spoke volumes. Angela translated what I had just said, and at that moment, she whipped off the blanket, dropped to her knees in front of me, and prayed in Aymara to God, Jesus, me, and Pachamama.

Angela said, "OK, Mr. Jimmy, she just promised what you asked." It was kind of funny, but sad as well—you had to be there.

I then agreed to fix her house for her and went outside to talk with Carlos, who was also a part-time contractor when work was available. He said just what I had been thinking: that it would be better to build a new house since the old one was too far gone. After we discussed materials, labor costs, the price estimate, and paced off the new corners, he said work would start in a few days with three other men he knew needed work and were available. Then, after we told Juanita that work would start in a few days, Carlos, Angela, and I drove off to a nearby village to order one thousand adobe blocks for Juanita's new house. We drove back to Tiwanaku, where I paid Carlos a deposit, agreed that he would complete the project within the next three weeks in time for Christmas, and text me when the house was done so I could come back and pay him. Just before falling asleep that evening, it was again confirmed: "Great job today, but continue south."

LITHIUM TRIANGLE

The following day, I left town and returned to La Paz, where I bought an airplane ticket leaving the following morning to Uyuni, a major stop on the international tourist trail, four hundred miles south. After a short taxi ride from the landing strip into the old dusty mining-town-turned-tourist-destination in the middle of nowhere, I checked in to a hotel that I found online, a few blocks from the center of town. The Uyuni salt flat is located at the northern apex of the so-called "lithium triangle," an area that encompasses part of southern Bolivia, northern Chile, and northern Argentina, which contains a substantial portion of the known lithium resources of the planet.

Since I've become interested in learning more about lithium, as it applies to the reduction of oil consumption and pollution of our planet caused by fossil fuel combustion cars, trucks, and buses, I signed up for a tour of the salar the next day (salt flats that stretch many miles, which were created by receding oceans eons ago). Our tour guide only spoke Spanish, so acting as a translator for the four

Asian tourists who didn't understand Spanish made for an enjoyable and fun day in our Land Cruiser.

One guy, in his late twenties or so, was a defector from North Korea who kept us entertained with stories for part of the day. While having our group lunch together, I asked him if it was true that people living out in the countryside frequently resorted to cannibalism. He momentarily paused, considering his response on a taboo subject, and replied, "Yes, but just occasionally. When they have no food for the family's child, they sometimes kill and eat them." I then told him that Kim Jong Un was looking for him, and when he answered, "He won't find me; he can't even find his socks," we all had a good laugh. Then he asked me, "Excuse me, do you have permission from Donald to be here?" which raised a few eyebrows, followed by a few light chuckles, until I replied, "Yes, he gave me a permission slip, and in the United States, we call it a *passport!*" The group went wild with loud laughs, moans, and groans, but we all had a good laugh again, and had a wonderful day overall. You should have been there!

Back in town that evening, I heard of an orphanage nearby, so the next day I found out the address, walked over, and introduced myself. The director showed me around while the kids were out at school, and I noticed one of the dorms hadn't been painted in about twenty years, so I offered to paint the room. My offer was graciously accepted, and the next morning, I showed up with a five-gallon bucket of paint, roller, and brush, and painted the room for the day. The kids were really excited when they came home from school and were extra happy with their "new" room two weeks before Christmas.

Having two weeks of extra time before I had to return to Juanita's new casita around Christmas, I decided to know the lithium triangle a little better by taking a bus to Chile and then over the mountains to northern Argentina. Traveling through the Andes in a first-class tourist bus with panoramic windows made for an enjoyable journey, with surreal scenery in remote places presenting vast expanses of barren wind-blown valleys and majestic snow-covered peaks. The backdrop of much of the extensive landscape appeared staged with a paintbrush, as the diverse colors brilliantly contrasted against the clear blue sky, with puffs of white cotton in between. The vast, open space made me feel very much at home.

After a full day's bus ride reaching fifteen thousand feet elevation crossing the mountains, five minutes before my Chilean bus pulled into the busy Argentinian bus station, I intuitively received, "Your duffel bag from the baggage compartment is about to get stolen." When the bus stopped, I quickly got off and positioned myself to the rear of the bus, with a clear view of the baggage handler unloading the bags and the crowd of people waiting nearby to retrieve their luggage. While I watched each bag get unloaded from the baggage compartment under the bus, I was able to determine who was going to steal my bag. I mentally and physically prepared myself to chase and tackle the guy at the moment he put his hand on my bag. My black bag looked similar to others, except it was clearly identified by having a bright-blue handle.

Rather than wait for the incident to occur, I was strongly moved to preemptively approach and confront the guy, prior to him touching my bag. I casually walked over to him waiting near the rear corner of the bus and let loose with the old New York Jimmy finger in his face, along with some extremely aggressive and vulgar language. He said nothing, immediately turned, and walked away. At that moment, I realized who was in on the whole scheme: the bus driver, the baggage handler, the thief, and the state police officer who was watching me from a distance; he instantly broke eye contact with me and turned and walked away at the moment I touched my bag. Inside the bus station, there was a centrally located and highly visible glass-windowed office with a counter, chairs, and a large sign over the door: "Lost Baggage Claim Office." The sign on the door read *Closed*, at three o'clock in the afternoon! The existence of a large lost-baggage office smack in the middle of the terminal's higher-rent district spoke volumes. I figured the office was there to keep the tourists out of the local police station, where travelers' missing property might potentially be seen.

Stolen baggage has obviously been, and continues to operate as, a major profit center for the criminal theft ring comprised of police and bus station employees, at the expense of primarily European, Asian, and American tourists. Even at only one bag per bus, ten or fifteen bags stolen each day, I would imagine they all have a nice little collection of laptops in their homes. Welcome to Argentina. The trip was both a cultural reality check and scenic overview for me, which afforded a firsthand look at the rampant, uncontrolled theft and corruption throughout their society, challenges of everyday tourists, and the overall burden on the honest people of their society as well.

After checking in to my hotel, I turned on the television to watch the news. Many channels showed live coverage of the bomb that had exploded several hours earlier in their capital's business district. Since I then had no desire to stay in Argentina for more than a day, I found myself back in Uyuni in under a week. When I experience things similar to that, it reminds me of why I love my country. Our Founding Fathers' intent was to live according to God's plan, and we should keep it that way.

Tica-Tica

With a few extra days remaining, that night I asked my Guides for a quick, fun project. When I awoke in the morning, I checked my map and accepted that I had a new mission to deliver five hundred pounds of food that day to a dreadfully poor, remote village in the mountains about an hour's drive from town. My first stop after breakfast was the local market, which was a square block that consisted of about one hundred vendors who sold regional fruits and vegetables. I bought five one-hundred-pound sacks each of quinoa, carrots, green beans, onions, and pasta, along with a box of smaller bags and a three-quart plastic drink pitcher to use as a scoop. Parked in front were the taxis, where I found the vehicle I wanted to travel in, and I asked the driver how much it would cost me for four hours. One hour to get to Tica-Tica, two hours there visiting with my friends, and an hour back.

"You have friends in Tica-Tica?" the driver asked.

"Yes, of course," I replied. "I am bringing them food for their Christmas presents."

The only thing I knew about the village was it occupied a tiny speck on the map about an hour away on a windy road into the mountains. Of course, I have friends there; we just haven't met each other yet! If I told the driver exactly what I planned to do, he wouldn't take me, because no one does that kind of thing by themselves; the driver would think there was something wrong with me and refuse to drive me there. We loaded the car, and an hour later, we approached the ancient, quaint little village when I stated that I would meet my friends in the central park in town. Driving slowly into the village along the narrow dirt streets lined with deteriorating adobe houses, I conveyed to the driver to stop near the corner so that I could give out some candy to a few little kids, that I had prebagged for distribution. As I threw the candy out the car window to each kid, I told them that I had a lot of food for their mother and grandmothers and to come right away to the central park.

"Run fast to your house and tell your mother that I have her Christmas food! Tell your grandparents to come *now, all* of them," I hollered.

Slowly we drove two more blocks, three more kids, same thing; next corner, two more kids, same thing. A few minutes later, we arrived at the small park square in the center of the deserted village where two cute teenage girls were walking past at the moment I stepped out of the taxi. With my Santa Claus hat on, in a white dress shirt and a big gold ankh hanging from a gold chain around my neck, I was not surprised that they at first appeared a bit puzzled before I spoke.

"Good morning! Merry Christmas! How are you? I was sent here to give this food to the children and elderly people here in this village, for Christmas presents," I said, while pointing to the large bags of provisions in the car. "I am a missionary, and I was sent here. [Of course, if I told them who sent me, they would have taken off running away as fast as they could!] Will you girls please help me for a little while, for about one hour of work helping me put this food into smaller bags, for the women and elderly people here, for Christmas gifts, please? I can pay you each fifty pesos?" (Fifty pesos was about seven dollars.)

Nobody pays that kind of money, so they were at first hesitant, thinking that's a full day's pay around there. "It's Christmas, and only for today. Will you help me, *please?*"

With big smiles, they approvingly looked at each other, said "OK,'" and were ready to start work, so I placed two Santa hats on the girls' heads and then hauled the heavy sacks of provisions into the park, in front of two benches, as the first donees began to arrive. One girl had the scoop, and the other held the bags open while they began filling ten- to twenty-pound bags for our new Christmas food distribution program in celebration of Jesus's birthday. After the first ten to twelve people arrived at the park, which turned into about thirty-five adults and as many kids within fifteen minutes, I couldn't believe what I had just gotten myself into. Old ladies, and a few men, slowly approached the park with their parents, some of whom were over *one hundred* years old, blind, deaf, crippled, couldn't walk all the way, in wheelchairs, on crutches, with a bunch of malnourished kids, some with no shoes, and others wearing clothes that hadn't been washed in a month.

While handing the first bag to the first old person, I heard from my Guides, "By the way, we forgot to tell you, Jimmy, that you are going to bless each person here today, and their food, every time you hand over a bag."

But I'm no preacher! I thought.

"You are now!" was the loving reply.

You never told me!

"Sorry, brother, we forgot, but you *have* to do it; you've been prepared for it!"

But what do I say? I demanded to know.

"Just open your mouth. You've had practice, and you're good at that!" was spoken to me in a jesting manner of love, appreciation, and reaffirmation of guidance. Each adult then was given, in Spanish, a fifteen- to twenty-second blessing to them and their Christmas food from Jesus, Mother Mary, and Santa Dorothea. (I was told that Santa Dorothea works with a group of women who assist Mother Mary helping elderly people, and children, among other tasks. Her lineage has been traced back to European royalty of the late 1300s.) Many older folks deeply thanked me and blessed me as well, some insisting that I was an Angel in human form. I always explain to people like them that it is the Angels for whom I work in partnership, and I am just the deliveryman. It was a lot of fun and also a very rewarding experience. I thoroughly enjoyed meeting all of the people from the village, and hopefully I am able to someday return there. I paid the girls and waved goodbye from the empty taxi, hollering "Feliz Navidad!" as we drove off through the mountains back to Uyuni.

The following day, I went to the local airline ticket office and bought my ticket for two days later to fly back to La Paz the day after Christmas. While sitting in a local café having my favorite *sopa de quinoa* (quinoa soup), I received a text from Carlos: "Your new house is finished," to which I replied, "OK, see you in two days."

Christmas Day I spent in town with my Santa Claus hat on at church; I watched some small celebrations and handed out candy to kids around town and at the local Christmas carnival in the park. While walking past a line of food vendors looking for a bite to eat that late afternoon, I ran into five of the kids and their teacher, whom I had met in the local orphanage the week before. We were, of course, happy to see each other and together enjoyed the carnival, but the excitement really raised when I told them they each could choose a personal Christmas present for a limited dollar amount from any of the many toy vendors nearby. Then we all went to a local restaurant for Christmas dinner: chicken, french fries, and Coca-Cola, and afterward we traded hugs and said goodbye. As I lay down on my bed that night, messages from my Guides expressed deep gratitude with joyful happiness and gave me a powerful knowing that many, many people in the community were affected by me, even though I hadn't even seen or met most of them. What a great Christmas!

I then flew back to La Paz the next day and took the bus later that afternoon to Tiwanaku. I was excited to see Juanita's new house, so Carlos picked me up at the hotel, and we drove up to see his completed project of the past three weeks. When we arrived, I was pleasantly surprised to find Juanita coming out of her new adobe block house to greet me. A finished house, with a roof, front window, and a wood door! Awesome! Carlos gave me the bill; we subtracted what I had already paid him, and I then paid him the balance while Juanita watched. She grinned ear to ear and gave me a big hug, saying "Feliz Navidad!" and other sincere blessings spoken in her native Aymara tongue. She insisted that we join her for a meal, so she quickly prepared some of her homegrown staples for us. I inspected the house, and then we visited and ate Juanita's naturally organic rations for a while with Carlos translating, and afterward we returned to the village just before sundown. The total cost to build her new house was about eight hundred dollars, the difference between life and death. A few days later, I returned to the international airport and flew home to Florida after a truly awesome Christmas adventure.

GO SOUTH, YOUNG MAN

After spending the summer in the Colorado mountains, the following fall, I winterized my cabin, covered the firepit, and closed up camp after hearing all summer underneath the pyramid, "Go south, young man, go *all* the way south." They meant it as a joking analogy to "Go west, young man, go west," as I did earlier in life, so I appreciated the humor and instantly knew, of course, who it was coming from. While driving from Colorado back to Florida, I mentally contemplated finalizing basic logistics of a potential trip that would lead me to the tip of South America, so I began to lay out a flexible plan. Continuing with internet research on Peru, Bolivia, and Chile, I decided to begin my journey in Lima and continue down the coast. My agenda included a visit to a small museum with elongated skulls on display in Paracas, and then down to Arequipa, where an old Franciscan monastery hosts an excellent collection of ancient and Amazonian artifacts. The city also is home of the old Convent of Santa Catalina that I wanted to visit. I would then decide to continue south from there as far as wherever I ended up—Antarctica, if necessary.

I flew from Fort Lauderdale to Lima, Peru, and spent my first day visiting the country's two best national museums of archaeology and anthropology. Their depiction of ancient life displays and models on exhibit were fairly accurate according to their artists' enhanced Hollywood perception of what the viewer should see. The huge collections of authentic, unretouched artifacts individually spoke for themselves, though, and offered this visitor a glimpse into historic life and culture without influence by the ones presenting or promoting the display. As I walked around inside the archaeology museum, I knew that I was absorbing vibrational, informational energy, but I was unsure of the content at the time. The collection of skulls there were fairly old (post–Ice Age), complete, and detailed, but did not exhibit the features of other ancient extended craniums to the extent I was looking for. I was told there were some in storage for "protection," and afterward returned to my hotel, bought a bus ticket for the following day, and headed out of the horribly gridlocked city of Lima.

I took a tourist bus south for a few hours to Paracas, a small town along the coast. The purpose of my visit there was twofold: to view the collection of hybrid human skulls and to see the area where they originated. After my arrival in the old fishing village with ancient roots, I checked in to a bayfront hotel (don't get excited, as it wasn't a resort on a white sandy beach, but an older, remodeled building with a nice view out to the boats in the harbor) and asked where to find the collection of skulls I had heard about. Although I got directions, I was told the small museum was closed since it was late in the day, so I wandered around the waterfront, had a bite to eat, and called it an early evening, as most everyone else did in that quiet village. That evening, while relaxing in my room watching television, I felt, "Tomorrow you will be pleasantly surprised, but afterward, continue south."

When the tiny waterfront museum opened its doors the following morning, I paid my one-dollar admission, then walked around a corner into a small room and stopped in front of an enclosed glass display case. On display were about a dozen, well-lit, first-quality skulls, which obviously appeared to be other than human as we publicly know. I stood alone in front of the display case, moving slowly side to side at times for different viewing angles, in order to get a clearer look at their detail, with my face two feet from the skulls behind the glass. They were almost speaking to me, and I was tempted to talk back aloud, but I thought the museum security guard might call the police and have me thrown out.

In another nearby glass display case was a skull that had been named the "Star Child." Its features indicated to me nothing other than the appropriate name given to it, specifying a most accurate description of its origin. Peering into the deep eye sockets of these skulls that seemed to be vibrating from their core was analogous to peering back into the depths of time, and they created a lasting impression for me to draw upon at a future time.

In front of the museum were a few taxis by the waterfront, so I asked one of the drivers to take me about ten miles out of town into the desert, to a newer museum and visitor center, which was located near where a few of the elongated skulls were found. The new museum was less than impressive, but the parking lot offered a nice view of the surrounding area from where many ancient remains have been found. The climate there was naturally perfect to facilitate long-term preservation of the skeletons buried in the sand, and my understanding is that there are thousands of them buried throughout the area. I returned to my hotel in town and the next day hopped the HOP bus to Arequipa.

I arrived in the white stone city the afternoon of the one day per week that tourists were permitted to enter the four-hundred-year-old Convent of Santa Catalina, at night. Gee, what a coincidence. It covered an entire city block; the interior maze of walkways and rooms of the old, small living quarters of the nuns were dimly lit with lanterns and small fires burning in their kitchens' fireplaces to afford light, since all electric lights were turned off in order to replicate what life was like in the convent before electricity. I was fortunate to have visited that particular evening, as other tourists were almost nonexistent, allowing my enhanced awareness of Spirit messages from the Sisters who physically inhabited the facility hundreds of years ago.

For about a half hour, I found a dark corner on a stone ledge inside the house of Sor Ana Monteagudo Ponce de Leon (July 26, 1602–January 10, 1686), where I sat while she explained in Spirit why it was acceptable for them to live with the extreme, tortuous, and brutal conditions that were commonplace in convents throughout that era. To sum it up, brutality was a commonly accepted practice, so they believed it was necessary and the right thing to live with, of course, oblivious to their misconstrued philosophical brainwashing. The concept explained to me was a direct relationship to the human mind's conditioning and acceptance of belief in nontraditional, altered states of truth, and it also enhanced my understanding of anthropophagy and other practices that psychologically coerce acceptance of one's participation.

The Franciscan monastery in Arequipa had an excellent collection of ancient Amazonian artifacts, that monks who had avoided being captured, cooked, and served as dessert had brought back with them from their missionary travels into the jungle. Their library is also home to one of the most comprehensive religious and spiritual collections in the hemisphere, containing more than twenty thousand very old books and manuscripts hundreds of years old, some dated pre-Columbian. One picture in the museum of an Amazonian tribe clearly spoke of cannibalism.

The next day, I made my way to Matarani, an old ocean port two hours away by bus, down to the Pacific coast from Arequipa. Translated from a South Pacific Indonesian dialect, the name "Matarani" means "Eye of God." It seemed the energy I picked up was similar to that around Tiwanaku and Lake Titicaca, and I felt there was a connection of sorts to ancestors of yesteryear who migrated there from the sunken continent of Lemuria. For the afternoon I sat in the park overlooking the ocean watching the world go by, while eating great ceviche, contemplating the ancient arrival of humans from the long-ago-sunken continent to the west. The most direct route from Lake Titicaca (where the Aymara, Quechua, Wari, and Inca believe they originated) to the Pacific, is across the Altiplano and through the canyon down to the port of Matarani.

Several days later, I traveled down the coast to Arica, Chile, where I had learned of a collection of Chinchoro mummies being the oldest on the planet, some which have been dated three thousand years older than mummies in Egypt. I walked around town the evening I arrived, and the following morning, I took a taxi a half hour out of town to a small museum operated through a joint effort of governmental agencies, with a Chilean university in Santiago being the lead curator. Shortly after the doors opened, I entered the compound with only a few others in attendance, likely due to its distance from town and it being an off-season weekday. Finding a perfectly quiet, dimly lit room with a viewing area separated by large, thick glass windows, I stood in front of a couple of dozen mummies laid out on tables in open boxes, the oldest dating back to around 9000 BCE. Realizing this peaceful setting was ideal for a meditation, I relaxed and tuned in to the collective intelligence in the room.

My understanding there again implied that God-Source "re-booted" humans at least a half-dozen times because of unintended faults, one earlier period of which allowed interbreeding of humans with animals and thereby created some of what we now refer to as "mythological" creatures. Humanoid "things" were also among those groups created on various continents as workers, as well as other similar humanoids who eventually interbred and formed our current basis and overall platform for humans' development. We advanced slowly, which enabled our progression to yield a more desirable and stable long-term outcome. Even with continued but subtle adjustments, there still remain errors, which will be overcome. There in front of me, I realized, I was then viewing descendants of the resulting class of humanoids designed and descended from a previously modified group of 50,000–70,000 BCE prior to the series into which we humans have currently evolved. They were a foundational part of the Lemurian bridge, among others, that enabled us to develop into the higher-IQ beings that we have become today, although a more refined and profound impact on human brain development was crafted in Atlantis after the second ice age past, which ended around 20,000 BCE.

On a long-distance overnight bus, I continued south to San Pedro Atacama, where I visited an interesting, ancient desert hillside fortress of a primitive tribe from several millennia past. The town itself is an old adobe village turned tourist haven of businesses and employees, that reeked with the most hideous energy of deceit, greed, theft, arrogance, and dog crap everywhere, of anywhere in any country I'd ever been. It made my blood curdle, so before getting sick and throwing up, I got the first bus out of town the next day to the airport an hour away and flew south to La Serena.

After checking in to my hotel, I made my way to the beach for the day, where, of course, I had to seek out a good ceviche restaurant and a cold beer. There were a few interesting places around, and I spent an hour in the local museum. I didn't come across any mummies there, but generally speaking, local museums frequently hold many interesting, prehistoric, and unique artifacts, as that one did.

PEERING BACK THROUGH TIME

Throughout Chile, astrotourism has recently become exceedingly popular, apparently because of a more educated, economically viable, international society desiring to visit the premier location on the planet for astronomical observatories. There were many tour agencies around town that each offered a half-dozen different programs, so I just chose one for that evening that would pick me up from my hotel a couple of hours before dark and return me afterward around 1:00 a.m. After the van picked me up from the hotel, two hours later, we arrived at the facility's parking lot under a clear, moonless night sky, with a dozen other vans already parked in the lot. Gathered at the central tourist meeting area, we were separated into two groups: English speaking or Spanish speaking.

I initially chose the Spanish tour, for my preference to continue improving my Spanish language fluency, until the tour guide said, "You can do what you want, but each group gets equal time on the eighteen inch, and right now there's only five others for English; with you, there'll be six, and that's the Spanish group over there," pointing to the sixty people behind me.

"OK, thank you. I got it; let's go," I smilingly replied.

The oversized Spanish group went inside the observatory dome first, with the eighteen-inch Cassegrain telescope, while we walked five minutes across the hillside to an open-pit viewing area with an eight-inch telescope in the center of the recessed amphitheater. After we all introduced ourselves, our part-time astronomy professor, Tom, gave us a great one-hour lecture under the crisp, clear night sky, as we took turns viewing a dozen objects, while the last of lingering daylight had fallen below the horizon. Having followed the ascension of the Southern Cross as I continued my journey south (from invisible below the horizon in the Northern Hemisphere) to my first sight of it from Lima, it had then risen to a fairly impressive elevation, which made a statement to me in itself.

One hour had passed, so it was time to trade places with the larger group. After they exited the dome, we went inside up a few short flights of stairs, and Tom then flipped the switch that opened the motorized roof panel of the observatory. He focused the telescope on many of the same objects we had previously viewed outside with the smaller eight-inch so we could see the difference in power, which was substantial. We zoomed in on popular objects such as planets, nebulae, the Andromeda Galaxy, several of Jupiter's moons, the Oort Cloud, and several star clusters. By the time he had shown us all of these objects, and each of us had our turn on the eyepiece, the group was more interested in naked-eye viewing and personal discussion with our astronomer tour guide under the open dome. After the last viewer before me finished his viewing and went to join the others, I asked Tom to realign and focus the monster scope for me into the deep southern sky, on 47 Tucanae.

With the giant eye centered and focused on "47 Tuc," I peered deep into the cluster of a half-million stars lying around seventeen thousand light-years away, just inside the outer edge band of our Milky Way Galaxy. The cluster was formed shortly after our galaxy was created, a little over thirteen billion years ago, so it is generally a system of older stars, in contrast to our younger sun of around four and a half billion years or so. With fascination and imagination, I could only wonder what other life-forms exist in that place, having an eight-billion-year head start over us. After about ten minutes of my undisturbed viewing, the incomprehensibly powerful external gravitational "edge field" surrounding our galaxy out in deep space ripped a star right out of the cluster! To view this event in real time with such a powerful telescope was nothing short of miraculously remarkable and was the most magnificent and mind-bending cosmic human experience for me ever in my life, to say the least! Since some scientists claim that no black hole exists in the center of 47 Tuc, no other known gravitational field nearby is strong enough, other than our galaxy's edge field, to rip a star out of its orbit and burn it up. The five-second event shook me and rattled my brain to its core.

Having seen in my life, on two separate occasions, two stars get sucked into the black hole in the center of our galaxy, I noted that 47 Tuc's accelerating star's path and color closely resembled my previous experiences. Although similar in color but a longer elliptical arc than the others, the brilliant, pure, deep-blue object appeared to move slightly slower (about four to six seconds, possibly because of my viewing the back end as it accelerated away from us) starting off in a brighter magnitude and dimming toward the end of its three-fourths elliptical path. Viewing an event that occurred around seventeen thousand years ago, at the same time of the setting of the first celestially aligned stones in Tiwanaku and construction of other massive sites around the planet was quite a coincidence, no? I hope by this point in the book that you know I don't believe in coincidences.

PATAGONIA

A few days later, I flew south to Santiago and then changed planes to continue south to Puerto Montt, where I had previously made a reservation for a bunk on a cargo ship that also carried up to one hundred passengers. The journey was scheduled for three days through the fjords of Patagonia to the small town of Puerto Natales, located about two hundred miles north of the Western Hemisphere's southernmost city of Ushuaia at the tip of the continent.

Having arrived in town two days prior to the ship's departure, I found a taxi driver who knew of the approximate location of Monte Verde, an archaeological dig site just over a half hour from town. Located in a remote wooded area along a small riverbank, the ancient site has been the location of many old artifacts excavated under the direction of an American professor in conjunction with the Chilean government's supervision. Hiking off on a trail into the forest, I came across the lead archaeological professor supervising several others who were digging, sifting, and sorting the dirt and residue from their three-foot-deep excavation. Nearby was a small visitor's tent with a few maps, displays depicting huts and primitive life in the area of ancient indigenous people, and it included a life-size replica mastodon. I found it interesting that the ancients used mastodon skins as walls to wrap their small huts, as the thick skins were not only waterproof and durable but also helped keep their heat inside.

The excavation has provided a wealth of evidence of the pre-historic camp, food sources, culture, and living environment of the time, with human fragment remains having been dated to ap-proximately 17,000 years BCE, with other artifacts of 22,000 years or more, indicating human occupation. Carbonized wood dated to 36,000 BCE and a small piece of animal skin dated to 43,500 BCE are unconfirmed as to a natural or human-created Source events. I was unable to create any worthwhile meditation time there due to several factors, such as a no-loitering policy in the woods in the middle of nowhere and an uninvited, irritating taxi driver. No big deal though, because I'm used to coming across egocentric, scientifi-cally educated jerks, and it was still worth the trip for me. I found it interesting that the archaeological findings of Monte Verde were similar in date to findings of the same pre–Ice Age dates determined at the Gault site in Texas, Paisley Cave in Oregon, the setting of corner stones in Tiwanaku, and other major sites from similar time periods all around the world. The difference appeared to be the advanced intelligence of Tiwanaku, possibly appearing so because of more detailed excavated remains that exposed a more established, civilized society that expressed an extraordinarily wide range of inhabitants' IQs, thereby possibly indicating multiple Sources of origin. My understanding is also that Teotihuacan, Mexico, origi-nated and jointly communicated with other humanoids from the same time period, such as Samaipata, Bolivia, and many remote civilizations of the Amazon, which have since been swallowed by the jungle. Pictures and artifacts that I have seen, which originated from the Tayos caves in Ecuador, appear to have predated all of them, though.

The next day, I bought a yoga mat at a sporting goods store in town and then made my way over to the ship's office for check-in to prepare for departure the following day. After last-minute errands in town readying for the three-day ocean journey south, I boarded the 380-foot vessel, along with eighty-five other passengers, that we would all call home for the next few days. Our cargo consisted of several sixteen-yard dump trucks, fifteen semis, a backhoe, a bull-dozer, a dozen pickups, 600 tons of cement, and 480 tons of fish food, and when loading was complete, we backed off and motored into the sunset. After we settled in and explored the ship, passengers attended the mandatory safety briefing held in the cafeteria just before supper.

The buffet-style cafeteria was situated in a large room on the center upper deck, with sufficient open-seating tables to feed about 150 people. It was lined with large picture windows on both sides of the dining hall, a few comfy chairs, and two couches. With a big-screen TV for movies, it was "social central" every day to meet and visit with fellow travelers. Many were recent European college graduates, some working on their master's and a few PhD candidates traveling the world before finding jobs, since they knew their worldly travels would abruptly end once they became employed and had families. One Japanese girl had finished her doctorate in Tokyo and was traveling the world for a year and a half. She frequently wanted to practice her English with me in the cafeteria, so I asked her one day, "Jennifer, why are you asking me all these different types of questions?"

"Ha ha. I give you IQ test, ha ha. Dat's OK, you smaht man! Ha ha." She grinned ear to ear, laughing at me.

I hit my bunk early the first night after supper and quickly fell asleep in the lightly rolling ship, but by 1:00 a.m., I awoke refreshed. Bundled up, I found my way to the top deck with my yoga mat, pillow, and binoculars. Finding a dark space on the bow under the stars, in front of the bridge, I stretched out and peered deep into 47 Tuc with the portable lenses strung from a cord around my neck. A short while later, I learned that 47 Tuc contains many, many ancient and advanced life-forms and is a major access point into and out of our galaxy. Having viewed the center of our galaxy from the Northern Hemisphere on many occasions, and then the outer edge of our galaxy high in the sky of the Southern Hemisphere, afforded me a deeper perspective from which to contemplate our place within as we spin around our softball-sized solar system off in a remote corner of our universe.

After I became thoroughly relaxed while sprawled out on the deck continuously gazing into the heavens, my Guides came through to finally say, "Congratulations, Jimmy, you are now south enough. There is no need to continue further south unless you really want to, and, of course, we'll be here with you, but this trip completes this side of the planet for you. You know we all have preference areas in which we work, and you have now sufficiently traveled in your physical body throughout your chosen area and have received your intended earthbound and off-planet energies affecting your total being, that no other physical place is necessary for you to experience in your current incarnation. Since this entire planet is your current home, you can, of course, freely travel to other hemispheres if you wish and broaden your horizons, as you say, and continue your work. All newly experienced energies may at first be perceived by you as different; however, they will all be just a variation of everything you have previously encountered. After this trip, you will probably be drawn back to spending more time on the Altiplano of Peru and Bolivia because of your strong sensitivity there of connection to origin, Spirit, and intelligent energies, besides physical health benefits. Your working with us is eternally appreciated, no matter where you take your physical body; we will always be with you." I don't even know where to start to tell you what I think of that. Thank you, God.

I dozed off for a little while and intermittently awoke to view the Southern Cross and 47 Tuc continually inching higher in the southern sky, directly ahead. By 4:00 a.m., astronomical twilight was coming quick, and my nose was cold, so I rolled up my mat, grabbed the pillow, and headed back to my bunk for a few hours until breakfast. After breakfast, I slept most of the day away in my bunk, gently rolling in the calm seas, even though there was beautiful scenery to enjoy. Sure, it was nice, but having lived in and traveled to many other beautiful places, it wasn't that important to me because all the mountains eventually look the same anyway, especially with snow-covered peaks. The scenery that matters most to me can only be seen on a cloudless night when it's really dark, since that's where my friends live!

Unfortunately, the following two nights were cloudy, with only a couple of hours of 50 percent cloudless sky. I saw a few shooting stars and was able to establish a familiar, profound connection with Source that mostly confirmed what had been previously downloaded to me. All humans receive downloaded information at various times, which slowly releases into our subconscious mind and beingness over the following days, weeks, and months. It is necessary for us and is an inherent design feature for progression and development of our species, in order that it won't be necessary for humans to be rebooted again (i.e., terminated and started over). Vast collective resources and energy have been utilized to get us to this point in our evolution, and although mistakes were made, we can and will be correctly molded to eventually evolve into the premier universal species.

On the last night of travel, the Southern Cross was almost directly overhead, so I knew we would be arriving in port later that day. Navigating the Patagonia fjords the third day was an exciting experience while our ship passed through waterways with just yards between us and the one-thousand-foot rock walls that shot straight up out of the water on each side, where each bend in the waterway created a beautiful new picture. Preparing to disembark the ship in port, we gathered our belongings and all wished our new travel acquaintances farewell, sending one another off with blessings of love and light on our eternal journeys. After completing my journey south, to just north of the Drake Passage, I felt a fulfilling state of wholeness, completeness, and totality consume my being with a more thorough understanding of God, consciousness, and the Source of our humans' origin in the stars.

THE ICING ON THE CAKE

I flew back to Santiago and then up to La Paz, Bolivia, where I initially planned my return to Tiwanaku. When I woke up in my La Paz hotel the following morning, my Guides suggested I find my way high into the Andes for the "icing on the cake." What this could possibly be, I had no idea, but I, of course, complied with my clairsentient message. Looking over my map while having morning coffee, I decided to take none other than the "Death Road." After all, with a name like that, it was calling me, so after breakfast I checked out of my hotel and taxied to the local bus station about a half hour away. I bought my two tickets (one for me and one for my duffel bag) to Coirico and boarded an old beat-up bus, taking my seat among the locals. One lady asked me in English, "Do you know where you're going?"

"No," I replied, as two men started laughing.

Immediately, a local indigenous woman scolded the men in Aymara, and the men became quiet until another said, "Don't worry, my friend; you will be fine. Just close your eyes, go to sleep, and we'll wake you when we get there."

I figured, *What the heck, we're all going to eventually end up in the same place anyway, right?*

I laughed with the others and said, "Thank you very much," while they reassured me that we would be fine because we were taking the new Death Road, and it was a "little safer." They were very friendly people with keen interest in my origin as well. Wearing my ankh tends to attract conversation with the locals who are more spiritually aware and aligned, as the majority of South Americans were whom I encountered throughout my journey. It also seemed they freely offered valuable travel information, in contrast to North American travelers.

The driver finally boarded and got the old clunker started, and off we drove on a windy two-lane cliffside road up into the mountains, with two hours of awesome scenery. Although it was the new road, it was obviously still a Death Road, and I definitely wouldn't take it at night. We arrived at the small park in the center of the old quaint mountain village of many small hotels, from where I walked about two blocks until I felt that "this one" was the right hotel. I opened the front door, and a walkway led me through the small lobby to a path out back with directional signs pointing to the dated two-story building containing the office, rooms, salon (common living room), and restaurant. The view from the three-acre cliffside perch was nothing short of spectacular, overlooking a fifteen-mile-long valley surrounded on four sides by massive eighteen-thousand-foot snowcapped peaks with stately condors soaring in the distance.

After settling in to my room down the hall from the shared living room with a few couches, overstuffed chairs, and a large television, I kicked off my shoes and stretched out on the couch in front of one of many large picture windows overlooking the valley, and I became mesmerized by the captivating view. As I was the only hotel guest there, the soundless peace and tranquility transported me to a place from where I didn't want to return. With the condors sailing in the distance, they soon made their way into the air current rising up against the cliff in front of my window. The endless air current provided the soaring giants with unlimited power to cover miles and miles of territory in the domain of their existence since the beginning of time. The few hours that I spent in front of the window that afternoon, I was in a euphoric state of existence, with no sense of time or place. When I regained my senses and returned to my normal self, I made my way into the village for supper. Afterward, I walked around for a while and returned to the hotel in darkness to find that the giant birds had called it a night. Since I decided to stay for three days, I paid the owner for two additional nights, went back to my room, and passed out into la-la land.

The following morning after breakfast, I found my way back to the ringside seat with a stunning mountain-valley view from the couch to watch the main event of graciously soaring condors in their eternal home. Falling into a relaxed, partly meditative state, my connection to Source was readily available and continued with my informational messaging. The condors are direct descendants and product of an offshoot species by creators worshipped by the ancients. They maintain a fundamentally embedded vibrational "bridge" (whose communication systems and abilities are mostly unknown and misunderstood by most humans) to ones long ago of another star system, whose group participated in human design and development. They have evolved as all other life has, but their primary geo-electromagnetic connection "frequency" remains wide open to Source, similar to many other animals as well. This aspect of functionality was well known, understood, tapped into, and worshipped by ancient people and races worldwide. People who claim to have this ability today are given drugs and sent to the loony bin.

I was led to Coirico for several reasons but primarily to confirm and solidify my comprehension and understanding of God's creation of human origin and my place within it. Our ability to mentally connect with God-Source remains a deeply embedded foundational feature in our DNA, as one aspect of our design that enhances spiritual awareness of our race by utilizing this subtle communication channel. I recognize that I also soar with the majestic condors, as well as other stately birds, in effortless flight from high above, unimpeded, in the winds of God. Freely sailing within the vibration of God-Sourced energy, absorbing light frequencies and geo-electromagnetic input with direction determined by simple awareness and instinct alone, the pulse of universal life-form is received from the highest order. The all-encompassing view from high above gives one an expanded awareness of deep within, enabling processing and comprehension with more clarity and in-depth appreciation of our ultimate destiny. I also am a bridge to our Creator Source like you, as all humans are, but it's just that I am aware of it a little more than most. After a most phenomenal and rewarding side venture into the mountains, I returned to Tiwanaku still vibrating with the ultimate sense of fulfillment and wholeness. On the bus, I then realized my cumulative three to four hours of time-slip during the previous two days. Thank you, God!

All aspects of pre-Inca and indigenous life incorporated the condor, jaguar, serpents, and other animal figures into their spiritual lives, as indicated today by their thousands of remaining pottery paintings, weavings, and stone carvings. In most all of their remaining art forms and design, expression of connection to Source through animals, gods, ETs, and rituals is a primary theme, which also indicates their understanding of the interconnectedness of all things. As far as I know, there are no currently available scientific instruments to verify this connection, but someday soon, even the most narrow-minded scientists will come around to admitting the truths of our Source when their colleagues explain the function and operational capabilities of, and in, dark matter. It's just a matter of time. Pun intended!

One year prior, I met three sisters about my age who have made a long-standing annual tradition of sharing their economic generosity with Aymara children living in the small villages and outlying rural communities near where they grew up. Rosa invited me to participate in distributing Christmas toys to kids with them and their half-dozen helpers. When I instantly heard from my Guides, "Absolutely," I replied to her, "Absolutely!" The Morales sisters each year purchase several thousand toys (trucks for the boys and dolls for the girls), and during the few months before Christmas, they wrap each one. I acquired two thousand small individual bags of chocolate vitamin milk, and two days before Christmas, we loaded into two pickup trucks filled with toys and Santa's helpers for the one-hour ride to Machaca.

Upon arrival, there were already hundreds of kids with their parents in two lines, one for the boys and one for the girls. To say "Feliz Navidad" one thousand times while distributing the milk was good practice for me—because the following day in Tiwanaku, I individually handed out the other one thousand bags of milk and repeated the same thing. I have experienced many blessed things in life, but this was definitely one of my top ten since I received many of the most powerful clairsentient messages that I have ever experienced, from the thousands of Spirit Guides in attendance accompanying the children. Most all said thank you (through warm, loving thoughts and smiles) and overwhelmingly reminded me how much my work was appreciated. Many angelic entities there included kids' Spirit Guides, Saints who worked for Jesus, Metatron, Mother Mary, ascended members of the Morales family, of course Santa Dorothea and her friends, and many other Archangels and hordes of unknown Spirits and Ascended Masters. It was one of my most powerful days *ever.*

On Christmas Day, I went back out in the countryside to a remote community near Lake Titicaca, where I brought two hundred pounds of pasta and lentils for distribution to parishioners of a small local Catholic church. My gift for the local Padre was a beautifully bound copy of the *Kollan Arunaka,* ("the word of God") Christian Bible written in Aymara. There were several dozen Aymara elders there, including several who spoke Spanish, which was great, so they were able to translate for me. I attended their Christmas service and afterward distributed the provisions while I joined in their celebration feast of local food, including coca leaves and quinoa cola after the service.

There was an old adobe garage-sized structure next to the new cement church, where several of the men opened the huge wooden doors for me to view inside. Against the back wall was an original, beautiful, exquisitely constructed wood altar with statuettes of Mother Mary and several Angels, with detailed gold leaf trim and adornment. It was covered in an inch of dust, having been abandoned there due to insufficient local resources to move it into their new church. I received intuitive messaging that offered the opportunity to move forward with that project if I so desired, maybe subconsciously reinforced due to the altar lacking an effigy of Jesus nailed to a stick hanging in the middle of it. I thought it would be a fun work project and thought aloud to hire several workers to complete the task.

The following day, I met Geronimo, a nephew of the Morales sisters, who is a Bolivian licensed civil engineer. We briefly discussed the project, and he offered to advise me on the best course of actions, since I ultimately would like to refurbish the old adobe building into an Aymara meditation center. It could be the source of badly needed tourism dollars. The original sagging doors needed to be rebuilt also, which appeared to be quite an ambitious project, so I had to let it rest for a while to see if it was meant to be. I will receive assistance from nature and the universe for whatever is supposed to happen—this is what I've been told—and I will move forward with the project "when the time is right," according to God's plan. On a hilltop overlooking a spectacular eighteen-thousand-foot mountain range of snowcapped peaks to the east and an expansive eighty-mile view to the west over Lake Titicaca to the shoreline of Peru, the spiritual and personal energy there was captivating and almost overpowering. It was a place where I preferred to remain, as I desired to continue my enraptured existence in such close proximity to God. But my Christmas journey was nearing an end, and I returned to La Paz for a couple of days to prepare for my trip home.

A New Mission

While relaxed on the airplane returning to Florida several days after Christmas, I received several powerful messages that expressed my need to thoroughly document my Spirit Guides' influence on my life and spiritual travel missions. I thought to myself, *Ha, that would have to be a book!* Then I affectionately heard, "Now you are getting the picture, Jimmy."

Oh no, no, please, don't make me do that! You know that I don't like to write!

"Why not? You've been prepared for this," was the good-natured response of one of Their favorite sayings to remind me of the many tasks that I had been prepared for in the past. Then, laughing to myself in disbelief while knowing that I would do it, I took a few minutes to let the thought settle in and realized that writing a book was about to dramatically change my daily life routine for a while. Slowly I began thinking of logistical planning and absorbed the concept as my truth of a new assignment.

At first, I felt as though I had received a prison sentence, but a few days later, I had fundamentally accepted the project and began to hear multiple times a day, "Get ready to write; are you prepared? Organize. Do you have all of your notes and journals together? Clean up and prepare your computer; you will start with an outline," every day, persistent reminders all day long, until New Year's Day, I woke up with a sense of urgency to begin my new project. After confirming to myself in the mirror that I was actually going to do this, I sat down and began to write, shortly thereafter becoming consumed with writing at all hours of almost every day, morning, noon, and night, for two months straight. Then I took a break so my head wouldn't implode. I realized that with only three-quarters of my book completed, there remained substantial missing information that I needed to acquire, so I again returned to Bolivia for several weeks in April 2019.

BACK TO BOLIVIA

My itinerary took me to visit acquaintances back in Uyuni, take an off-road tour for a few days in the remote mountains, continue my goodwill projects in the countryside near Tiwanaku, and resume spiritually based study of Lake Titicaca's ancient culture.

Upon my arrival in Uyuni, I found a tour guide with one spot open for their three-day journey into the mountains along the Chilean border, with an evening planned at some hot springs, which

I had long wanted to visit. The following morning, six of us loaded ourselves and our baggage into an older Land Cruiser, and we lumbered off with two bald tires first to the expansive salar (a huge, old salt lake bed) and the next day onto four-wheel-drive roads leading deep into the remote mountains. The spectacular scenery of the dry, desolate terrain gave one ample space to contemplate all that is. At fourteen thousand to fifteen thousand feet of elevation, the air was thin and cool, but the beauty of the distant snow-covered mountain peaks suppressed any temporary physical concerns of discomfort. Energies always seem lighter and less dense when viewed and sensed from more open and expansive less populated locations, and that area indeed qualified as a place in direct alignment with God-Sourced energy.

We traveled over two hundred kilometers on rough four-wheel-drive roads through the mountains all day until we arrived at a roadblock an hour before sundown. The twenty-five local residents collected twenty-five pesos (about $3.50) from each vehicle that passed through in order to pay for their nonexistent road maintenance. All tour vehicles in front of us paid the fee, but our driver/guide didn't want to pay, so he got out of our truck and began an hour-long argument. I offered to pay it, but our guide refused, even after I argued with him to get us out of there. None of our weenie group members backed me up with one word, so we were stuck at the gate with our jackass driver. The men guarding the gate adamantly refused our entry, even when our idiot driver an hour later finally offered to pay. The gatekeepers said our guide was a bad man and we were not coming in, period. As darkness set in, the dipshit driver got back into the driver's seat and said, "We'll just have to go another way." At that time, it would have been appropriate to abandon our guide, pay our entry fee, and leave him at the gate, but the docile group allowed our being held hostage. I would imagine that just the threat to our driver to ditch him would have likely engaged his cooperation, but no one backed me up.

We turned around, and none of the wimpy tourists in our group said a word for the first five minutes that we drove off into the darkness, until someone asked, "How long?"

"Two hours," was his reply. After a few left- and right-hand turns at many forks in the road around the back side of a mountain, a half hour later, we came to a complete stop. The driver got out to look around and then realized we were lost in the dark in the most accurate description of the middle of nowhere at fifteen thousand feet in the desolate, windswept Andes Mountains with no trees, no shelter, and little food or water. Of course, a quick thought passing through *my* mind was previous airline passengers stranded years ago in the nearby mountains with no food. You know what they had to do for survival, so you begin to look at your party members very differently. Here we go! Ha!

Finally, our driver made the best choice and turned around, where we arrived back at the gate an hour later. The guards reluctantly accepted our payment, and we were allowed to pass through to reach the next gate manned by official government personnel. They collect a "national park fee" of twenty-one dollars per person. For what? The right to breathe the air, that's what. No visitor center, no water, no maps, no picnic tables, no trash cans, no bathrooms—nothing but a big joke. We eventually arrived at the private hot springs around 9:30 p.m. They closed at 10:00 p.m., so there wasn't sufficient time to enjoy a well-deserved soak under a cold, but clear, southern sky. We checked in to our hostel and had supper, and we were told the hot springs would open at six o'clock in the morning. I set my alarm for 5:30 a.m., bundled up, and walked a half kilometer to the pools, only to find no water in them. Nobody said the pools were emptied at night for cleaning, and then refilled at 7:00 a.m. We had to eat breakfast, pack, and leave for Uyuni by 7:30 a.m.—so much for the hot springs.

I had contemplated this trek for a few years and went to great lengths of time and expense to incorporate my plans for this particular experience. Sometimes when things don't work out, I know they are just not meant to occur for me at that time, and although disappointing, it typically works out in the long run for my benefit. When an unexpected cause or event of the universe derails my plan, I typically find out why weeks or even months later, well after the event. I learned the reason there was due to "less-than-desirable occupants in the hot springs, among other things"; to me, that meant there was just no reason for me to know.

An exciting bonus of that trip was when I left Uyuni and flew back to La Paz in a seventy-passenger jet. After takeoff, the captain leveled us off at two hundred feet above the salt flat, for approximately five minutes. Screaming over the salar at three hundred miles an hour looking out from my window seat was bonus!

I had previously located, purchased, and thoroughly studied a copy of the most authoritative work published on Tiwanaku (*Tihuanacu, the Cradle of American Man*, by Arthur Posnansky, 1945). It not only added to my in-depth understanding with scientific proof of occurrences and physical progression of the area's multiple phases of construction, but it also gave me some insight as to the culture and knowledge dating back 17,000 years BCE. Posnansky was a Bolivian archaeologist who dedicated most of his life surveying, excavating, and studying the areas in and around Tiwanaku. He held several university degrees and was appointed to sit on some of the most authoritative scientific boards of professionally recognized universities and government agencies in the Western Hemisphere. Sharing his work with other international research scientists brought him confirmation of data and status as a most authoritative resource on the ancient history of South America.

Due to its location off the main tourist route, a specific intent must be made to allow time and resources for one to enjoy a fruitful and rewarding visit there. Most visitors arrive on tour buses and get whisked through the site in an hour or two, hardly long enough to stretch their legs, snap a few photos, get back on the bus, and then say, "Oh yeah, I've been there." Similar to some tourists on cruise ships that stop for an afternoon in the port of a foreign country, they are convinced that they "know" the culture, food, and other aspects of the place because everything was explained to them by their tour guide, when the truth of the matter is that they barely have a clue. To fully absorb and understand any foreign culture, one must talk with locals, eat what they eat, walk a mile in their shoes, visit local museums, and hear their music, history, and legends to acquire a basic comprehension of their culture.

Although the two hotels and half-dozen hostels in town are a bit rough for an extended stay for this older guy, one of the benefits that I enjoyed by staying in a hotel there was meeting the fellow travelers who passed through on their spiritually aligned journeys. Due to the energetic, spiritual, and historical significance of the area, an uncommonly high percentage of single and independent small-group travelers have overall more in-depth knowledge, personal connections that afford higher vibrational awareness, empath abilities, and spiritual wisdom as compared to most other types of tourists. Information exchange among lightworkers, star-seeds, empaths, mediums, channels, and the like is helpful for all to continue connecting, elevating, and enhancing the vibration of each other, their abilities, and the understanding of all that is.

In the hotel restaurant, a recent breakfast conversation with three middle-aged European ladies touched on the following subjects for several minutes each: Tiwanaku, Lake Titicaca and other Peruvian high-energy sites, energy and souls trapped in massive nearby stone/rock formations, underground groups of nonphysical Beings working on humans' behalf, a nearby extraterrestrial ancient landing site that is still occasionally active, comparison of ancient energies of the Uyuni area as compared to Tiwanaku, the manipulation of our DNA, and the remaining Spirit presence of Sor Ana in the Santa Catalina Convent in Arequipa. This was a typical and normal discussion with the type of travelers who frequently remain in the area for more than a few hours. After our enjoyable visit, we said farewell, and my three breakfast acquaintances went out early to the Kalasasaya (site of the infamous Doorway to the Sun, just a ten-minute walk from the hotel) since they had to return to the hotel later that day to catch a 3:00 p.m. bus to Copacabana (the takeoff point for Isla del Sol in Lake Titicaca).

I went to a local fiesta for the day about an hour away by bus, watched a good soccer game, talked with some locals, viewed a short parade, and sampled some of their local foods while I listened to a local band play in the village square. There was something strange about my visit there, in that I didn't care too much for anything about my whole day. I was "off course" somehow but couldn't identify any specific issue. I just got a really weird feeling being there, so I finally got back on a bus and returned to my hotel around 5:00 p.m.

When I opened the front door and entered the hotel, there in the lobby greeting me were the three ladies from breakfast. "Hi, what happened? You were supposed to be on the bus two hours ago," I said.

"We lost a little time," was the first reply.

After a brief silence, while I looked at each of them, I knew right away what happened. I asked, "Do you remember any of it?"

"Not much," was one response.

"We sat down to meditate after lunch," another gal said. I proceeded to explain to them that it was very common for people to time-slip there, including myself on several occasions, one in which I lost over two hours there several years ago, and more recently in Coirico. Lacking any explanation and having absolutely no memory of what, when, how, or where, other than knowing you had experienced a catatonic state, are typical. During these time lapses, powerful energetic Source entities download to us encoded information for our benefit that slowly seeps into our subconscious minds and bodies over the following days, weeks, and months. My understanding is that unexplainable time loss is a frequent and common occurrence not only there, but also at many other sacred sites and random places as well all around the world, particularly at points along the Earth-energy grid.

Throughout the region, there are significant remnants of past civilization, but locals say 90 percent is still buried underground and also under the lake. Identified remains in the ancient communities of Sicuya, Chiripa, Pariti, and Huacullani indicate occupation of approximately two thousand years before the known commencement of Tiwanaku, which time frame is scientifically recognized as 17,000 BCE. Of course, the oldest time periods of human occupation offer the least amount of remaining evidence. When the South American continent was a lower elevation, the ideal climate provided the average-sized four-foot-tall person with superb nutrition through more quality food sources than exist on the Altiplano today. The rich soil of years past is a distant memory, and the slow, methodical rise of the continent continues, in contrast to the decline of the Aymara race.

It is interesting to note the frequency at which modern-era excavations have identified artifacts originating from the time period of approximately 17,000 BCE, from Tiwanaku, to Paisley cave, Monte Verde, Gobekli Tepe (disputed), Oceana (Nan Madol), many statues buried in Sierra Leone, and the Tarahumara of Mexico. The Tarahumara incidentally, who also primarily lived in a vast underground cave system (which some continue to inhabit), claim they are the most direct descendants of the Olmec, who occupied regions of Mexico near Teotihuacan and also shared similar gods of the Tiwanakans. I was told by a local, nearby tour guide that he was a descendent of original Olmec and Toltec of 17,000 BCE. Around the world, it seems that humans more rapidly populated the Earth after the second Ice Age past, when more coordinated development occurred circa 17,000 BCE or so.

After three weeks in Tiwanaku delivering basic foodstuffs and blankets to elderly in outlying areas, studying their ancient culture, and visiting small local archaeological sites, I returned to Florida for a well-earned break after hiking every day at over thirteen thousand feet.

CHAPTER 10
ECUADOR

This past Christmas, I was unable to visit Charlie due to two miserable distant male relatives of his that belong to a violent gang of kidnappers and extortionists in Guatemala City. Of course, the entire extended family all know how I have supported Charlie and his immediate household over the past fifteen years, but now I have been informed that the distant scumbags also want some help—all they can get through whatever bank accounts that can be drained—by kidnapping me. Through the chain of approximately three hundred various relatives, they are privy to the detailed information of my flight arrival, route of travel, and length of my stay, so Charlie has projected to me to find and assist another quadriplegic similar to him, with a close family of loving caregivers.

Although I was informed that the two problem men could each be the recipient of a five-hundred-dollar one-way ticket to an alternate dimension, and I can hire several legitimate well-armed bodyguards to protect me, Charlie and I don't feel that's the appropriate solution to the problem. They also will be dealt with swiftly and decisively by the correct authority of Source when they cross over in the future, most likely after being murdered themselves.

Knowing that I have enjoyed my travel in South America over the past several years, Charlie implied to me through projection that I should travel to Ecuador instead of visiting him for the holidays, so I went online and bought my round-trip ticket for the better part of December. I packed my backpack and small duffel bag with some clothes, my netbook, a few Santa hats, some candies and small giveaways (some of which help quiet the crying babies on a long plane or bus ride), and left my pitifully low-vibration condominium community behind.

I arrived in Guayaquil, where the US dollar is the Ecuadorian national currency. The cost of living there generally costs about a third of what it costs in the States, so I quickly learned why so many expats have relocated to Ecuador. Besides the country being generally safe during daylight hours, some of the coastal regions boast white sandy beaches, and other areas of the country are the ideal elevation and location for great weather, situated there on the equator. Some of the mountain scenery is breathtakingly beautiful and also conducive for creating vast areas of year-round lush, green countryside. With a continual rotating harvest of farm animals and fresh fruits and vegetables, the availability of quality protein was clearly evident in their society, as compared to many other places that I have visited in South America.

Exploring Guayaquil by foot and bus, one afternoon I found the national museum in the city center, just a few blocks from their internationally acclaimed *malecón* (and rightfully so). Comprising two floors of the two-hundred-foot square building, there were many collections of artifacts from recent history, ancient history, and a loft area jam-packed with bugs, birds, stuffed animals from the Amazon, a shrunken head, and a dozen well-presented large birds of prey. I enjoyed wandering around for an hour until my back started to bother me, so then I began finding my way back to the main exit until I was just about to reach the door. I heard a message tell me, "Go back; you missed something." I hesitated, turned around slowly, and walked back into the museum down the hall from where I just came from. Totally oblivious as to where I was supposed to go, I methodically followed instinctive energy around the corner and was drawn to the back wooden stairway again, up to the stuffed animals in large display cases lining both sides of the oblong loft. I didn't quite understand it since I had just left there five minutes ago, but from the top of the stairs, I again gradually walked by and viewed each display as I felt I was being pulled to the back corner, where there were perched a half-dozen large birds of prey. I had seen most of them a few minutes prior, so I was a bit perplexed, wondering what I was going to find.

I previously didn't walk all the way to the last case in the back corner because I was thinking about leaving and finding a park bench to rest for a while. But as I approached the last-in-line magnificent, stately bird in the corner, it sat there balanced securely on a tree branch staring at me eye to eye from the well-lit clear glass case, with the utmost power and dignified authority as I stood there frozen in time. It was a huge white eagle-hawk, projecting its self-confident connection to all that is with piercing eyes, which encompassed my being for an undetermined amount of time. After I regained my senses, I looked closely at the faded paper tag attached to its foot. It clearly stated the donor's name and the date it was given to the museum. Written in numbers and letters incredibly similar in style to my father's handwriting, the month and day was my father's birthday, with my year of birth. When I saw that, I felt a sense of divine nature overcome my physical being and thought to myself with humor and amazement, *How did you do that? Thank you, just thank you!* In all my life, my father had one known affinity in nature, and that was with birds. He had never been to South America while he was alive. As my dad once said in one of his many corny sayings, put *that* in your pipe and smoke it!

After almost a week on the Pacific Coast searching out fishing boats for a potential future marlin trip, I headed up into the mountains over the Andes through the clouds, on a four-hour bus ride to Cuenca, where I coincidentally found a very nice bed and breakfast hosted by a very spiritual lady. The accommodations were wonderful, and the assistance of Margaret and her daughter Jenny was invaluable for providing local information and allowing efficient planning and use of my time.

The three of us visited an old-folks' home one afternoon, where I was introduced to a middle-aged lady borrowing the use of the kitchen facilities to support her independent missionary work, helping kids with malnutrition. On the outskirts of the city, there are several poor neighborhoods, and one of the local churches has offered her a room for use in their annex to establish a new neighborhood after-school program. I may possibly work with her in the future but have no plans at the current time.

After our brief introduction, Margaret, Jenny, and I walked a few blocks to the cultural art center, where Jenny participated in a Christmas concert hosted by her piano instructor. Students of various ages each played several Christmas songs, with all the parents proudly clapping after their kids' performances. When Jenny played, the entire room of one hundred people was vibrationally lifted to another level by her most penetrating and fantastic performance. She clearly had divine guidance while playing, as well as when she sang, you would have thought you were in Carnegie Hall. Just incredible. Of course, her mom had tears, and almost me too as well!

PADRE CRESPI

Several years ago, I learned about a Catholic priest by the name of Carlos Crespi, who lived in Cuenca for over fifty years until he passed over in 1982. His hobby was collecting ancient artifacts as brought to him by indigenous people from remote places in the mountains, caves, and jungle. His indigenous jungle friends told him that many of the relics originated in the extensive cave system running underground for two hundred kilometers from the eastern mountains near Cuenca down into the Amazon. Several legends claim that many bands of short-statured humanoids lived primarily underground for their security to avoid ending up on the menu of the giants that roamed above. There also are vast cave systems that run south to Peru, under Lake Titicaca, and into Bolivia.

Over the course of his life in Ecuador, Crespi accumulated a massive hoard of rooms full of intricately carved solid gold plaques,

panels, carvings, unknown ancient tools, and high-quality artifacts that were brought to him by distant Amazonian tribespeople.
University educated in Milan, he stated and showed to many people
the common origin and similarity of artifacts identical to ancient
Atlantean, Chinese, Egyptian, Sumerian, and Assyrian gods prior
to his museum being burned down and losing much of his collection. The contents of his collection distinctly revealed the interaction of Atlanteans from the east and Lemurians of the west, most
likely after the worldwide cataclysm sank their continents around
the same time, 3200 BCE.

While he was hospitalized deathly ill, the government's military and police raided, looted, and stole what remained by hauling
off many large truckloads of his life's work of what was once most
probably the world's greatest collection of ancient artifacts in all of
human history. Several museums throughout the country display
some of the remaining pieces, excluding the most significant, of
course, which reportedly ended up in the Vatican, and many others
that secretly remain in private collections.

MUSEUMS

The first week I spent visiting typical tourist sites around town,
knowing I would eventually stumble upon the city's well-publicized
large, modern Pumapungo Museum. To me, logic would have it
that some of the remaining collection would be housed in their
oversized modern museum, but I found nothing of the sort, nor anything else that really moved me. Although there were several quality displays of earlier periods of life throughout the varied nearby
climactic zones, the most significant attraction was the remaining
stone foundation knee walls of pre-Columbian occupation of the
ten-acre hillside site along a nice tree-lined river. I saw no ancient
(pre–Ice Age) anything, but it was a nice family-friendly facility to
accommodate typical tourists.

I finally found the small Museum of Aborigines, where I viewed
many hundreds of high-quality various-sized artifacts claimed to

have originated in the lower Ecuadorian mountains and upper Amazon basin. Much of the pottery displayed designs common to indigenous peoples throughout the Western Hemisphere and implied awareness and location of interdimensional entities and realities. Many of the most ancient stone figures and head carvings that I have viewed in the Western Hemisphere indicate they were wearing some type of helmet. I viewed two metal helmets in a display case there, which were found with other artifacts displayed and stated to be unknown thousands of years old, presumably originating from the Crespi collection. The voluminous numbers of figurines and pottery designs clearly expressed to me a comprehensive and thorough connection of integral familiarity of Source and alternate dimension Beings, both good and bad. There were many artifacts similar in design to Egyptian, Asian, and African figures, also with elongated heads and both slanted and goggle eyes, comprising an extremely diverse collection. I believe most of the collection are what some of remains from Father Crespi's life's work.

The new building that houses the Guayaquil Anthropological Museum is located on the city's fabulous three-kilometer-long waterfront malecón, in the shadows of La Perla, the largest Ferris wheel in South America. The most extensive collection of Valdivian culture artifacts, and many other unknown origin artifacts displayed there, include a dozen or so exquisite, intricately detailed masterpiece busts of individuals most likely revered by their society. Hundreds of ceramic and stone-carved faces, figurines, artifacts, and pots are laid out in timelines of the local cultures that thrived along the coast of Ecuador, Peru, and Chile around 4,000 to 6,000 years BCE. Some items clearly demonstrate their connection with interdimensional Beings, as indicated by designs, symbols, and the several triangular shaped heads identical to others that I've seen throughout Central and South America. Here again also, most all are wearing some type of helmet. Only a few collections move me enough as something to write home about, and this was one of them.

There was one ceramic pot I found particularly interesting, with two pyramids toward the bottom of the pot, under which there was an arrow pointing downward. Above their peaks appeared to be a tsunami wave design, with smaller waves above, and the waved lip of the pot above that. Similar to several other stone carvings found in Peru, the only thing missing on that piece was a guy in a canoe on top of the water, which indicated his origin. Designs and stories told on pottery don't necessarily mean the event occurred the day before the pot was made. Most often, legends that have been recorded for posterity are recorded on cave walls, stone tablets, and papyrus, but many have also been presented through pottery inscriptions recovered from ancient undated burial sites.

The many glass-enclosed displays collectively presented artifacts of similar design features and materials of composition on the same shelf. In several situations, however, there was an artifact or carving completely contrary to all the others in the immediate collection with which it was displayed. Even though the item may have been excavated or recovered in the same location at the same time as the others, there is high probability that many of those figures and carvings have previously belonged to a collection that were ancient to the ancients. Just as we collect old things and have an interest in our past, it appears the ancients were no different in that regard.

Several stone carvings of bird heads and faces had fine detail and were surely most intriguing to view with contemplation. Without explanation, they were displayed along with other unsimilar artifacts but were grouped together, leaving space for insightful thought as to their significance, age, and origin. The Guayaquil Anthropological Museum is the best in the country, easily accessible, and well worthwhile to make time for a visit.

Just a quick note on the new national museum in Quito, which houses their anthropology collection and art museum. I felt there was limited education value and a cockamamie layout presentation, which, to me, defied logic. As admitted by an employee, the bulk of the unique and valuable collection relating to ancient history and human origin is kept for themselves, hidden from public view for protection. The phrase "for protection," according to some, is curator's lingo for "It's hanging at home on my living room wall." Some of the items that I am referring to have been exposed to natural climatic influence since before the Ice Age, and they have survived since then just fine. The several large rooms in which they so proudly display their selected stolen and looted remains of a Catholic priest's private collection (while he was sick in a hospital bed) is appalling, immoral, criminal, and disgraceful. The anthropological presentation most appropriately calls for renaming the facility to "The National Museum of Disgrace." But admission is free! Welcome to Ecuador.

It's not only Ecuador, but many European countries also proudly display many of their stolen artifacts of inestimable age and value originally obtained throughout South America. National museums all around the world possess innumerable artifacts that they refuse to return to the rightful country of origin. Talk about bullying?

INGAPIRCA

With another unplanned day available, one morning I hopped a bus to visit Ingapirca, one of the oldest remaining ruins of pre-Inca origin and archaeological significance in the country. The hundred-acre site, with various foundation remains and stone agricultural channels lining the hillside, lies in the scenic mountains about two hours north of Cuenca. The main event there is a smaller, centrally located pre-Columbian four-sided stone structure with a round dome on top. It was built on a hilltop and exhibits a few similar construction techniques as those found in major ruins of significance, such as Machu Picchu and Tiwanaku. The construction is in alignment with the Earth's rotation and pitch so that the solstices and equinoxes are identified when beams of sunlight penetrate specific points through window openings of the building. Although it was interesting, the site pales in comparison to the extent of other ruins in nearby Peru or Bolivia.

I did feel as though a higher vibration energy emanated from the immediate and surrounding hillsides but was unable to identify anything in particular. In a tiny local restaurant where I had a delicious bowl of *caldo de pollo* (chicken soup) for lunch, an elderly woman told me that she and many locals live in harmony with the Earth's energy, and for many years had frequently seen UFOs at night over their valley. It was an interesting day trip and added to my overall pleasure of travel. With the weekend quickly approaching, the two-hour trip back to the city gave me time to contemplate the choices for my next excursion.

SARAGURO

Since most businesses in the city are closed on Sundays, it was a good day to explore another out-of-town village somewhere. I decided to visit the popular Sunday market in Saraguro, a nice indigenous mountain village about two hours south of Cuenca. Many centuries ago, several thousand ancestors of the current resident Saragurans were relocated to their new valley from northern Peru by the powers then in control. Its beautiful setting is located in a region of lush mountains with substantial streams and rivers at a median elevation, conducive to year-round agriculture.

Instead of taking a bus, I took a ten-minute taxi ride from my hotel to a local tour operator recommended by my hotel, and shortly thereafter, I was off in the front seat of a van with six other passengers for a two-hour ride. We raced south out of the city, dodged a few pedestrians, and then headed up into the mountains on a wide two-lane paved highway with little traffic.

The driver continued to drive way too fast as we climbed the winding mountain road up into the clouds with light, drizzling rain. He continued to cross over the yellow center line, passing other vehicles in dangerous curves, until I became annoyed enough and decided to influence and correct his driving behavior. I waited a few more minutes to see if possibly one of the other passengers would say something, since my limited Spanish vocabulary would only suffice at the minimum.

I then strongly felt that it was time to say something, so I firmly told the driver he was not driving safely and was being disrespectful to all of us passengers. He gave me a confrontational dirty look, said nothing, and continued his unacceptable behavior as if I hadn't said a word. I continually felt an internal reactionary force building within my physical body as we closed in on an unknown serious event that was about to occur at any moment. I then decided that if we were to spin out in a slippery curve, I was going to punch him as hard as I could the moment prior to impact. I would rather fight this guy in the van or on the side of the road and hitchhike the rest of the way, rather than fight for my life in a hospital bed.

Then I forcefully heard, "That's not going to happen because you are going to speak more, strong, and follow through." (Oh boy, here we go—that sounds familiar!) As I contemplated my lecture, I continually felt the force consolidating within me. While I stared him down, the only thing that occupied my mind was a crash, and the feeling kept getting stronger by the second as he continued his wild driving. When we rounded our three hundredth curve five seconds later, he quickly hit the brakes as we approached three vehicles that had crashed in front of us, with car parts strewn all over the highway. He dodged between the wrecked cars, people, and parts on the road by veering through and around the crash site, and then he immediately stepped on the gas again.

That's when I heard "OK, *now*," and let lose big time, with the old Jimmy finger crossing the center of the front seat, pointing at his face. I began firmly hollering that he was just like the other driver who was probably dead in the head-on collision, and he was next because he was a freaking idiot with the IQ of a jackass. "If you want to kill yourself, *do it!*" I demanded. "But we have families," I loudly exclaimed. "If you want to die, commit suicide, and kill yourself, stop right here and go jump off the mountain, now!" I yelled at him while pointing off to the cliffs alongside the highway.

At first, he didn't know what to say and gradually slowed down to a more normal pace, and then irritatingly responded in a timid tone of voice in order for him to save face and defend his nonexistent credibility to the other passengers. I didn't understand what he said, but it wasn't important anyway, since he drove normally for the rest of the time I was in the van. He stopped on the side of the road in front of the Saraguro market street an hour later, and I quickly departed without a word. I arrived alive, so mission accomplished!

I first came upon what appeared to be the weekly main event: men's volleyball with three-man teams. I bought a tortilla to snack on and watched the game for a while with a few dozen locals, since the players were pretty good. The four-block-long market consisted of local vendors selling everything from hats, shawls, shoes, indigenous clothes, tools, music, and local handicrafts, to chickens and rabbits and tons of fruits and vegetables. As was typical in South American village street markets, on a side street were parked the larger farm trucks with thousands of pounds of rice, corn, flour, sugar, and other bulk foods.

Many centuries ago, several thousand ancestors of the current resident Saragurans were relocated to their current valley from northern Peru by the powers then in control. Their Kichwa language, some designs, and native dress indicated to me that they are clearly descendants of the original Aymara culture (pre-Wari), since their overall lifestyle in the surrounding rural countryside appeared to reflect many ancient habits and ways typical of the indigenous of the Altiplano of southern Peru and Bolivia. When asked from where they originate, they point to the sky.

Walking slowly through the crowd of locals, I occasionally encountered another tourist, most often having a quick chat. Lunch was with the locals under the community tent, around forty feet square, near the twenty or thirty vendors selling some of the largest and most colorful fruits and vegetables I have ever seen, although almuerzo (lunch) was nothing to brag about. From the market, I made my way a few blocks into town, where I walked around the sleepy village and checked out their old central park church and several surrounding blocks. It was a sizable church for the town that it served, with a modest wooden altar. I didn't view anything architecturally special to occupy my time, so eventually I found my way to the bus station, and after a nice snooze on the bus, I returned to Cuenca around 5:00 p.m.

CUENCA

As I took various local buses and walked around exploring the city on my daily adventure, it was clearly obvious as to the extent of the numerous homeless, Venezuelan refugees, everywhere. The situation was replicated in the city of Guayaquil and outlying areas from there also, which I became aware of when I first arrived and spent a few days in the country's second-largest city. There were hundreds of thousands of them. The bulk of them were young people (i.e., in their teens, twenties, and thirties), with a significant percentage of new babies. At the bus stations and almost every street corner, sidewalk, park, alley, and niche were refugees holding cups, asking for money. If they weren't begging, they were selling bottled water or local street food (hot dogs, hamburgers, empanadas, and tortillas), ice cream, or snacks.

Many had also obtained local employment, which had put a substantial squeeze on the native Ecuadorians due to the rampant abuse of businesses taking advantage of the cheap labor. Many folks whom I spoke with told me that refugees generally earned ten dollars a day for ten to twelve hours of work. The Ecuadorian government does not feed the immigrants as the United States does so freely, so many of the destitute homeless are on the verge of starvation. Many said that was one of the main reasons they left Venezuela to begin with, besides the fact that the government continues to execute thousands of its citizens who disapprove of and voice their opinions against their dictator, President Maduro. I wanted to tell them they should go to Florida, because they are eligible to receive thousands of dollars' worth of food for free, and they can sell any extra. When I spoke with my son on the phone in California, he said, "No, Dad, tell them to come here because, along with the food, they'll probably get some cash too!"

In the city center of Cuenca, there are dozens of huge, impressive churches that were built with the stones of pre-Columbian Inca palaces and house enormous, ornate gold-leaf altars, some of which are over four stories tall. Most churches are open daily, and I found it a worthwhile hike around the city center to view many of them. One early evening two days before Christmas, after a long day of walking around to many churches and also a huge local market on the south end of the city, I was relaxing in my hotel room watching the television. After a half hour I heard, "OK, rest time is over; let's go. We're going to the central park across the street from the cathedral, just a few blocks from here."

I instantly thought to myself, No, *rest time is* not *over; it is just getting started!* Of course, knowing better by now than to ask questions, I took a minute to mentally prepare, got up, got dressed, and headed out from my hotel room down to the park at around 8:00 p.m.

ANGIE

I passed alongside the largest cathedral in town, which was built with the original intention to accommodate ten thousand people, so it's quite architecturally impressive to say the least, both inside and out, as the mainstay cathedral of the city. There were lots of lighted decorations, music, and vendors selling Christmas-themed everything throughout the city, which added to the harmony and ambience of the evening. After crossing the street in front of the cathedral, I slowly entered and strolled into the nicely laid-out park with various wide paths of stone pavers winding through the many well-maintained gardens and trees in the peaceful one-block-square setting. The large, smooth pathways were much appreciated by skaters and small kids on their kick scooters, too, while their parents sat nearby on one of the many benches enjoying their ice cream. Wondering what or who I was looking for, with many paths to choose from, I veered to my left on the second path, where three women were sitting together on one of the larger concrete benches with a young girl in an old, well-used, beat-up wheelchair. I continued to walk past them out of sight, around to another garden area while my eye zeroed in on an ice cream store across the street. At that exact moment, my Spirit Guides influenced me to stop walking, turn around, and go back to talk with the women, which I did.

I slowly approached them while I said, "Feliz Navidad," and asked who was the mother of the young girl. I introduced myself and explained that I have an adopted son named Charlie who is quadriplegic, living in Guatemala. Lorelly then introduced herself as Angie's mother, and we exchanged some small talk before she told me that seventeen years ago, her daughter was hit by a bus when she was four years old, which also killed her brother and father. She is just four months younger than Charlie; what a coincidence! Ha!

Similar to Charlie, Angie diverted her attention above and to the side of my shoulder, where I felt that she was viewing some type of Spirit, Angel, or energy field, and then broke out in a big, happy smile. Although she is unable to speak, I immediately knew she was connected, and I directed my questions of Angie's awareness to confirm with her mom some comparable qualities similar to those of Charlie, in particular inquiring about indications of spiritual connection and participation. While silence then momentarily overcame our physical space, I intensely focused on her energy and immediately sensed her soft and loving connection of a divine nature.

I was quickly engulfed in complete silence by a powerful white bubble of light, into which I was freely drawn and encompassed, and then realized that I was in the presence of Divine Spirit. It was a most incredible and indescribable experience! At first, I was frozen as I "looked around" inside the bubble and noticed several small, concentrated signature fields of small white energy bubbles and orbs hovering inside, off to one side. I understood them to be angelic assistants to the all-encompassing powerful light, and although I did not visualize the appearance of any physical Being, I *knew* that

I was with Angie in the presence of Jesus and/or Mother Mary. It was at the exact moment of my asking Lorelly if Angie connected frequently with Mother Mary or Jesus that I was overcome into the light. I felt that it was a phenomenal privilege, and for a few moments, I was speechless while smiling at Angie with amazement. I was unable to read, see, or hear her messaging, but it was clearly evident to me that she had just experienced the same thing as I. I've experienced very few other incidents similar to this during the course of my lifetime. A true blessing! Merry Christmas!

As indicated by their facial expressions when I returned from my ten-second experience, Lorelly, her sister, and niece all seemed to know that I had "left" or was momentarily diverted. They were pleasant and friendly while we all talked for about a half hour until three men returned to the park bench—her son, brother-in-law, and his friend, who were all fairly big dudes around thirty years old. They sensed my apprehension at first but were very cordial after the women explained who I was and why I was sitting there talking with them, since they all had knowledge of Angie's interdimensional connection with Spirit and Angels. I was informed by my Guides at that time that "this was my Christmas host family."

They explained to me that their family had left Venezuela four months prior with only a few suitcases, Angie's wheelchair, and the clothes on their back. I picked up on the shock of them fleeing as refugees and the unity and closeness shared by the nine of their direct family. After five days on a bus, they arrived in Cuenca to begin a new life. They all worked daily, selling bottled water, empanadas, ice cream, and newspapers, while Lorelly's sister cleaned a private house ten hours a day, six days a week, for two hundred dollars a month.

Since it was then getting a little late, we felt it was time to part, so I invited Lorelly and Angie to join me for lunch the following afternoon. I wanted to visit with Angie in a less hurried atmosphere so I could practice telepathy with her and hopefully connect with her Guides to ascertain more information. We agreed to meet the following day at the same location, all said good night, and we went our separate ways.

The following afternoon, Lorelly, Angie, and I met again in the park, where we relaxed and chatted for a short while before crossing the street to a local restaurant. We enjoyed a nice conversation, more in-depth than the previous evening, and although we spent an hour together, I was still unable to mentally receive direct projection from Angie, but I felt she was accompanied by many personal and angelic Spirit Guides that influenced me on her behalf. Feeling prompted to ask about Angie's general living conditions and resources, I became aware of her more immediate need of food and clothes.

Knowing that any Christmas celebration would be out of the question due to the lack of resources, I suggested that we throw a big party for Angie if Lorelly and her family could cook. She happily responded with a big smile while Lorelly nodded her head yes and explained that their kitchen had a large gas stove, able to cook two large pots at the same time. Since they lived in an area with many other poor refugees, I asked Angie if she would like a party big enough for all of her neighbors and friends. She gave me a big smile, and I agreed by saying that we were going to have a *fiesta grande* for her and to celebrate Jesus's birthday. Since it was the day before Christmas Eve, I suggested to Lorelly that I accompany her back to her house so I would know where she lived, and then two men could come with me to the market to help carry provisions for the party.

We took a taxi twenty minutes back to their house, where her son and brother-in-law, of course, joyfully agreed to come with me to the market. The huge local market sold everything necessary, and we returned to their modest home with forty pounds of chicken; one hundred pounds of various vegetables, potatoes, spices, and seasonings; a few cases of beer; and a big teddy bear for Angie, for a total cost of around $250. Everyone in the house and neighborhood knew that Santa Claus had arrived for Angie! I said good night and agreed to return Christmas Eve around 6:00 p.m.

On Christmas Eve around suppertime, I taxied back to the house, where I received an overwhelming, warm reception from the family and their friends, as I sensed Angie express her deep-seated joy. When I entered the house, there were several long tables end to end with thirty-five chairs stretched through the combination living-dining room, where we visited and told stories about our lives, our families, and where we were from. Little by little, more people began to arrive for dinner, until we had forty people seated and celebrating Christmas! Prior to our feast, I stood and spoke for a few minutes to tell everyone we were celebrating Jesus's birthday for Angie. After I introduced myself, I relayed some basic spiritual and angelic information, said a short prayer, and then expected everyone would repeat "Amen" after me when I was finished. Instead, I received a lengthy standing ovation from all, hollering, "Woo-hoo, right on, yeah, Jimmy!" It was totally unexpected, very funny, and quite a moving experience! Thank you, God!

CHAPTER 11
CHARLIE TODAY

The last time I returned to Guatemala City, my personal body-guard met me at the airport, and Charlie's uncle drove us back to the house for one of my more recent weeklong visits with him and his family. Charlie lives with a dozen family members in a small gated community about an hour with traffic from the city center, with armed security twenty-four hours a day, seven days a week, so residents walking around the neighborhood at any time are very safe. Walking in slippers to the corner store after dark for ice cream, or kids going in their pajamas in the morning to buy milk or cereal, is the common way of life in the family-oriented, peaceful neighbor-hood. Retired local government and business men enforce their own rules of community law and justice, and they make for a pleasant neighborhood in which to live. The area between the airport and the community is the problem, and one particular area that I have to pass through has been the subject of a North American television documentary on extortion and violence. It is most likely this area would be the location of any nefarious activity initiated against me, but I have no intention of finding out.

Charlie has stated on many occasions that he and I were in-troduced to each other by angelic design. Since his natural father abandoned him shortly after he was born, the male figures in his life before me were his uncles and two grandfathers. Although they offered a limited level of security for him, he still deeply wanted a dad who understood him and would play with him like other kids, so he persistently insisted and asked Jesus until I was led to him and came into his life.

One of the things he enjoys most is a good fireworks display, and for the holidays, I also enjoy legally acquiring some large pyrotechnics. The flat roof of his house was an excellent launch site, with a commanding vista over the countryside of massive amounts of evening fireworks brilliantly lighting the valley and hillsides below. Buying in bulk directly from the manufacturer, I was able to acquire a taxi load for an ultracheap bargain. One Easter was extra special, since Charlie wanted "double last year" with a lengthy finale; it was just awesome! I, of course, graciously paid for all damages to the bakery down the street on the corner when a stray rocket flew in the front door, ricocheted off the back wall, and blew up inside the pie case. There was cake and whipped cream *everywhere*! Thank you, God, nobody got hurt! Although the owners initially refused any compensation, it was I who sponsored the community fireworks show that Easter weekend, and the *panaderia* owners were appreciative of my reimbursement. That was the last pyrotechnic party that we had.

During some of my first discussions with Charlie after we first met, I showed him pages of pictures with Jesus, Archangels, Angels, and Ascended Masters. While I slowly flipped through the pages, he stopped me on Jesus and Metatron and told me they both have been with him since before he was born. Metatron is a nonphysical entity of geometrical shape whose mission is to assist children and disadvantaged humans on this planet. He says Metatron is originally from Mars and elsewhere "more than ten thousand years ago" and can frequently be found working in elementary schools with children, assisting adults who help kids, and influencing teachers as well.

Charlie has always said for many years that he worked for the Angels, until I arrived and asked, "So have you been working hard with the Angels?"

"No."

I just froze, shocked along with a few other family members as we looked at him, waiting in suspense to hear more. I asked, "What?"

"No," he again replied with a big smile. "*I am one* now. I got promoted."

We all sighed in relief, laughed, told him that he scared us, and gave him a big hug. "I do what they do, just like them," he said.

It had been several months since my prior visit with Charlie, and I quickly felt that he was mentally uncomfortable with himself. I received telepathic messages from him all day long, and although I refused to discuss it, that evening we continued at bedtime. While lying on the bed next to him, I held his hand as usual, so that when I don't understand his telepathic response, he can easily squeeze my finger to answer my question for confirmation. At first, I was, of course, sad and disappointed that his priority of discussion was to clearly state that he wants to die. This has been a prior topic of dialogue on several previous occasions, and it had been his primary thought all day. He has technically died a half-dozen times in the past, where he has risen through the light, only to be told by Jesus that he can't stay because it isn't his time yet. He still had lessons to teach other family members, and me also, but his time was "getting closer," Jesus told him.

Charlie told me he has clearly had enough of this life and is absolutely beyond sick and tired of his skeletally twisted, dysfunctional body, and after twenty-two years, it is now torture to him. He told me that he spends most of his time in another place, where there is no violence, theft, or corruption, and when an occasional "dark entity" is identified, it is dealt with swiftly, and they all return to living in a world of only love. He firmly asked me to jointly petition Jesus with him to allow him to go there and stay. I responded verbally that when I returned to Florida, I would consider asking Jesus; however, he instantly knew by his mind-reading ability that I was only thinking of considering asking, because we could've done it right then and there. Sure, just what I want to do—ask Jesus to terminate and remove from the planet the person I love most. There's a brain bender for ya! I do pray to Jesus, asking for His mercy in considering His disposition of Charlie.

Playing games on people when you're telepathic is funny and entertaining, especially when it's a spoof on your mom. One day from another room, he telepathically told me though IPP that he wanted pizza for lunch from Pizza Hut, but I responded to him that I wanted Little Caesars, with pepperoni. I then verbalized it by asking everyone else in the house "Pizza Hut or Little Caesars?" All eight each agreed by hollering back throughout the house "Little Caesars!" except Marcy, who was outside. When Marcy walked in the door five minutes later, although he already had given in to have Little Caesars, Charlie telepathically projected to his mom, "Tell everyone we're getting Pizza Hut!" and with her not knowing all of us had been through this for the past five minutes, she hollered out, "Charlie wants Pizza Hut for lunch!" thinking she was the first to tell us. It was absolutely hysterical, and everyone roared, but I guess you had to be there. Uncle Jorge came home a short time later with Little Caesars, and Charlie was very happy.

Another example was when we had just finished playing with our r/c car in the street, a longtime neighbor friend came home from school on his 250cc dirt bike motorcycle, parked it across the street, waved hi, and walked up the steps to enter his house. Charlie always enjoys seeing a fast car, motorcycle, or anything of the sort, so "coincidentally," Jose immediately turned around, put his helmet back on, got back on his bike, and pulled a wheelie ten feet in front of Charlie sitting in his wheelchair on the sidewalk. "Gee," I projected to Charlie, "I wonder where that idea came from?" while he grinned at me a certain way and laughed, knowing that I was on to his mischievousness! Of course, Jose thought that it was all his idea to do a wheelie.

As we lay on the bed before bedtime the next night, I asked Charlie to ask Carolina to play with us before going to sleep, in that we wanted her to help us play a joke on Marcy. Charlie told me that Carolina agreed, so verbally I asked if she would flicker the bedroom light on and off when Marcy came in to say good night to us. Charlie said yes, that she would play.

Five minutes later, Marcy came into the room with us, where the light was on as normal, and I asked her, "Has the light bulb been flickering? Is there something wrong with the bulb?"

"No, there's nothing wrong with it. Why?" she answered.

"Maybe it's Carolina playing with the switch," I said.

Responding with a dirty look, she asked, "What's wrong with the two of you? You're just both crazy." She laughed while sitting on the end of the bed, making fun of us.

At that moment, through IPP, Charlie told me, "Now," so I asked aloud, "Carli, is there anything wrong with us, or is it the light bulb?"

The light bulb instantly flickered on and off about ten times in three seconds. Marcy screamed and ran out of the room while Charlie and I laughed so hard we almost peed in our pants! That was probably the funniest joke I have ever experienced in my life while playing with Spirit. You just can't make this up! I still laugh to this day when I think about it, but Marcy fails to find the humor in it.

He and his Spirit friends have games they play too, one of which is with fast remote-control toy cars in the street in front of his house. Since I also love to play, Charlie and I are often the first humans out the door after supper, with the r/c car and remote in his lap. I or others physically operate the remote control, and we race the car fifty to a hundred feet in each direction up and down the narrow street from our fixed location in front of his house (where I stand next to Charlie in his wheelchair). His friends in the astral race and jostle for position while flying and hovering directly above the car and instantly turn direction when the car changes course. They can also momentarily increase the speed and extend the battery life, but I don't know the specifics other than they all love to play, and it seems as though they are addicted to it. Charlie is the host, and he can watch but doesn't fly with them (during the game). I believe their excitement is partly created when the Spirits' energy fields rapidly pass through one another, causing a "rush" of some type.

We most often used rechargeable batteries, but sometimes they weren't charged or were unavailable for some reason or other, so regular ones were used. Charlie's Spirit friends often come by and tell him they want to play and that he should ask someone to drive the car for *him*, because if he asks someone to drive for his friends in the astral, no one will do it for them except me. They all had so much fun one day; the new batteries were flat dead, even with their extended life, but they all wanted to continue playing, so Charlie asked his mom for another set of batteries. She said no, because he is allowed only one set of new batteries per day. He was so mad at his mother that he telepathically drove the car across the living room floor to piss off his mother (with help from his friends), in front of everyone watching television. At that moment, the house cleared out when his four cousins, aunt, grandfather, and Marcy all ran out the front door of the house freaking out, laughing and screaming at the same time! It was another one of our absolute funniest moments ever, and Charlie and I couldn't stop laughing until our stomachs hurt!

The next morning, we had breakfast and played with the r/c car in the street, and I returned him to his favorite pastime of all time: watching anime girls (computer-generated Asian teenage electronic/dance girls) on his YouTube television. Watching anime is a mental retreat and escape from human-influenced souls, thoughts, and actions since there are no actors' or entertainers' personalities attached to distract from his mentally relaxed state.

Over the past five years or so, family members say the biggest change in Charlie is that he is much more intelligent, using words and concepts previously unknown to him. He doesn't go to school, nor does he watch television news or educational material other than sometimes Animal Planet or the History Channel. Previously, his sole interest of entertainment was cartoons, and now it's anime. He says several of the cartoon programs currently on television are based on real characters and animals from another world.

Most of the family members living in the house with him, except his aunt Lucy, have little idea as to the extent of which he influences their daily, routine lives and thought decisions through mind control. For example, when Charlie wants a certain person to push him in his chair around the neighborhood, he implants the idea into that person's mind through projection (IPP), so they ask, "Charlie, do you want to go for a walk around the neighborhood?" as if it was their idea. It's really funny, and when he knows that I know when he does that, we make eye contact and laugh at the "victim," while the others in the room always want to know what's so funny. It's even funnier when we are in a public place when a soda dumps into the lap of a stranger who just yelled at or slapped their kid for something. It's great, because absolutely nobody knows that Charlie did it, and he can't get in trouble for doing it! He can also make someone momentarily choke on their food or trip over their own feet. He is a force to be reckoned with for sure, but only for defense or to defend someone who can't defend themselves.

While we sat on the couch one midafternoon, he just looked up and away as usual when there were Spirit-Beings present among us in the room. The conversation went as follows:

Me. Charlie, who is here?

C. Carli.

Me. Hi, Carli!

(*As he looked to the other corner of the ceiling, I knew there were others.*)

Me. Carolina is back from the light? Who else?

C. Yes, with las muchachas [*young or teenage girls*].

ME. How many and how old are they?

C. There are five of them, different ages, some children.

ME. Five! Where did they come from?

C. They are just passing through. They followed you here.

ME. How is that? Through Carli?

C. Yes.

ME. Are they nice Spirits and good girls?

C. Yes.

ME. Would you like to light a candle for them?

Charlie physically responded with an overwhelming yes, so I lit a candle, and we had an official welcome for the girls into the house as new Spirit friends of Charlie. Carli left quickly, but the five muchachas stayed for a couple of hours, watching anime with Charlie. He said they also enjoy the computer-generated entertainment, and I responded they were welcome to return at any time, as long as they work for Jesus, Mother Mary, or Angels of the light.

ME. Do they spend other time here in this colonia [*neighborhood*], at other houses?

C. Yes, many.

Me. Have other Spirits passed through here to watch anime?

C. Yes, there have been a few, and they come back to visit me from time to time.

Me. That's wonderful, Charlie, to have nice friends like that who come visit you.

(*C. agreed.*)

During another typical day of Charlie receiving the most love and attention imaginable, after racing his r/c car up and down the street, we returned to the living room, where he told me the following: he now works from the other side with a group of three friends in Spirit, helping similar people who currently occupy bodies resembling his. The teenage boys in Spirit also had bodies comparable to Charlie while they were alive, two of whom lived in Guatemala, and one other who had just passed over three years ago, unknown from where.

With the assistance of Metatron for powerful support when necessary, this group of Spirit boys seek out quadriplegics, paraplegics, and elderly with disabilities, primarily in the cities and sometimes in the jungle throughout Central America. Charlie and his buddies each "work" on a person who is responsible for that disabled person's care and influence their thoughts both while sleeping and awake, to produce resulting actions favorable to the disabled person, who sometimes also communicates with the boys. Examples of ideas and thoughts they implant into the caretakers' minds range from giving someone an extra blanket or water, to bathing them more than once a month, to throwing more food into their cage (or prison room to prevent their escape), or stopping severe, daily beatings and physical abuse. Brutal stuff, but no one ever said the work of Soldiers for Jesus was like joining the Girl Scouts. *They* are truly "special forces."

Each situation is unique, and their ability to effectively penetrate the minds of responsible caretakers varies as well.

He also explained that Angel "De La Guarda" helps the homeless living on the street, particularly those who are open to acceptance of thoughts to do something nice or good. Those in harmony with universal energy receive favorable influence of even the slightest things, but those who resist and refuse to accept God-Sourced, wholesome thoughts are left to continue absorbing dark energy and evil-influenced thoughts, which lead to their eventual demise.

Before going to sleep one night, he told me that Carli's father was an evil spirit on the other side and stated that he clearly saw Carli running from her dad in the ether, who was trying to "kill" her with a knife. Charlie's physical reaction was fairly extreme, exhibiting body twists and contractions during the occurrence, similar to convulsions. I immediately called upon Jesus and Archangel Michael for assistance, so he was able to calm down after a few minutes, and eventually we fell off to sleep. The following morning, he told us about Carli's evil father and of a massive fire burning in hell, but I do not ask him about or discuss dark or evil forces. Our conversations are held almost always in the light, with the powers of protection.

His grandmother phoned yesterday, asking for Marcy to bring Charlie with several other family members to their home because Franco was deathly sick and he was expected to pass within the next several days. Franco and Charlie have always been close, and they both wanted to be together when Franco made his transition, which occurred about a week later. It was an honor for Charlie to assist, because if anyone died and went straight to heaven with Jesus, it was Franco, and knowing Charlie, he pleaded to Jesus to allow him to stay as well. Charlie said that Franco's sickness was initiated by nearby jungle Spirits of deceased evil men.

Lying on the bed with Charlie the night before I was to leave to come back to Florida, I told him that early the following morning after I got home, I would be going fishing in the ocean on an open-seating local party boat that usually takes about twenty-five men. It docks near my condo, a few miles up the road, and leaves every day at eight o'clock in the morning, so it's easy to access on short notice after checking the weather that morning to see if it's a go. Before leaving his house that next morning in a taxi to the airport, I reminded Charlie to please help me catch a big fish, exactly twenty-four hours later, when I would be out on the boat the next day fishing in the ocean. He smiled and said OK, and after hugs and kisses, I was off to the airport.

I got back home and went out fishing the following morning, and for the first three hours, I watched twenty other guys catch a lot of smaller two-to-three-pound fish, while I caught absolutely nothing. After the excitement of my travel, relaxing on the ocean was peaceful until a few of the guys near me were making fun of me because I wasn't using the correct pole, hook, or bait, let alone was I wearing the right fishing shirt or shoes! An hour later my lure got a solid hit, and whack! I sank the hook, and my sixty-to-eighty-pound-rated pole practically bent in half. All of a sudden, the half-dozen guys who had been laughing at me for the last two hours because I hadn't caught anything became quiet. Twenty minutes later I landed a forty-four-pound cobia, the most prized fish to catch around here, due to its fight and quality of meat, let alone its five-hundred-dollar value.

I won the pool of about $150, and while holding the money high in the air, I smilingly said, "Thanks for the cash, guys," and had the fish filleted at the dock. You think they were mad at me then? At thirty dollars per pound in the fish market, how do you think they felt watching me give away half of the best fish fillets to the poor and old Haitian people waiting on the dock to buy fish heads and scraps for their dinner for fifty cents or a dollar? Actually, the giving-it-away part felt better than catching it! I love you, Charlie! It was ironic that the most arrogant guys on the boat were the most irritated and pissed off back at the dock. It was definitely another great day fishing for me, though!

⇌╫╪⇌

A few weeks later while I was driving down a Florida highway one afternoon at fifty miles an hour, all of a sudden, the Spirit apparitions of Charlie and Carolina appeared above the front passenger seat inside my car.

All I heard was, "Bye, Jimmy. Bye, Jimmy. We love you! Goodbye!" while one of the Spirits was waving at me, but I didn't know who.

At that moment though, I thought they were telling me that I was going to die, so I slowed down, thought to myself, *Son of a bitch,* and pulled over to the right lane.

"Bye, Jimmy! We love you!"

I thought to myself, *Damn it, today's not a good day to die!* I was pissed. I told them, "Wait! Tell Jesus that I said *no,* and to hold off just twenty-four hours more, please, because I have important things to do, and I'll talk to Him when I get there. Not today! Absolutely not!"

I was quite disturbed for a couple of hours while waiting for whatever to happen, powerless to completely understand what the heck had just occurred. I called Marcy that night, and she told me that Charlie had been crying continuously all day because Carolina had departed the astral and returned to the light. They both came to me together to say goodbye. I knew that she had been the love of his life for every day of the past ten years; he again was alone in his deformed body all by himself. Charlie's mental anguish was incomprehensible, and his heart had been broken. He was allowed by Jesus to go through the light and visit her in heaven, but Jesus again disallowed him to stay because it was not his time yet, the same as the last five times Jesus told him he could visit, but only for a short while. My heart really hurts writing this. When we eventually visited a couple of months later, Charlie and I hysterically laughed so hard talking about the car incident with him and Carli, we both laughed continuously until we cried ourselves to sleep!

He says that we all come from space and that our ancestors continually watch over, interact with, and help us, but also, there are other unfavorable groups that want our planet because of our reserves of valuable resources. They are a continuous threat and serious problem, which he is often concerned about. He also says that there is a mixed experimental colony of more than ten thousand people/Beings living harmoniously in massive underground facilities operated by extraterrestrials inside the moon and on other planets as well. Many occupants are the humans who have disappeared from Earth and are integrated into the joint experimental colonies consisting of thousands and thousands of children, adults, and animals. Our military also maintains an operational base there, and in other locales as well, where earthbound officers and workers frequently visit for a few days and then return to Earth. An Earth-orbit station is the staging platform for the several-hours-long one-way journey, currently utilizing multiple types of ultrafast "secret" craft with advanced propulsion systems. Longer journeys reaching to planets farther out in the solar system originate from those platforms as well, but with different craft.

There are many other colonies in the outer solar system, besides the millions of extraterrestrial hybrids that live here in our "colony" among us, already integrated into our government, military, media, and society in general. Just watch the television news anchors and Hollywood actors, or look at the politicians, and you will see some of them. We are currently being psychologically prepared by them en masse for "official" government disclosure of our joint secret space programs working with extraterrestrials, both in space and here on Earth. Many government officials want disclosure ASAP and will eventually expose a half-dozen other countries that have been working with them also—for an exceedingly long period of time.

He says that most importantly, love and forgiveness are foremost, and we must only pray to God, Jesus, and Mother Mary. It is OK to recognize and thank other Spirits and Ascended Masters in appreciation of their work and contribution to this planet, but it is not OK to pray to them. Charlie said that God's plans for humans have been altered and misaligned from His original intended plan. Many, many energies, off-planet powers, and Spirits from Earth and beyond continually attack our planet, and many continue to unfavorably influence mankind, in opposition to God's plan.

Charlie also told me that some of the highest-IQ humans make up a secret think-tank group, who are the targets of extremely dark, powerful forces. This has resulted in the masses of us dummies being utilized as expendable pawns of slavery, solely for their personal narcissistic endeavors. Without them following dark-force influence, they and their families would have among the most rewarding human life experiences of all mankind, but they choose otherwise.

When we first met twelve years ago, his interaction with the other side was about 50 percent of the time. This percentage has gradually increased over the years not only in frequency, but also in breadth and depth. Currently, he is "living" on the other side around 95 percent of the time, also indicative of his desire to terminate occupancy of his physical human body. He has become proficient in separating and staying alert in both dimensions simultaneously. He says he travels with me frequently, along with a group of other Angel Guides that accompany me, as they do with many travelers, but he doesn't know their names. He identifies with Spirits by their energy signature.

Overall, Charlie has recently appeared to accelerate his abilities of ESP, telepathy, and interdimensional travel since being deathly ill for a few weeks. Three months ago, his longtime doctor, Dra. Gloria, told the family to prepare for his death, as his passing within a few of days was likely. Being deathly sick for three weeks had taken a dramatic toll on his fragile twenty-two-year-old body.

A couple of days after my last visit with him, he imparted into my being through IPO, his feeling of the most intense, deepest sadness imaginable. It lasted for about an hour until he removed it from me. I believe that he presented me that experience in order that I may fully comprehend how deeply saddened he feels himself, regarding our inability to continue our physical visits. Also, at the time of his permanent physical departure, I will be more accepting of his choice to leave. Something tells me that even after he makes his transition permanent, that doesn't mean I won't visit with him anymore!

CHAPTER 12
SPIRITUAL AND TELEPATHIC PROJECTION

RECOGNIZING CONTACT BY PROJECTION

- There is an internal feeling, either through the whole body or the mind alone.

- There may be a disruption of normal thought process at first before you recognize a deeper awareness of knowing.

- There is a desire to follow an inspiration or thought, not knowing the reason or source.

- You experience a rapid change in thought process or subject matter.

- You may feel a sudden sense of urgency, yet it is subtle and indefinable.

- When it is Spirit initiated, it feels denser and occupies more rear depth, as compared to a person's projection, which occupies more frontal space.

- On many occasions, rapid, unsettling thoughts raced through my head, as if I was preparing to leave my body, when something extraordinary was about to occur.

- Sometimes it was a specific message, but more often, I sensed a feeling to leave a particular location that I was in at that time, not knowing why.

Time spent visiting with Charlie has enabled my understanding of the functionality and frequency of the concept of mind and thought control. I have taken classes, attended a seminar or two, and read several books on the subject, but my knowledge is limited to personal experience and practice with Charlie. Implanted thought can be extraordinarily powerful, so much so that the person often knows it subconsciously but is unable to overcome or suppress the deep, embedded force or feeling causing action from within. Knowing this has enabled me to now more fully grasp and see the origin of many implanted thoughts received by the serial killers with whom I worked a few years ago. Although there may be unpublished methodologies in which to electronically or magnetically manipulate a human mind, I have found that either another human or a Spirit has the ability to extensively influence or control another through one of four ways:

Inter-Personal Projection (IPP): The act of one human imparting and implanting predetermined pictures, thoughts, or feelings into another target person's mind, creating the impression that the target themselves is the singular origin and source of the thought. The message seems to be less dense, more in the frontal, shallow region of the mind, as opposed to the rear, denser, depth of ISP.

Inter-Spiritual Projection (ISP): When a Spirit implants a target human's mind with pictures, thoughts, or feelings, similar to IPP, but the Spirit also has the ability to see or read the target mind at the same time, and more rapidly adjust their transmission according to the reception.

Inter-Personal Occupation (IPO): A person may transmit to a target and implant their personal energy field so powerful that the target mind may be consumed by it and feel powerless to stop or change it, even when they know it has occurred.

Inter-Spiritual Occupation (ISO): Spirit walk-ins have similar effect on a human brain, but the walk-in will also take complete muscle control of the body, such as when a person is possessed or talking in tongues. More often, the host human allows the occupation.

It seems that walk-ins desire a more permanent occupation and total control for the medium or long term, whereas projection is for temporary brain influence, such as for a short-term request, mission, or action. I understand that some walk-ins of ISO have been powerful enough to completely and permanently "steal" a human's life and existence. I believe future research will cause a major clinical breakthrough to be learned, proving that ISO is also the cause of many split-personality disorders. The subjects occupied often agree and adapt to their living in a shared body, such as an adult neighbor acquaintance of mine. After a person experiences a traumatic event, it is an opportune time for an uninvited Spirit to take advantage, as the shock that has occurred to the host body creates opportunity to enter under the disguise of emotional comfort.

Easy targets for them are weaker people with low values, low self-esteem, or low IQ; those under the influence of alcohol or drugs; or generally broken, greedy people. Many children's souls remain in the astral to enable them to play with each other; hence, they also become targets of dark forces as well. Through projection and occupation, dark souls take advantage and continue to perpetuate dark deeds against humanity as well as other vulnerable souls.

Almost everyone is vulnerable to a certain extent, but more sensitive people are more susceptible. The psychiatric medical and prison communities will someday in the future identify criminals by the vast difference of a population's mental/genetic imbalance versus both projection and occupation. It can be safely surmised that substantial research occurs in this field, but in-depth studies of effective mind control techniques, I would imagine, remain classified and secret.

Many souls, however, remain in the astral remain in the location of their physical death after parting ways from their physical body. Their souls linger due to their failure to ascend to the light, which ultimately prevents their reintegration back to the one reality of God-Source consciousness, hence the term "lost souls." In the astral, souls frequently unite with other souls similar to themselves, and unfortunately, many of them unhappily remain there in limbo. Since there are an insufficient number of human bodies to accommodate the excessive number of souls wanting to occupy them, one common phenomenon is for a Spirit entity to attach their soul to a vulnerable human without their permission, frequently with children.

PROJECTION IN CHURCH

Inconsistently, I attend various church services here in Florida mostly on Sundays, but sometimes during the week as well. One Sunday morning I decided to go to a metaphysical church near where I live, which I have attended on many occasions over the past seven or eight years. The minister is well known as one of the premier intuitive mediums in the country today since he has developed his ability to clearly receive and interpret messages from Spirit. I was familiar with this minister's service and teaching format, and toward the end of each service, he would usually give several brief open-message intuitive readings to a half-dozen randomly chosen individuals in the congregation. Church that Sunday began as normal, leading to a soulful sermon sprinkled with a little humor that resonated with the fifty or sixty parishioners. This service was different than most other Sundays, though, as he openly stated from his podium while appearing a bit overwhelmed. He stepped down from the podium, seemingly taken back for a moment. While gazing above as he usually does while "seeing," he addressed the congregation as follows:

"I had intentions of closing our service today in the usual manner, but as you know, Spirit often changes things at the last minute, which is exactly what is occurring right now. I'm being guided now to do something a little different today, so we're holding a very special celebration service of recognition. It is being coordinated here in our physical world at this moment in time to participate simultaneously with the corresponding celebration service being held by a huge number of Spirits on the other side, right now, at this moment. I can't tell you how many of them; there are hundreds and hundreds of them gathered in attendance in an enormous grand celebration hall, all kinds, with numerous Archangels and Ascended Masters also watching.

"This special celebration today is being held in recognition of you, Jimmy, for the work you have done and what you continue to do. The hosts of this service, Jimmy, are your father, grandfathers, great-grandfathers, and lineage before them, along with their relatives and friends, going back who knows how far. They are all so very proud of you, happy for you, and have incredible appreciation for all of your work and what you have done. They are all saying thank you, each one of them. With a long line of family members and many others standing on both sides of an aisle three to four deep, they ask that you now approach and accept that which they all present to you here now, this medallion of spiritual honor." He raised his arms in motion, as if placing it to hang around my neck. The minister paused, speechless for a few moments, appearing to recollect himself, and said, "I have never seen anything like this before, and I also am proud to have been a part of this service today, as I know you are as well, Jimmy. Wow."

As he spoke a clear description of the ceremony and circumstances, I strongly felt projected spiritual energy encompass my body as I visualized the event. Momentarily, I also was speechless, until I uttered, "Thank you very much. Thank you." It was all I could say. Good thing I was sitting down for that! The minister was equally overwhelmed as was I, and he needed a minute to absorb what had just occurred. To maintain continuity of the remaining service, he then led us to immediately sing our closing hymn. After church, many people just looked at me, wondering what to say, but mostly I heard, "Wow, Jimmy, that was so cool!" and "Amazing!" and "I'm glad that I came today to hear that," and many other similar compliments.

That experience was another one of the most significant spiritual events of my life, and it also highlighted my attention as to how fortunate I am compared to many others who don't comprehend the depths and functionality of interdimensional realities. My knowing with confirmation that my relatives are with Divine Beings on the other side of the veil is very humbling and reinforces my awareness of continuity of life after death with the ability to rise into the house of God.

SPIRIT CHILDREN

One condo that I lived in for a while was a duplex, built on the site of an old Indian encampment in the western Colorado mountains. It was located higher up on a plateau near the confluence of two rivers, with a beautiful panoramic view off the back deck of the surrounding countryside and distant mountain peaks. There were many stories told over the years of wagon trains that were attacked in the area and scores of settlers who were slaughtered by the Indians.

After returning from the supermarket one afternoon, through my living room common wall, I heard what I thought was my neighbor moving furniture around and then some kids laughing and giggling. During the course of my first few months living there, I heard these types of noises dozens of times but never said anything to my neighbor. Then I figured they must be Bill's nieces and nephews and the adults must have been out for a while, because the kids were being extra rowdy and having a whole lot of fun! I was glad they were happy kids and were not yelling at one another. The raucous noise continued for about a half hour and got really loud, until the kids finally quieted down after their last pillow fight. I thought it was odd, though, that I had never seen the kids outside, either being dropped off or picked up, because my neighbor Bill lived there alone.

A few days later, I saw Bill and asked him if his nieces and nephews were visiting again. He looked at me as if I had two heads, and started laughing when he asked what in the heck I was talking about. It turned out that he had no visitors or company, but he had been meaning to ask me the same thing for a few months! It seemed those kids were lost souls from previous wagon train battles that were fought in the valley nearby.

One afternoon I "opened" sacred space in my living room and held a prayer session, while projecting my energy at the common living room wall between my neighbor's house and mine. I first called the Spirit children and then called upon Jesus, Mother Mary, and their assistants of the highest order to assist them to return to the light. I felt there was discourse between the angelic Beings and the children, although I was not privy to the specific contents of the communication. A few minutes later, I felt my mission was a success, although no message or vision was received by me. Never again did I hear any noises from the kids, and neither did Bill.

HOMELESS PEOPLE

Over the past fourteen years of encountering and counseling homeless street people, and others with less-than-good intentions, many had often verbalized their lack of understanding the cause of their poor actions. "I don't understand it. I just don't know where the thought came from. I don't know what made me do it; that wasn't me" and "I knew I shouldn't have done it, but I did it anyway" were among the common responses of many I have spoken with. Before I was able to partly identify the true Source and cause of many of these people's poor choices, I originally believed it was all just part of their makeup, or drugs, but now I know otherwise.

Besides illogical brain processing due to faulty brain connections or unbalanced chemicals, many of them behave that way because of increased brain sensitivity. Enhanced sensitivity frequently amplifies their awareness of alternate dimensions, thereby expanding their influence by unwelcome thought from a stand-in reality, causing many to become confused as to which is their true existence. The truths they live are often contrary to what they have been told. This also results in excess, uninvited Spirit-originated thought input by projection, in contrast to their subconscious truths, that also adds to their confusion, which leads to irrational decision-making. After all, how many university-educated professors understand the natural concept of living in two dimensions at the same time? Unfortunately, we have an insufficient number to educate the masses. Eons past, many of the intelligent ones had enhanced mental abilities and transcended as interdimensional Beings, and were referred to as gods—which at the time was recognized as a privilege and was generally perceived by society as special.

Due to an insufficient number of professionals who truly comprehend the underlying origin and cause of many potential problems, incorrect diagnosis often leads many to become convinced they are incurable and left without hope, but their situation can be "controlled" with drugs. Part of the problem is that the licensed wacky ones prescribe drugs for the other wacky ones, give "special" new drugs to realign their brain, and effectively terminate their natural being, all due to an incompetent "professional analysis." Often, street people believe that they are mentally ill because they have been told so by inept, ignorant counselors who don't believe their story, when, in fact, they often know more than their counselor does. Many know that frequently, the counselor or psychotherapist needs the drugs, and they should switch sides of the desk.

Failing to recognize and understand some humans' abilities to live interdimensionally while occupying a human body is mostly due to the archaic nature of our "modern" psychiatric institutions and universities. Misdiagnosis of a person's telepathic overload by projection occurs because most doctors, counselors, and institutional professors don't understand it themselves, which then, by default, leads to the permanent, legal destruction of that person's brain. Starting out with a controllable (misidentified) problem turns into a disaster that could have been used for their, and society's, exceptional benefit. Sad.

I have met and spoken with many homeless people, and telling them my story of previously living in a luxury suite cardboard refrigerator box gets them to listen. While recently driving to my favorite coffee shop, I passed one of many homeless people, a woman, standing on the corner. I rarely help them, but after driving away, I was intuitively told to go back and talk to her, which I did. After driving around the block, I pulled the car over to the side of the road, where she came to the passenger's side after I called her over and gave her a dollar as an excuse to talk with her. While trying to figure out what I was supposed to tell her, I asked her a few questions, and she soon subtly revealed that she was a suicide candidate in an advanced stage. I realized my priest finger had work to do, fast, and I performed accordingly. As you know, sometimes I just open my mouth, and my Guides do the talking. Several minutes later she cried and thanked me with all her heart, as my words resonated with her core thoughts (little did she know that I wasn't the one doing the talking). She needed to return to her support system and promised to travel there to restart her life. Ten minutes later I drove away, after I knew she would continue to live—at least a little longer anyway. I went to Harold's and had some green tea with lemon, and while sipping my tea, I heard, "Good job, Jimmy."

When a person refuses their time to alter the course of their life for ten minutes in order to save someone else's life, it's time for them to reevaluate who they themselves really are and what they are doing here. It's part of our fundamental obligation of primary responsibility to assist in overall elevation of vibration of humanity. There are some real basket cases, both on the street and in the boardroom, and sometimes it's impossible to connect with them. Then I hear that it's OK because "you can't help everyone," as some people are too far gone for the type of help that I provide. A most truthful fact that I have seen, though, and which is true beyond the shadow of a doubt is written as Psalm 34:18: "The Lord is close to the broken-hearted and saves those who are crushed in Spirit."

Throughout my travels, I frequently attend church services at various impromptu times in both large cities and small villages, regardless of the religious denomination. Since Catholic religion is predominant throughout Central and South America, I've attended numerous services and gatherings and have had the opportunity to meet many priests. The numerous old stone churches of exquisite architecture are impressive, as well as the energies and Spirits occupying those buildings. Although the massive old buildings were constructed as a result of the Spanish Inquisition, when millions of men tortured, raped, and slaughtered untold millions of indigenous women and children and kept some for slaves, it was done "in the name of God." This appears to me as massive and powerful evil mind control at the highest level, seemingly implemented by a dark impostor utilizing mass projection to deviate and fight the intended loving world of Jesus.

It takes knowledge and understanding of the concept and functionality of projection prior to a person having the ability to intelligently respond to its influence. After all, if you don't know that something exists and you are told otherwise by a so-called "educated" doctor, counselor, or teacher, in some other bogus line of reasoning or excuses, what do you have to compare the information to? Nothing, so therefore you believe the line of BS handed to you. Forget the fact that you may have a gift; it seems to me the attitude of higher educational institutions reflect this message: "We think we're the smartest, we don't know about it, and we are in control so that certain people can capitalize! Screw you." It seems to me, and Charlie as well, that it is another form of dark-force influence and egoistic stupidity.

Don't forget that now, it's all about the money, and it's easier to extract from a social system that thrives on greed under the disguise of sympathy and goodwill to improve the lives of the less fortunate. If half the people in society understood that their alleged problem originates from an understandable source, and they are taught how to naturally deal with it and correct it, a permanent issue would then be resolved. I imagine that half the shrinks, counselors, and drugs would then no longer be needed. We certainly can't have that, can we? With issues resolved, afflicted ones are highly likely to return as productive members of society, and many of them could go on to teaching the homeless shrinks themselves after half of the licensed ones become unemployed due to a decrease of new clients. Keep the masses dumb—it's better for the economy, and they're easier to control, until the time arrives when the masses become enlightened and the offenders will be held accountable. It will be interesting and entertaining to watch, I'm sure.

CHAPTER 13
MY OBSERVATIONS AND UNDERSTANDING

CREATIVITY

Creativity is the most critical aspect of our fundamental makeup, because without it, we can't advance as a race. All actions we take collectively determine our ultimate path, since our unified vibration manifests our destiny. With humans having an infinite number of choices that contribute to our progress, it is obviously in our best interest to make the wisest choices available then, leading to a most favorable outcome of our future and assimilation into more advanced, peaceful vibrational Beings. Actionable choices compound off one another and collectively create our future reality. We are continuously and persistently advised of, and offered, Source-aligned choices on a daily basis. It is necessary to recognize and acknowledge these, and follow this input when derived from light.

With independent abilities to think creatively with emotion while utilizing wisdom, we are able to progress, improve, and advance our species; these choices collectively determine our destiny. By looking around us here at other life-forms, on the surface it appears that we humans are the most intelligent of all. How many of us are really that narrow-minded, egocentric, and obnoxious to believe there are *no* other life-forms currently existing both on- and off-planet, in an elevated state of energy, occupying alternate aspects of consciousness right here among us? If you raised your hand, go to the back of the line and reread the preface.

TRUST

You are what you believe. By the conscious and subconscious self-implantation of visions, desires, personal truths, and feelings into yourself, your reality is created by the energy of the universe, which supports your desired outcome. Trusting yourself to follow your instinctive, intuitive thoughts of truth through your heart energy will lead to your living a most rewarding life with guidance of your highest Spirit Guides. The old saying "be careful what you wish for" is an example of this concept, since it is eventually what you become. Hence, the law of attraction is also a fundamental attribute of our reality.

In any walk of life-energy, however, TANFL, as my economics professor so clearly expressed in giant letters written across the chalkboard the first day of class: "There Ain't No Free Lunch!" he hollered out. There is no such thing as something for nothing and no substitute for hard work (contrary to unfortunate beliefs of many politicians), so execute a positive personal plan, and trust that the rewards returned to you will be more than you can ever imagine. Have faith from the core of your being.

SPECIAL NEEDS CHILDREN AND ADULTS

Often parents of special needs persons (SNP) are unable to identify causes of emotional and dispositional variances in their child. One Source that frequently escapes identification by the parent is when a new Spirit entity, or a group of entities, introduces themselves to the child. With communication being a major barrier, SNP will most likely abstain from any attempt to explain to the parent, knowing the parent or caregiver is functioning in linear reality and most often doesn't have a clue. They are unable to explain the in-depth details of a currently abstract phenomena, and they know the concept of human interaction with the Spirit world is currently considered unacceptable by most people. The child's underlying fear of being designated crazy or mentally insane suppresses disclosure—and rightfully so, even though it sucks not having another human to talk about it. After all, they think, *Stupid people only make fun of me, and I can't defend myself,* or *What if they give me drugs and cut my access and connection to the Spirit world?* Cutting them off from the world in which they currently live in God would be the equivalent of a death sentence, permanently condemning them to living in a torture chamber, but psychiatrists will swear the drugs are good for them. Society overall, legally and permanently, allows the destruction of SNP brains as a result of narcissistic incompetence and personal fears of many mentally deranged psychiatrists and psychotherapists. We must expand our capabilities to identify those who are gifted versus those who are mentally bananas.

To enhance the lives of special needs children, their education must be more spiritually focused to enable and enhance their connection with Source, without religious bias. To assist them, primary subjects necessary to teach are science, biology, astronomy, astrology, geology, and the basic mental and breathing concepts of Kriya Yoga, to the extent of their mental and physical ability. A class on Spirits and Angels would be helpful as well. To a SNP, language, grammar, and history are mostly irrelevant and a waste of time, not only for the SNP but also for the educational system in lost opportunity cost. Spiritual and scientifically aligned instruction is the most useful. Teaching these specific classes will more rapidly accelerate the special needs person's connection by setting the foundation upon which they may internally learn to connect—if they have not already done so.

Just as there are groups of humans bound by a common cause, so are many Spirits working for the same cause on the other side of the veil. For example, let's say a human who has transitioned to the other side may have been a financial advisor in their most recent human incarnation. So now, they may work with a group of others who, like themselves, had similar lives, and now as a group, they influence financial decisions that will favorably affect humans who operate in alignment with God's plan. Or maybe someone always had the desire to assist or donate to a certain humanitarian cause but never had the resources or time while they had a body, and now they work for that cause from the other side of the veil. Maybe someone who had killed another human works off his eternal karmic debt with several others resembling themselves to help prevent further human violence, suffering, and premature death.

So, if someone has been paralyzed and is now confined to a dysfunctional body, they may also work with such a group in the ether, as Charlie does. In direct alignment with Jesus and Metatron, Charlie and his friends in the ether carry out nightly missions to the benefit of many people. Frequently, the group of boys finds a handicapped person who is mentally receptive and communicative with them, and thereafter sometimes maintain a strong etheric bond, which continues into a permanent relationship of them working together in the ether. The choices are infinite in number for those who choose to work for God. As a parent of a SNP, wouldn't it be nice for you to know who your kid's friends are? If you believe your child is connected, be sure to tell them that you appreciate their friends' accompaniment and assistance. Keep in mind that many SNPs are much more perceptive than you can comprehend, and many of them are unlikely to disclose any acknowledgment or information that could potentially be used against them by a mentally unstable psychotherapist, oblivious rehab counselor, or a low-IQ parent.

TIM

During my travels, I met a lovely couple with a quadriplegic teenage son, so, of course, I had a bunch of questions for them after introducing myself and explaining my relationship with Charlie. They told me that seven years ago while on a family vacation to a well-known ancient ruin site in South America, Tim Jr. was a typical, happy-go-lucky kid who went a short way off the trail into the woods and quickly returned with a walking stick. That was the only abnormal event that occurred for Junior that day. Continuing an enjoyable day, the family then returned to their local hotel to rest for the night. That evening, Junior began to get seriously ill, and by morning, he was rushed to the hospital with half his body unable to function, and he became fully quadriplegic within a week. His parents and grandparents thought of every single thing that happened that day and came up with nothing except that stick.

A slew of examinations by doctors, specialists, neurosurgeons, and diagnostic tests resulted in finding no cause, cure, or explanation. His body is healthy, and he maintains normal mass, but he is unable to communicate in any vocal or physical way. The following day, the four of us visited together for a couple of hours while exchanging information with each other. During the first hour of our visit, Tim Jr. was mentally present and happy, making verbalized sounds of laughter while looking at me. I had no proof at the time, but a very strong suspicion told me that Charlie had something to do with Tim Jr. laughing at me! When I am sufficiently confident through spiritual confirmation one way or the other, I will first speak with Tim and Tammy before writing it herein. Tim Jr. also has a lot of other stuff going on "on the other side"; he just can't communicate it. The thing that hurts Junior the most is his inability to express his appreciation to his mom, dad, and entire family for the profound love and care they give to him on a daily basis.

Tammy told me that Tim Jr. has been happier than usual over the past two months of February and March. I found that interesting, since I last visited with Charlie in February and told him that I would be traveling back to South America in April. What a coincidence. Charlie, of course, had previously told me that he was always aware of my detailed travels and people I meet, and that he accompanies me everywhere I go, along with several other Spirit Guides who do work similar to us. Sometimes the work includes assisting the parents with information for mental comfort and deeper understanding of their quadriplegic children.

Around that time of year (April), Tim Jr. typically gets abnormally depressed. According to his parents, usually near the anniversary of his bone marrow transplant, his disposition reflects an underlying sadness, which lasts for several weeks. Tim mentioned that the bone marrow was nowhere near a perfect match, but it was the best available, and it came from an unknown donor. It is difficult to determine the donor's influence because of Tim Jr.'s inability to communicate.

Current science has proven that all *living* cells, cellular structures, bones, organs, and beings possess an energy field that retains specific quantum information related to the unique source of its origin. When combined with another human, it incorporates into the new energy field and creates a new, unique, combined energy signature. Just one medically verified example: A forty-year-old woman, after a heart transplant, began to suddenly crave Snickers bars. The woman's daughter also then accused her of beginning to walk comparable to a man. The donor was an eighteen-year-old male killed in a motorcycle accident who loved Snickers bars.

NATE

Walking through Walmart one early evening, I met a lady pushing a quadriplegic man in his wheelchair. I stopped to introduce myself to Renee and Nate and then explained that Charlie has taught me amazing things over the past fifteen years. Renee said that Nate knows "an incredible number of things" and indicated that she knows he is connected to unexplainable information. After I mentioned the names of several angelic Beings, she asked Nate if he knew them, and he positively indicated his awareness and interaction with them. Revealing that Charlie works with Jesus, Mother Mary, and also with groups of disabled people similar to him on the other side got a strong positive reaction, and Renee confirmed his interaction with them also. It was interesting to me that Nate had visitations of other spiritual entities as well. We didn't have much time to chat, but I confirmed many similarities of his experience were the same as other quadriplegics whom I have met. Renee reminded me of Charlie's mom in that the subject matter was just "a little too far out there" for her and preferred to pleasantly terminate our conversation. I felt bad because Nate wanted to continue our visit for a while longer, as the subject matter was of utmost importance to him. It is mostly a rare occasion when a connected person meets another human who understands where they actually live. I sensed that Nate could see I was being accompanied by a Spirit entity at that moment, but I didn't get a chance to ask him who it was. Gee, I wonder who was there with me!

After learning the interdimensional connectedness of a half-dozen quadriplegics, it is only now that I realize the degree of vast ignorance of society as they relate to incapacitated people. I believe that most of them are connected, and the complete lack of understanding this group of people is not only sad but is unacceptable in an educated society.

ENERGY FIELDS

Source energy emanating from the ultimate consciousness supports an attribute of the cosmic field where Angels, Spirit Guides, and Ascended Masters manifest. Influenced by a combination of these entities working in harmony, I've been led to places to help various people both prior to, and after, them needing assistance. Thankfully, I have been delayed or diverted from moments in time where my original intended path would have put me in a most deadly situation. Many instances of physical travel occurred in my life where most men would not have made it back alive, because there frequently seemed to have been a helping hand that utilized a higher power to protect and guide me. Spirit has also changed other people's thoughts and actions on my behalf in an instant, to avoid the hindrance of my welfare or freedom to move forward in this material dimension in order to continue my mission, as previously mentioned. As a recent example, I almost got shot and robbed in a local gas station the other night. A worker taking out the trash made eye contact with a guy twenty-five feet in front of me, at the exact moment I saw him reaching for a gun on his front seat while looking directly at me, and he quickly sped away the instant our unexpected witness appeared.

Aspects of the God-Source consciousness of ultimate reality hold all life with the highest intentions of favorable outcomes, with the desire that our contribution helps to elevate all that is. Powerful groups of Spirit Guides are working for God and Jesus to influence humanity and our planet, for not only our benefit but also for theirs. Humans open and willing to participate with this force are encouraged to do so, and most often are rewarded with living and loving their life in a more favorable way than if no spiritual path had been followed. *Listen* and *trust* are the key words here.

There are energy fields pervading our universe that host and maintain a higher vibrational field of entities in various stages of existence. Information itself is also stored in an aspect of one of these fields and is accessible not only to us, but also to other interdimensional entities and nonphysical Beings. Recently disclosed scientific experiments at MIT have proven that light in itself has the ability to store information, as well as droplets of water, and in the power of crystals, which has been known for millennia. I think that many humans have long been aware that other fields of energy contain numerous interdimensional entities and have existed since the beginning of time, and science is finally figuring it out. As quoted by my friend Roy Eugene Davis, "An enlivening power is nurturing the universe, and we can learn to cooperate with it."

Energy signatures of each individual human are unique to their entity. When more than one individual signature acts, behaves, sings, dances, or meditates in unison in the same location and proximity of one another, a new signature is created by the merging of those energy fields into a new, unique entity comprised of that group in which each of the contributors remain a small part of the whole. Although each contributor leaves with their complete energy signature, particles of that new signature remain in that location and are detectable long after the matter that generated them have gone. They can be picked up by sensitive people and scientific instruments, similar to odors and scents recognized by tracking dogs.

At times, I sense more powerful energy signatures in locations where certain localized Spirit forces have imparted their energy signature in harmony with off-planet sources and with other entities that effectively transcend interdimensional realities. Some energy signatures just "feel" ancient, such as near Paracas and the Sacred Valley near Cusco, Peru; the Chinchoro mummies in Arica, Chile, Tiwanaku; and areas surrounding Lake Titicaca, including Isla del Sol, Isla Patiti, and the Uru-Chipaya region of southern Bolivia; along with many sacred indigenous sites of the American southwest, just to name a few. Those locations seemed to emanate the most powerful and direct connections to the ultimate God-Source Creator, on this side of the planet, as perceived by me. Authoritative jungle energies are also an example, although less frequently for humans' benefit because they often felt denser to me and not of the higher light order.

During an extended meditation in a sacred place in South America, I was taken by my highest Guides to the edge of all universes, and all consciousness, into the origin of time in infinite space. It seemed to me an incomprehensibly distant, extensive journey through escorted teleportation (extensive compared to a normal five-second trip) and then from the edge, turned and looked back at all that is. In Aymara, the existence of that state is referred to as *anapudaka.* Our language doesn't contain the appropriate verbiage to describe the phenomenal experience or the distance, but if it does, I've never heard it. The distance is probably something like ten to the ten-billionth AU or something like that! While the location of our universe was pointed out to me, it was also made known that we are the future of all that is, but yet unviewable because we were less than the size of a neutrino off in the farthest distance imaginable. Current science has just begun to disclose the existence of much more distant space beyond our neighborly "wall" of our visible 13.7

billion light-years. Utilization of wormholes and attributes of dark matter are what take us both inside and beyond.

OUR DEVELOPMENT

While we currently use only around 20 to 25 percent of our brain's capacity to process, analyze, and function as human beings, do you really think the other 75 percent was incorporated into our design solely to take up space? Of course not. Development of our species in the recent past (i.e., ten thousand years) has been dictated by our progressive discovery and utilization of various scientific principles, as well as energy technologies with their corresponding storage facilities. Expansion of our brains' processing power is necessary to advance our abilities to effectuate increasingly complex concepts, which elevate our race overall. It is the unused and unknown 75 percent of our brain capacity into which we expand, paving the way for our continued advancement to an elevated level of more intelligent function.

From the basic forces of nature's wind, gravity, and fire, combustion, compression and thrust, nuclear reactivity, instantaneous communication through the "cloud," to now playing with teleportation and time travel, we have historically advanced physically at a proportional rate equivalent to our technological expansion. With the assistance of higher-order intelligent entities, we're now on the cutting edge of understanding the attributes of dark matter and our place within it, with current generations of "light workers" and "star-seed" children helping to bring about accelerated stages for a long-term beneficial effect on humans' development. It appears, however, that our technological abilities are now logarithmically accelerating more rapidly than our physical growth exhibits, causing a growing disconnect in human society. Does this lead to the future departure of higher vibration humans to a new off-Earth home, who develop into an entirely new species of exceptional intelligence with modified DNA? Then when 144,000 of us disappear instantly and many others ascend to an Earth-orbiting complex on modern flying machines, or dematerialize into a cloud, or thin air, are *we* looked upon as gods by the ones remaining? You can see some of the stone ascension chairs used the last time remaining behind the church in Chinchero, Peru.

Each and every human is a unique hybrid entity, part of the whole. Since we are all matter and connected to each other, each one of us contributes influence to the whole. The more attention we pay to making choices that contribute to elevating humans' vibration in alignment with God's plan, the better off all of our lives will be, so be nice to yourself. The Bible says we were created by God in His own image. We are a part and product of everything that exists within an energy field that has manifested its unique combination of aspects from Source consciousness, thereby creating highly intelligent energy, and then manifesting terrestrial biological entities such as us.

Recognizing and opening one's awareness and understanding by choice, enables access to expanded channels of God-centered light, love, and information, as well as increased levels of natural telepathic communication. These are initial effects of our current multigenerational, interdimensional shift of humanity. For now, it may be suppressed by mass mind control utilizing drugs, media, movies, electronic diversionary entertainment, genetically modified food, or maintaining a balanced level of violence in society, but eventually, there will be no stopping it as truth *will* prevail.

WHO WERE THE GODS?

Some of the first groups of humans in the Western Hemisphere and Southeast Asia originated from extraterrestrial groups seeding of the continents of Atlantis and Lemuria. Working for God, a highly intelligent intergalactic collective design group worked harmoniously to create us with the preeminent features of their individual specialties, and created us from the best available biological, chemical, and neurological resources at that time. There are many theories, of course, one of which is that the builders originated from approximately twenty-two of the thirty or so galaxies in our local group, here in our far-off corner of our known universe. They materialized in different locations around the planet to seed their unique versions, with slight variances of the groups' collective creation over the course of millions of years. The remains of various-sized humans who lived eons past reflect the slightly differing design characteristics of their respective designers' distinction. When one series was unable to sustain themselves, they were wiped out before a new, modified version was seeded several hundred thousand years later. Eventually, after a half-dozen restarts, we took hold with more advanced design and continue to thrive. The variant physical features of Chinese, Indians, Africans, Europeans, indigenous Westerners, and Pacific Islanders give testament to these differing traits.

Extraterrestrial and interdimensional entities appearing as humans have the ability to transcend dimensions from their home locations and star systems and adapt their physical bodies at will, in order to function in and continually develop our race and Earth environment. Intra- and intergalactic travel is not new at all; it's only new to you and has been utilized for billions of years before we showed up. While manipulating the DNA of humanoids, enabling them to develop into all they can be, the ETs' technologies were also utilized in smaller construction projects in numerous locations around the planet, which helped to enable a kick-start of our race.

Shortly after the second Ice Age past (19,000–17,000 BCE or so), many massive construction projects were implemented by unknown constructors, utilizing currently unknown energy technologies. From Teotihuacan, Tiwanaku, the Bosnian pyramids, Nan Midol in the South Pacific, Egypt, Angkor Wat, underwater Mediterranean cities, and Stonehenge—they all seemed to possess the ability to cut, levitate, and mold stone.

Large groups of short-statured beings, averaging four feet tall, were created as workers all around the planet to mine resources and construct the massive projects directed by the gods. Several groups of very large-stature humanoids were initially created worldwide as well, where excavated skeletal remains prove their heights were well over fifteen, twenty, and twenty-five feet tall during various epochs. With those groups of giant meat eaters having DNA embedded-survival instincts, the oversized humans apparently looked at the four-footers as appetizers, but consumption of our own species for a food source was absent in the original plan. Maybe that's when it was figured out that all men need to be created equal!

The gods materialized and dematerialized in small groups as well, according to their predisposed work plan of their originators. Utilizing Earth-grid energy fields, some Beings materialized in pyramids, on earthbound stone formations, some in our atmosphere in physical craft, while others were grounded in their particular home base locations. Many sites in South America remain clearly visible where this has occurred, although discussion is scarce due to the bulk of our population's narrow-mindedness and personal fears; also, it's probably suppressed due to it being classified information. The pyramids around the planet offered them an Earth-based headquarters with unlimited free natural power to support their missions, one of which was to mine gold and other precious Earth resources. They possessed and utilized abilities that appear "supernatural" to us, although in fact they are common, natural technologies utilized in harmony with *their* known laws of physics. Different dimensions have different laws. We modern humans now travel elsewhere in the cosmos to mine resources, just as the ancients came here and did the same eons ago.

The Australian Aborigines claim to be the oldest, most continuous direct human lineage on the planet, of sixty to seventy thousand years, although there have been many discoveries of humanoid remains from vastly differing periods of existence—from two million years ago in Africa; 640,000 years ago in China (Peking man); and, more recently, 240,000 years ago as a detailed account written in stone by Sumerian kings, and the South Pacific remains of a recently excavated 67,000-year-old human. We have obviously been wiped out a half-dozen times in the past and then reseeded with newer genetic upgrades. Evidence of this is found worldwide, and the remaining narrow-minded scientists living in denial need to retire with their teddy bears, to allow the bulk of us to advance naturally into a higher vibrational level society as intended.

Physical evidence found throughout the Western Hemisphere lies in the story told in numerous stone carvings, statues, and artifacts left by survivors that describe their race's origin, along with much evidence of interaction with Atlantis. It seems that when people of Atlantis expanded to the west, prior to Lemuria sinking beneath the Pacific Ocean, they expanded simultaneously and met common ground in between, on both continents of North and South America. At the time, South America was much lower in elevation prior to the Andes geologic upheaval; the Bering Strait was also exposed. The massive amounts of worldwide evidence collected over hundreds of years by hundreds of researchers indicates that humans of North and South America have primarily descended from the combination of Atlanteans and Lemurians, albeit with modification.

CONTROLLED DISCLOSURE

I have learned to withhold putting much faith in the accuracy of some "officially" dated artifacts since I discovered several years ago the rampant fraudulent information published by a well-respected American university and other government-sponsored sources. Their dates were only off by about twelve thousand years or so; maybe they consider that was their margin of error. What's the difference between an ice age or two among friends? A 600 percent margin is unacceptable to me, as well as any other reasonably intelligent person, and is outright insulting to the indigenous people affected. Many educated indigenous people look upon American university researchers as educated idiots. It's fraud, as far as I'm concerned, but that is what makes their story work. The suppression of truth and offense to intelligent people, Source, and the natural progression and development of the human race by promoting untruths and deception of God's will and making, under the disguise of an educated and trustworthy authority, is unacceptable. These actions indubitably earn them the well-deserved title of the ultimate dirtbags. The intentional deceit will eventually be held accountable to karmic debt—they will be unable to escape it, guaranteed.

ANTHROPOPHAGY

Numerous species of carnivorous animals around the world have been consumed by humans as a nutritional food source for millennia. It is my understanding that in the first several "rounds" of ancient human design, consumption of our own species was as normal then as it is now for those who consume cow meat, bear, elk, horse, alpaca, rats, llama testicles, sheeps' brains, and the like. It's only after several restarts of DNA adjustments that evolved our brains' development into a more intelligent species, which has socially suppressed consumption of our own. Many anthropological findings of bones from dig sites of thousands of years ago clearly indicate that humans' consumption of one another was a common occurrence. Legends of the Paiute of North America admittedly claimed they were tired of being on the menu of the prehistoric races of giants. Many also believe the four-foot-tall "Things" of Lemuria and South America, primarily lived underground beyond the reach of humanoid giants to avoid their demise as tasty little morsels. Public research and disclosure of those fifteen- to twenty-five-foot-tall beings has been suppressed, with many skeletons of the giants having been destroyed and disposed of for a long time.

In life-or-death situations, the mind is instinctively conditioned to accept and perform acts that would otherwise be thought impossible, thereby instructing and leading the body to perform accordingly. Cannibalism is just one example of a human's psychological acceptance of the effect caused by the recognition of impending death to one's physical body should a particular act not be performed—in this case, consuming protein. History has documented extensive practices of anthropophagy worldwide, including Europe in the dark ages, Brazil, and on many islands in the western South

Pacific. As recent as the late Middle Ages, conquering armies frequently consumed their opponents, providing the protein necessary to move forward with their conquest. There are unverified reports of modern-day soldiers who also consume their enemies due to the psychological trauma of war.

In modern society, however, it seems less known due to the progressively less frequent occurrences en masse. There are current-day accounts, though; the most well-known is the Donner Party in North America, some serial killers, and more recently, the passengers of a downed airline in the South American Andes. From what I know, cannibalism is also still alive and functioning well, in the jungles of Central America and the Amazon, besides North Korea and other unpublicized or remote places around the world.

It was explained to me thirdhand in a city park under a shade tree during a game of chess, by my homeless opponent who grew up and lived in eastern Bolivia. His good friend had grown up deep in the Amazon jungle and said it was normal and customary for them to consume humans, regardless of race, gender, age, or status as a tourist, missionary, or explorer. He stated there are still over one hundred uncontacted tribes and villages living deep in the jungle, which don't communicate or interact with the outside world. Apparently, many of them have been contacted, and it's just that the contactees never made it out to tell about it.

In the Amazon, it's normal for them to cook and consume a human, as it is a crocodile, monkey, jungle rat, or a victim of an opposing, conquered tribe. When several or more bodies are cooked at the same time, a ceremonial feast consists of dance, prayer, and music rituals. They believe that consuming outsiders' bodies has the same effect as our taking an antibiotic, to prevent them from becoming victims themselves of the diseases and evil Spirit that occupy those bodies. For the short time that I was there, I heard several stories indicating that tourists are a delicacy because they have more meat on their bones. It is common local knowledge that frequently, people never return from independent or small group trips into the Amazon, although there were reportedly documented accounts of fourteen hundred soldiers going in to the jungle and never coming out. I haven't been there, so I don't know for sure, and I have no intention of finding out for myself!

From working in the jungle, I know about anthropophagy as it relates to men's survival instincts. Other reasons that motivate an individual's desire to kill and consume another human in modern society is obviously due to deviant mental issues. A close analogy of thought might be comparing modern-day hunters who kill a bear for fun or food, return it to camp, cook, and eat it. When skinned, a bear appears amazingly similar to a human.

KILLERS

Many killers lack the naturally embedded brain function of emotion, so therefore they don't think, process, relate to, or feel what a logical person considers normal. They have aligned themselves with evil and have adapted themselves to live in alignment with the dark force. Others subconsciously deny their capacity to comprehend the extent of their actions until they themselves, in a coherent state, are facing imminent death. That way, it suppresses living with the nightmares and mental pain and also will fortify their denial of guilt. The potential consequences (death by state execution), for which they have no defense, reinforce denial. When they finally face our Creator and realize the deep-seated truth that their consciousness originated in the same place as the person they killed, many then become aware of their common origin and permanent connection with them, *especially* if they look into their victims' eyes at the moment of death. I believe many subconsciously cover up their feelings of guilt and responsibility by various methods, for primarily one reason: facing the fear of God. Unfortunately, hundreds of thousands of them have absolutely no remorse whatsoever and are incapable of any rehabilitation or spiritual association, due to their committed relationship with pure evil.

Incarceration initiates a desire in many of them to understand more of the concepts of spirituality; as a saying goes, "All prisoners find God." I'm not justifying anything here and only state for the reader's awareness that most all of our modern society, particularly administrative and institutional workers at all levels, are misled as to the underlying cause of killers' inquisitiveness to understand God consciousness, because most of them don't understand it themselves.

REALIGNMENT PROGRAMS

"New thought" programs of brain enhancement and reprogramming through intense relevant education should be implemented in our junior high schools and juvenile rehabilitation systems forthwith. Establishment of "new thought" programs exposing and teaching our underlying fundamental design concepts of interconnectedness, and how certain mental pictures and thoughts can transcend voice transfer, could significantly elevate the overall vibration of humanity.

Junior high schools and high schools teaching the basic concepts necessary to identify, suppress, and discharge mental positions that have been negatively implanted rather than personally derived, and that are out of alignment with their (or society's) best interests, would be the place to start. Such classes hopefully will someday become standard, in prisons, psychiatric institutions, homeless shelters, and particularly in juvenile detention facilities. Implementing "new thought" programs at age eleven would have a dramatic, positive long-term effect on human capital and society. By the way, adult education class has been in session since you started reading this book.

To implement such a new program on a wide scale, of course, would encounter fierce resistance from the legal system, judges, media, politicians, prison operators, and owners of rehab centers. The largest group of those opposing societal reform are the ones who need it most because they are mostly the parasitic ones capitalizing and surviving solely at the expense of pain and suffering caused by continued dark or evil acts and policies perpetrated against hard-working, innocent, God-loving society.

BURY THE TRASH

The evil souls occupying human bodies that are unable to reform need to return where nature's natural order of systems and structure provide for karmic disposition and processing, which mankind is unable to perform. Are we that hardened by the daily news to be unconcerned when we hear of the slow, methodical extermination of Christians, Jews, and other religions and races of God-loving people? "God said it's OK for me to kill you because you worship a different god than us." Humans are easily brainwashed into believing and accepting anything as a way of life; whether it is moral, sensible, or socially acceptable is irrelevant. We are currently living this way, whether you know it or not. As a race, we can't figure out the difference between killing God-loving people over their beliefs in God versus terminating those that commit evil actions against God-loving people.

Traveling throughout Central America, I met a semiretired doctor who worked in a hospital and whose self-imposed job was to perform the best he could with his life to contribute to society for the benefit of all mankind. He has been exterminating gang members at an average of one a week for almost twenty years. Hundreds and hundreds of them, over decades. Sounds unacceptable to you? It seems to me that he's an outstanding member of society and should be elected into some type of recognized authoritative policy-making position. He could be the head of a new division of the freedom fighters or something similar to that. Psychopaths with a heart, who only kill other psychopaths, in the interests of maintaining the core values of Soldiers for Jesus…hmmm…maybe we're onto something here. Do you think he is the only one that does it for the sake of elevating humans' wholesome advancement of society? I hope not.

NONPROFITS

Of the many small, independent, legal nonprofits that I came across, my experience was that few of them were honest, whether it was in the Bahamas, Honduras, Mexico, the Dominican Republic, Belize, or the rest of Central America. Their location was not a determining factor other than being near a tourist destination in a severely corrupt country. Although some of the money raised by these people does get used for its intended purpose, it's the bulk percentage of funds that get diverted to build their million-dollar beach houses along some of the prettiest beaches in the world that's the problem.

After thoroughly explaining my experience to a large south Florida nonprofit, I offered to assist in building a house in Central America for a very poor family, as they had promoted their work on a website. "Oh, no, you can't go there; you just send us the $8,000, and we have people who build them. We send you pictures!" I could only imagine from where they got their pictures. Many, many groups that I came across had fraudulent or nonexistent financial statements, foreign bank accounts in multiple countries, or million-dollar beach houses in another family member's name—you people suck big-time. The agencies and foundations based in tourist destinations seemed to be the most irresponsible, because when people are on vacation and they see poverty across the street behind their beautiful resort hotel on a beach, their emotions and cocktails kick in to open their pocketbooks, freely writing checks to the organizations' directors. Up yours, you freeloading, fraudulent bastards.

GOING FORWARD

Through projection of influence on humans' thoughts (ISP) resulting in action, and providing advanced scientific information to humans in a position to utilize it effectively, our race is guided forward on a path to advance not only favorable to us but also in the interests of our designers. When the groups of "gods" of millennia past ascended for the last time, it seems as though they put the final touches on readjusting our fundamental DNA but also left the door open for future readjustment when necessary to allow humans to evolve "naturally, with influence" into an intelligent race that would someday become them. It doesn't take a quantum physicist to figure out that we are *all* alien hybrids, *Created in His Own Image.* Many people need to quit freaking out about it, go hug a teddy bear, face the facts, and get over it, or take an aspirin and a nap. Denial not only suppresses you but also the collective advancement of our race as a whole.

In structured organizations, corporations, and government, many entities work behind the scenes to influence the outcome of a particular event, without the bulk of their group knowing about their mission or plans. A clandestine mission's success is more efficiently attained without the interference of ignorant or arrogant legal or media commentary, or questioning of the entities' intent, which may result in the delay, or defeat of, the intended beneficial outcome. Highly intelligent Beings of extraterrestrial origin operate the same way, often creating a more favorable outcome to humans.

Mind control may be a new area of study by our clandestine governmental groups, but the concept is obviously a component of our genetic design, embedded within the construct of natural law, having existed since the beginning of time. Exposing natural abilities that can be utilized for the benefit, advancement, and survival of our species on our prized terra firma is a good enough reason to implement a positive change to society, no? To get this going will take a powerful group to collectively work at the same time on all the irresponsible and narcissistic humans in control. Maybe Charlie, his friends, and the armies of Saints and Soldiers for Jesus should discuss it. I'll bring it up at the next meeting for a discussion and vote to be presented to our universal command.

GOVERNMENT INFORMATION

How was it possible that I was occasionally privileged by introduction to know, see, and experience some of the most secret, advanced scientific concepts prior to their existence being declassified or released to the general public? Some of the stuff is way more than a hundred years in our future. At first, I used to think they were just coincidences, because there was no rational explanation of how I should come to know certain things. From new military movies to advanced transport "ships," to really cool tools and machines, the average person would just think that it's all science fiction. Personally, I never liked science fiction anything, but I saw a *Star Wars* movie once.

Understanding that it's all the real deal gives me comfort in knowing there are Soldiers for Jesus working at the highest levels of control, who inform humans like me of their work. I don't even know where to begin to express my thanks appropriately for what they have presented to me, but for now, "Thank you, thank you, thank you!" will have to suffice. Sometimes, I feel as though it's a big brother looking after their little brother, giving me a treat. There is no need for me to know details at this time, so most of the specifics are withheld from me. I also realize that although much has been declassified and disseminated, the general public remains in denial! That's pretty funny to me, because people are always complaining (including me) that the government withholds from us too much information, but when they disclose it, the public doesn't take it seriously or believe it anyway! Fear, I guess.

GOD

When I enter a church and view a replica of Jesus's dead body hanging up on the cross, I can only wonder why in the world people choose to remain spiritually suppressed and depressed. Praying to an effigy of Jesus nailed to a stick hanging on the wall with blood dripping out of his mouth clearly causes many of the devoted congregation to individually exhibit mental disturbances. When they kneel and pray, opening their mindset allows enhanced sensitivity and emotions to take control of their incorrect physical and psychological perceptions. I believe their illogical expression of misinterpreted concepts also results in disparaging, emotionally damaging mental effects in babies and children. This is not Jesus's intent. You *do not* pray to a dead body. Pray to God and His Spirit.

EVERY MAN FOR HIMSELF?

Bless the egocentric human souls that are too spiritually immature, or too obsessed with their social or economic status to assist organizations, light workers, or independent missionaries like me because of their perceived lack of receiving anything in return. Their shallow lack of understanding is most often due to their personal fears. May the winds of God carry and guide you on your eternal journey. Go forth in God.

CHAPTER 14
CONCLUSIONS

Is Jesus God?

There are many who claim that without a shadow of doubt, Jesus has since reincarnated in other, more ancient, and more recent lives. If He died, rose again from the dead, and then on the third day ascended into heaven, why should we think that was His first time? What about spiritually gifted ones who walked our Earth before Jesus was born? I don't believe He waited fifty thousand or one hundred thousand years before deciding to come here for His first teaching mission. And knowing this, rest assured, He'll be back.

If Jesus is God, as many people believe, do you think He comes only to this planet? I don't believe that He would come only here, and that means He currently exists in Spirit and form on other planets in other solar systems as well, in various states of intelligent energy. It is difficult to comprehend because we humans have a deficit of mental abilities, and therefore, it's incomprehensible to many. The lack of our understanding is the root of our disbelief, based in fear, due to the limitations of our physical and scientific knowledge. If you're an open thinker, wrap your brain around the fact that different dimensions have different laws, since they are based on higher intelligence of other-than-human understanding.

Jesus has the all-encompassing power of God. If the power of God is Source, then Jesus is Source, and manifests Himself in our image in order to enhance humans' acceptance of Him, and to guide us on the path of love and righteousness that is the fundamental basis of His creation. One thing is absolutely certain, though—we all find out when we get there! When your soul arrives, just hope you don't hear the words, "Too bad for you; you were told, and you knew better!"

We have all sinned, so are we all screwed and doomed to hell? No, not most of us, because Jesus forgives but, of course, does not forget. Be prepared to take the consequences of your karmic debt, since no one gets a free pass. There is no such thing as something for nothing—TANFL, remember?

Regardless of what organized religions want you to believe, it is *you* who holds the ultimate power and ability to learn the truth of Jesus's will, and desire, for His intended way of life for us and our preferred outcome. You can easily connect with Him anywhere, the easiest and most powerful place, of course, is in His own house, obviously any Christian church. There are also other religions that profess and practice similar teachings of core values and lifestyles to those of Jesus. To me, He obviously has a connection and relationship with billions of other humans, albeit under a different umbrella.

MY PERSONAL TRUTHS

As I look back on my lengthy series of travel adventures, life-work contributions, and learning experiences, several core truths surface when reviewing the development parameters applicable in my life. I present some of those for you below:

1. I have learned the most about myself and all human life, Spirit, and God, from a teenager who never attended school; can't walk, talk, or feed himself; and can barely speak.

2. Conviction and truth to God from the core of your soul will result in living your life in the light, by rewarding you with living the richness of a soul's human experience far greater

than any economic value can ascertain. By working with Source in harmony according to God's plan, even just a little bit, you can have a wonderful life, as though you're living in heaven here on Earth. The law of attraction prevails.

3. Spirit assists you by allowing your benefit from other people's karmic losses (debt), when your proceeds are directed and utilized to help others in need.

4. The brain accepts anything, and any way of life, when a condition is consistently experienced and required for survival. Humans are designed to be creative, adaptable, and versatile in order to ensure their survivability.

5. Energies and Spirit occupants of many ancient ruins sites in this hemisphere don't hold the highest of God-Sourced intention (i.e., lower vibrational entities of dark forces occupy much of the lower earthbound dimensions).

6. When death is about to cross my physical path, I am often made aware through ISP.

7. I was recruited by Spirit to explain and teach through my travels and enhanced life experience, our direct connection to God-Sourced interdimensional, nonphysical entities and energies.

8. All of my near-death experiences and interactions with killers on the run, cannibals, and dying people subconsciously connected and increased my higher vibrational awareness of interdimensional realms, forces, energies, and entities for multiple purposes of:

A. Understanding and knowing there is only one true God above all that is.

B. Understanding that our soul has eternal "life."

C. Opening my intuitive channels to work in harmony with God, Jesus, and Angelic entities to locate, assist, or counsel others in need, and contribute to the enlightenment of all humans.

D. Counseling street people who unknowingly allow dark entities' piracy of their minds or occupation of their bodies, by my understanding the human influence of nonphysical entities.

E. Educating and confirming thoughts of others who lack understanding or comprehension that they can return to lead a normal life, regardless of their previous actions or experiences.

F. Knowing that all humans create their unique reality and live in their physical realm according to their perception and acceptance of the societal norms in which they occupy.

G. Acting as an ambassador to other Spirits working in harmony with God's overall plan.

9. Either one of five sources originate a person's conviction to consume the flesh of another human:

A. Knowing their natural order of progressive death due to starvation will occur without consumption of protein.

B. Evil Spirit has entered and occupied the mind and body through occupation (ISO) to control and motivate consumption.

C. The thought has been implanted and reinforced through telepathic projection (ISP, IPP).

D. Cultural acceptance and/or ceremonial practices.

E. Mental illness.

10. Origin

A. Working for God, extraterrestrials have seeded and modified us in various locations around the planet, and as the humanoids migrated and interacted, we evolved into who we are today.

B. *Oeaohoo*, the sound of the root of all that is; known as;

C. *Anapudaka*, the universal Spirit-soul endowed in man in its latent state. Before creation, the universe in its formless state, God.

D. God.

11. Sum it Up

If you have only the ability to physically see so far, does that mean nothing exists *beyond* that point?

If only our *visible* universe is 13.6 billion years old, but there are possibly other places ten times older than us, does that mean other life-forms could be ten times smarter than us?

So is it possible, then, we are actually a giant planetary experiment formed by our Creators that made us look like them? Now you get the picture.

IN CLOSING

While working on various volunteer projects over the years, I have asked my Spirit Guides many times why I haven't been given an assignment that would positively affect millions of people, instead of just a few hundred. Responses have been "You have to walk before you run," "You have to set a solid foundation to support the castle," "Your ripple effect will impact untold masses," and "When the time is right, you will."

"Now that you have been prepared for this, your writing will incentivize many others to write about themselves as well, incorporating spiritual content to elevate the masses" and "We need your writing account to be entertaining as well." Does "off-the-beaten path" (or to some, "off-the-wall") content count as entertaining? I hope so! If I have succeeded in helping to open your mind's awareness by expanding your understanding and commitment to God, it was well worth my time and effort to tell my story!

To some readers, however, a few powerful events of my life's story may be too incomprehensible and difficult for them to fathom as truth. But as time goes on, they will slowly realize the truth of their personal depth of connection to consciousness, which will result in the gradual awakening of themselves, and then will understand that God and Jesus are at the core of every being and everything. I strongly suggest that you continue your personal development by reading any of the publications listed in my reference pages in the back of this book, or pursue other sources of similar subject matter that are readily available to you. Your continued success and happiness is God's plan, and know that you signed up for all of it before you even got here!

Namaste.

FAVORITE QUOTATIONS

The unknown has never let me down.
—Dr. Joe Dispensa

Read a little, meditate a lot, think of God all the time.
—Paramahansa Yogananda.

A life spent redefining yourself to others around you, seems unproductive
unless you are interested in staying there.
—Sophia Love, *Inclusion*

THE TWENTY-THIRD PSALM AND HOW IT HAS APPLIED TO MY LIFE

1. The Lord is my Shepherd; I shall not want.
Throughout my life, I have always had His help.

2. He makes me lie down in green pastures; He leads me beside still waters.
I have rested and rolled in the lushest green grass fields in most serene places and rested in peace along rivers and oceans surreal, calming my life during times of turmoil.

3. He restores my soul; He guides me on the path of righteousness for His name's sake.
The times I have fallen, been tempted, or been lost, He has returned me to wholeness.

4. Yea though I walk through the valley in the shadow of death, I shall fear no evil, for Thou art with me, thy rod and staff comfort me.
Years of physically entering the most dangerous neighborhoods, villages, and jungles inhabited by brutal, evil killers, teaching the ways of Jesus was an impenetrable shield to me.

5. You prepare a table before me in the presence of my enemies; You have anointed my head with oil; My cup runneth over.
I have broken bread at many tables with ones who have committed the ultimate sin. My extra resources were mostly used to teach and turn those dark entities to follow the light of Jesus.

6. Surely goodness and loving kindness will follow me all the days of my life, and I will dwell in the house of the Lord forever.
I've been blessed with much goodness and kindness by Jesus's favor, and I intend to continue this path. Forever is still being written.

And so it is.

APPENDIX:
ANGEL GUIDES AND
ASCENDED MASTERS

At one point or another in my life's experience of physical or astral travels, I have learned of and received informational input and assistance from, or interacted and communicated with, the following nonphysical entities:

Of course, Jesus and Mother Mary are my most powerful God-Sourced connections.

Archangels: Michael, Melchizadek, Metatron, Raphael, Raziel, Gabriel, Uriel, Zadkiel, Saint Germain

Ascended Masters: Kuan Yin, Apollo, Ashtar, Kuthumi, Osiris, Babaji, Merlin, Sanat Kumara, El Morya, Neptune, Poseidon, Archimedes, Yogananda, and Max (the crystal skull)

Ashtar Command: where humans work with extraterrestrials to maintain peace.

Ascended family and friends include the following: All four of my grandparents, my parents, uncles, and many other Earth-departed relatives; Christopher L.; Todd K.; Keith M.; and Debra W.

Many souls have reincarnated here on Earth with the agreement to support and accelerate development of the spiritual nature of humans through sports and entertainment, due to their audience and influence stretching far and wide. Their effect on humanity is exceptional; several of them are Walt Disney, Magic Johnson (presented to me in the ether for a powerful, personal lesson) and Whitney Houston, with whom I also have a very special connection.

Attending churches, spiritual groups, metaphysical fairs, lectures, presentations, and visiting spiritualist camps (such as Cassadaga) has led to my acquaintance of many people who communicate with the other side of the veil. I know many empaths and mediums with various specialties in communicating, relaying, and channeling information and messages from Spirit. They tend to favor connecting with nonphysical entities in the specific areas of which they are proficient, such as communicating with deceased loved ones, Angels and Ascended Masters, groups of nonphysical intergalactic energy Beings, individual Guides, animal communicators, medical intuitives, readers of akashic records, or intuitive astrologers. One medical intuitive may connect through Jesus or God, while another intuitive may connect through a collective group of four thousand intelligent doctors volunteering to help humans, whose home base is a star system 190 billion light-years from Earth. Choices are available to every human and entity with a unique mind originating in Source consciousness. Miles and light-years are only human things.

REFERENCES

Barnes, Peggy. *Psychic Facts: A Series of Fifteen Lessons on the Laws Governing Mental and Physical Mediumship.* New York: National Spiritualist Association of Churches, 1999.

Blavatsky, Helena Petrovna. *The Secret Doctrine: The Synthesis of Science, Religion, and Philosophy.* Vols. I and II. London: The Theosophical Publishing Co., 1888.

Budge, E. A. Wallace. *The Egyptian Book of the Dead: (The Papyrus of Ani) Egyptian Text Transliteration and Translation.* New York: Dover Publications, 1967.

Bueno, V Roberto Millán. *Maravilloso Tiwanaku.* Bolivia: Sistemas Graphicos, 2016.

Carlson, Richard, and Benjamin Shield. *Healers on Healing.* California: Jeremy P. Tarcher, 1989.

Cotterell, Maurice. *The Lost Tomb of Viracocha: Unlocking the Secrets of the Peruvian Pyramids.* Vermont: Bear & Co., 2003.

Davis, Roy Eugene. *Absolute Knowledge that Liberates Consciousness: An Explanation of Higher Realities.* Georgia: CSA Press, 2007.

Davis, Roy Eugene. *The Path of Light: A guide to 21st Century Discipleship and Spiritual Practice in the Kriya Yoga Tradition.* Georgia: CSA Press, 1998.

Davis, Roy Eugene. *Seven lessons in Conscious Living: Philosophical Principles, Holistic Lifestyle Guidelines, and Effective Meditation Routines.* Georgia: CSA Press, 2013.

Day, Christine. *Pleiadian Principles for Living: A Guide to Accessing Dimensional Energies, Communicating with the Pleiadians, and Navigating these Changing Times.* New Jersey: New Page Books, 2013.

Dispensa, Joe. *Becoming Supernatural: How Common People are Doing the Uncommon.* Hay House, 2019.

Fairchild, Alana. *Crystal Angels 444: Healing with the Divine Power of Heaven & Earth.* Australia: Blue Angel Publishing, 2013.

Fortune, Dion. *Psychic Self-Defense: The Classic Instruction Manual for Protecting Yourself Against Paranormal Attack.* California: Red Wheel/Weiser, 2001.

Gawain, Shakti. *Living in the Light*: *A Guide to Personal and Planetary Transformation.* California: Whatever Publishing, 1986.

Goldman, Burt. *Quantum Jumping: The Inter-dimensional Quest for a Better You.* Text companion to CD module.

Hawkins, David R. *Transcending the Levels of Consciousness: The Stairway to Enlightenment.* Arizona: Veritas Publishing, 2006.

Hicks, Esther and Jerry. *The law of Attraction: The basics of the Teachings of Abraham.* California: Hay House, 2006

Jones, Aurelia Louise. *Telos, Volume 3: Protocols of the Fifth Dimension.* California: Mount Shasta Light Publishing, 2006

Jones, Martin. *Unlocking the Past: How Archaeologists Are Writing Human History with Ancient DNA.* New York: Arcade Publishing, 2016.

Joseph, Frank., *Atlantis and Other Lost Worlds: New Evidence of Ancient Secrets.* London: Arcturus Publishing Ltd., 2018.

Kaku, Michio. *Parallel Worlds: A Journey Through Creation, Higher Dimensions, and the Future of the Cosmos.* New York: Anchor Books, 2005.

Kapleau, Philip. *The Three Pillars of Zen: Teaching, Practice, Enlightenment.* Boston: Beacon Press, 1972.

Katz, Debra Lynne. *You Are Psychic: The Art of Clairvoyant Reading & Healing.* Minnesota: Llewellyn, 2004.

Kenyon, Tom, and Judy Sion. *The Arcturian Anthology.* Washington: Orb Publishing, 2013.

Laremy, Robert. *Spiritual Cleansings: and Psychic Defenses.* New York: Original Publications, 2001.

Laszlo, Ervin. *The Akashic Experience: Science and the Cosmic Memory Field.* Vermont: Inner Traditions, 2009.

McCune, Shirley, and Norma Milanovich. *The Light Shall Set You Free.* Arizona: Athena Publishing, 1996.

Montgomery, Ruth. *The World Before.* New York: Coward, McCann, & Geoghegan, 1976.

Orleane, Pia Smith, and Cullen Baird Smith. *Remembering Who We Are: Laarkmaa's Guidance on Healing the Human Condition*. Indiana: Balboa, 2013.

Posnansky, Arthur. *Tihuanacu: The Cradle of American Man*. Vol. I. New York: J. J. Augustin Publisher, 1945.

Prabhupada, Swami A. C. Bhaktivedanta. *Bhagavad-Gita As It Is*. California: The Bhaktivedanta Book Trust, 1983.

Prophet, Elizabeth Clare and Mark L. *Saint Germain on Alchemy: Formulas for Self-Transformation*. Montana: Summit University Press, 1993.

Roman, Sanaya, and Packer, Duane. *Opening to Channel: How to Connect with Your Guide*. California: H. J. Kramer, 1987.

Satori, Judy. *Sunshine before the Dawn: A telepathic transmission*. Illinois: Corporate Disk Co., 2011.

Virtue, Doreen. *Healing with the Angels: How the Angels Can Assist You in Every Area of Your Life*. California: Hay House, 1999.

Virtue, Doreen. *Archangels and Ascended Masters: A Guide to Working and Healing with Divinities and Deities*. California: Hay House, 2003.

Virtue, Doreen. *Messages from Your Angels: What your Angels want you to Know*. California: Hay House, 2002.

Virtue, Doreen., *The Lightworker's Way: Awakening Your Spiritual Power to Know and Heal*. California: Hay House, 1997.

Webster, Richard. *Communicating with Archangel Michael for Guidance and Protection.* Minnesota: Llewellyn, 2004.

Webster, Richard. *Communicating with Archangel Raphael for Healing and Creativity,* Minnesota: Llewellyn, 2011.

Wingate, Richard. *Atlantis in the Amazon: Lost Technologies and the Secrets of the Crespi Treasure.* Vermont: Bear and Company, 2011.

Yogananda, Paramahansa. *Autobiography of a Yogi.* California: Self Realization Fellowship. 13th edition, 1998.

www.ingramcontent.com/pod-product-compliance
Lightning Source LLC
LaVergne TN
LVHW051456080426
835509LV00017B/1778